Building

open

Relationships

Your hands-on guide to swinging, polyamory, and beyond!

Dr. Liz Powell

A Dr Liz Powell International Publication

Copyright © 2018 by Dr Liz Powell International LLC

Book Layout & Cover Design: Tracy Lay / digivisualdesign.com

ISBN-13: 978-0692151594 (Dr. Liz Powell)

ISBN-10: 069215159

To the people who love me, exactly as I am,
to those I love, exactly as they are,
and to the future we are building together.

Thank you.

Contents

Why this book?
A note from Dr. Liz

● ● ● ● ● ●

As you open this book, I'm sure you're wondering why it is that I would sit down to write an entire book about something so "fringe" in our culture. Honestly, if you had asked me a few years ago if I would ever write a book, any book, I would've told you that wasn't my thing.

You see, as a TOTAL extravert, I'm a person who wants to be with people. I want to feel their energy, see the looks on their faces, hear their laughter at my jokes, and feel their sorrow and excitement and nervousness and arousal. I like to be in the thick of the people I'm helping. (Well, I mean, not "the thick" since I don't have sex with clients, but you get what I mean.)

To me, I always imagined writing a book as a solitary, lonely, isolated experience. You throw some words out in to the ether, and someone somewhere else reads them. Maybe they never see you, maybe you never see them. Maybe it changes their life, maybe they think it's hogwash.

It's an experience where I cannot alter what I'm saying based on the reaction I'm getting. Where I can't see if I have to explain more or if I'm explaining too much. I can't gauge where I am because I can't see you reading this in order to know how you're doing with it.

And yet, I know that there is so much that needs to be said on this topic. As of this writing, there are but a handful of prominent books about non-monogamy in circulation. When we think about how many books exist about how to have good relationships, and how few about how to have good non-monogamous relationships, it's clear that people like us are shunned.

In some ways, this book is a letter to my past self. In these pages are stories of some of my worst mistakes, my greatest heartaches, and my most serious relationship blunders.

When I was a young person trying to figure out how the hell I fit into this monogamous world, I had one, maybe two books to read about polyamory and open relationships. Compare that to THOUSANDS of titles telling me about how I had to settle down and be monogamous if I ever wanted "real love." I had people I cared about telling me that I want too much and that I would never be able to find what I thought I wanted.

I'm a little scared to tell you that I'm crying as I write this, thinking of all of the years I spent trying to be someone else, all of the heartache I brought on myself and others. Remembering all those people who saw me - this bright, shining, hopeful, young slut - and told me to be someone else. I mourn for the years I spent hating who I am, resenting the way that I love, and berating myself for not being "normal."

If I could have one wish, it would be that you never have to feel that way. That everyone could find a community or a book or a website or something to help them know that who they are is perfectly wonderful. That we all deserve love and belonging, even—and especially—the slutty queerdos like me.

I wish I could reach back through time like a pervert fairy godmother to grant all the wishes of all the non-monogamists who found themselves struggling to shove their very round-peg selves into society's square hole.

I guess, then, that in some ways this book is also my love letter to you. Yes, you, the person reading this paragraph. I may never meet you or know your name or shake your hand or kiss your lips, but I want you to know that someone out there loves you exactly how you are. I hope that in these pages you find the belonging and acceptance that so many of us have struggled to find. I hope you find at least one sentence in here that makes you feel seen and understood and loved.

I also hope that you find in these pages a way to avoid the mistakes I made. Mine have been pretty spectacular sometimes, and I wouldn't wish that hurt on anyone. I hope that you find a set of ideas and questions and exercises and worksheets that guide you to the person you want to be and the love you want to build and the sex you want to have. And I hope you find something in here that you didn't know you needed to think about. Maybe it's something you don't think you need now, but you'll come back to it when you find yourself facing something unexpected.

Most of all, I hope that you USE this book. Unlike a lot of books, this one isn't designed for you to just sit down and read. I want you to make notes, scribble, sketch, and engage with this material. I want you to turn to some pages so many times the spine cracks, showing the exact worksheet you found most helpful. I hope when you're facing something tough, you feel an urge to run to your bookshelf and look up the resource that can help you right then. I hope this doesn't just gather dust for you, but instead that you wear it down with much use.

So, with that, I will leave you with this guide, this love letter, this wish, this gift - direct from my heart. May it serve you as I wish it could have served me.

How to use
this book

● ● ● ● ● ●

Unlike a novel or some other books on non-monogamy, this book isn't meant to be a read-it-once-then-put-it-on-the-shelf kind of book. Nor does it have to be a start-at-the-beginning-and-read straight-through kind of book. Instead, I'd like this book to be like your live-in relationship coach; available when needed, full of resources and knowledge, and devoted to helping you work through the stuff that comes up. Here are my recommendations on how to tackle this book:

If you're brand new to non-monogamy or pretty recently starting it:

💜 Read through the whole book once, focusing on the Section 1

💜 Highlight, take notes, put flags on parts that seem important

💜 Download the fillable PDFs

💜 When you notice a conflict or you're having some uncomfortable feelings, pull out the book or scan through the PDFs to see if there's anything that might be helpful to you

♥ Every year or two, scan over the chapter and section titles and see if there's something that's more applicable to you now than it was when you first got the book

If you've been doing this non-monogamy thing a while:

♥ Download the PDFs

♥ Skim over the first section, flagging any worksheets or parts that seem relevant to the ways you're moving through your non-monogamous journey

♥ Read the second section

♥ Highlight, take notes, put flags on parts that seem important

♥ When you notice a conflict, or you encounter something you hadn't before, or you're having some uncomfortable feelings, pull out the book or scan through the PDFs to see if there's anything that might be helpful to you

♥ Every year or two, scan over the chapter and section titles to see if there's something that's more applicable to you now than it was when you first got the book

That's it. Pretty straightforward, but oh so important. When used this way, this book becomes a valued and trusted resource to help you navigate your open relationships more authentically.

Section 1:
Getting Started in
Non-Monogamy

● ● ● ● ● ●

If you're reading this, you're at least curious about what relationship options you might have beyond standard monogamy. Non-monogamy is any form of sexual or romantic relationship that does not require exclusivity. I like to think of non-monogamy as expanding from a set, limited menu to a huge buffet of options. When we explore the world of non-monogamy, we open ourselves to all kinds of new possibilities - some might be exciting, some might be intimidating, some might not be for us, but our options are nonetheless expanded. While you may be tempted to jump all the way in as fast as possible, the information in this section is devoted to helping you figure out how to approach your exploration with information and kindness, both for yourself and anyone you're exploring with.

Throughout this book, I'll be using a lot of terminology you may not have heard before. At the end of the book is a glossary with full definitions for all of the terms that you might not know. If you run across an unfamiliar word, check the glossary to help you out.

Reasons to Be Non-Monogamous

● ● ● ● ● ●

One of the most common questions I hear from monogamous folks is, "Why would you agree to this non-monogamy thing? Why do you want it?" A companion set of questions sounds like "Why are you so greedy? Why isn't one person enough for you?"

For me, these questions are important to address, but they don't necessarily get at the important parts of non-monogamy. Is non-monogamy greedy? Well it can be, but so can serial monogamy. And the idea that one person could be "enough" for someone seems odd when you think about how everyone has friends and family and other connections outside of their partner, even in monogamy. As for why I would "agree" to non-monogamy, well, it's generally my idea!

But why do people decide to venture from the "safe" shores of monogamy land to see what else is out there? There are as many answers as there are people who do it!

For example, here's why I'm non-monogamous:

To be honest, I'm a slut. I like to have a lot of sex with lots of different people. More than that, my heart is slutty - I fall in love with lots of people, usually falling in love with someone new while I'm still in love with someone else. In addition, there's nothing I love more than introducing the people I like dating and playing with to other people who they would enjoy dating and/or playing with. Compersion is my super power, and hearing about the hot sexy date my partner had with someone else gets me as hot and bothered as hearing about the sexy things they want to do with me. While monogamy for me felt at best like a scratchy, slightly too tight sweater, non-monogamy for me feels like a dress that hugs every curve perfectly, showing me off to my best.

Many other people have reasons that are totally different than mine for being non-monogamous. Here are quotes from a few people explaining why non-monogamy works for them:

"*It's how my heart works.*   *- Anonymous*

" *My marriage had ended and I was reflecting on how to *fully live my life. A friend introduced me to The Ethical Slut and what I read resonated. A new relationship I was in was getting more and more serious and we had some discussions about if we were going to do "the big R" relationship thing and what we'd want that to look like. Neither of us felt the need to be exclusive. Just because I found my favorite dish didn't mean I wanted to shut down the rest of the buffet. Even just having the option felt so much freer. Monogamy felt stifling. I didn't necessarily feel it at the time, but looking back on my life - even in high school - non-monogamy just fit me.*

I don't like doing things 'just because that's how it should be' with no logical reason behind it. I love being able to talk to my partners about other folks I find attractive. I don't feel guilty for finding others attractive. I know now just because I feel the pull toward another person doesn't mean I'm currently with the wrong one. Wish I'd known that decades ago!

I love that we're modeling possibilities to our children.   *- Josie*

❝ The reason why I have polyamorous relationships is *because it turns out that I really suck at monogamy. I just keep falling in love with new people before I'm done being in love with the old people.*

I'm polyamorous because I find it really difficult to manage other people's emotions regarding what I do with my body, mind, thoughts, and feelings. I'm sure there are monogamous people out there somewhere who don't need someone else to manage their emotions for them by controlling their behaviour, wants, or feelings, but it's way easier for me to find people like that in the non-monogamous communities.

Plus, keeping track of everyone's massive unspoken, implicit lists of rules and regulations for monogamous relationships (and all the *different* lists, because not all monogamous people do monogamy the same way, apparently. Only, everyone seems to *assume* everyone else does it the same way as them.) was just too much effort. I have poly relationships because I find them to be much simpler: I love who I love and my partners love who they love and everyone gets to manage their own selves because of the trust, consideration, empathy, compassion, and self-security that comes with respecting the agency of others.

- Joreth Innkeeper of The Inn Between at ·TheInnBetween.net

❝ I never understood monogamy. Since freshman year of *high school, I would ask people why we follow these seemingly arbitrary rules, but no one would take me seriously. When I found out about* *polyamory, it was as if everything in my life clicked into place. This is what I have always been and always tried to explain to others. - ADM*

&& *WSOD: Wrong Side Of Door... Like when your cat clearly needs to be on the other side of the door, no matter what side they are currently on. When I'm in, I need to be looking. When I'm out, I need the stability. Poly is my cat door.*   *- Nomi Jade*

&& *It's not so much that I am constantly looking for new people to fall in love with. It's that when a new climbing buddy, dance partner, or knitting friend appears in my life I want to see where it goes. For me, poly is about relationship without ownership. The only part of the relationship I own is how I treat my others. I want them to live full lives that are meaningful and fulfilling to them. If their lifestyle includes risks I'm not willing to assume, then we have the freedom to renegotiate our boundaries without the threat of the loss of relationship. Let relationships grow and change as they will or need, don't just throw them away because it's not how you envisioned it in your mind.*
- Eric L. Bale

&& *I did monogamy for 30 years, and somehow always ended up a 50s housewife in my relationships. Each time I would realize that I had become someone I didn't want to be, and leave. Finally I stopped to take a look at why. I realized that I had both given up my own power and chosen men who were particularly controlling and wanted to take my power. Now, I am polyamorous so I have the space to work on myself and still have love, and so that no one person thinks they have a right to control my life.*   *- Anonymous*

&& *I choose non-monogamy because I do not want control over my partner's relationships with other people. This also allows me the freedom to choose how all of my relationships with people grow and develop. I get to choose friendship, casual sexual encounters,* intense loving relationships, or any other type of connection. All of this within the bounds of a healthy relationships based on communication and consent."   *- Arizona*

❝ Polyamory, to me, reveals the true potential of an independent yet interconnected relationship. While monogamy is not a fallacy, I feel the modern societal narrative of monogamous relationships force upon us a false concept of 'intimacy' that muddies up and limits the idea of connection and bond.   *- PhilipJP*

❝ In a world with so much cheating, infidelity, and adultery, I feel more secure in a polyamorous relationship than a monogamous one. In a polyamorous relationship, if either my partner or I are attracted to someone else, we've already agreed that it is okay to talk about that and explore it, and that means there are fewer reasons for either of us to be dishonest with each other. While cheating is possible in a poly relationship, I feel like people are more likely to cheat in a relationship that is fundamentally based on monogamy. I have been cheated on by a partner in a monogamous relationship, but never a polyamorous one.

I also feel like polyamory encourages a healthier approach to jealousy than monogamy. While jealousy is sometimes idealized as an expression of romantic love in monogamous relationships, in a polyamorous relationship it is typically regarded as a problem that should be worked on, either individually or together. I feel like polyamory is more beneficial for my own emotional growth and development as a result of this, because it does not simply accept jealousy without examining it.   *- Anonymous*

❝Before society impressed upon me the 'right' way to have relationships, I always felt open to more than one connection and didn't like my generation's push toward exclusivity rather than dating a few *people at a time. But, I went with the flow and didn't realize there was another way until my twenties.*

Once I did learn there were other people like me, I was ecstatic! Since then, I've appreciated the flow of relationships and, at times, chosen monogamy for a time or reason or both. Monogamy doesn't feel as constraining when it is a choice rather than a default expectation, and when the option to move to another choice is always open for discussion.

While I prefer having a foundational partner to 'do life' with - share living quarters, expenses, and future plans - I choose to do non-monogamy because I don't want there to be limits imposed on any relationship in my life. I want to love openly and freely and if that love becomes sexually intimate, I want to be free to explore it. I want my chosen family to be expansive and to know that my foundational partner's network is just as expansive. As I get older and reminders of my mortality increase, it is so comforting to know there will be others who love my partner and will be there for him if anything should happen to me. I do believe that love is without limits (even though time is not) and by allowing more love into my life I have even more to give. - Jennifer Rahner of geekysexylove.com

66 *It took me a while to realize that I don't need to limit* someone else's desires in order to feel secure, nor do I want things that are healthy and positive for me to be restricted based on others' comfort.

The security that I thought monogamy provided was just an illusion. My partner's ability to feel affection, love, or desire for others in no way diminishes how he feels those things for me. Fear of him "straying" was so much more limiting than the joy of us mutually deciding every day to return to each other.

Once that clicked, it allowed me to question all of my default expectations; not only about my relationships but about every aspect

of my own identity. Now everything that I choose to be and for my life is an active choice and that feels more liberating than anything else I've fe lt.
- Josh

The rest of this chapter explores three of the other common reasons why people practice non-monogamy: having a lot of love to give, exploring yourself, and the excitement of seeing your partner with others.

Reason #1 – A lot of love to give

Some of us, including myself, just fall in love a lot. Some of us see the beauty and kindness and wonder in more than one person. If you're like this, the idea of not sharing love with someone because you already love one person can feel restricting.

If you've ever wondered why or how some people can love so much, here's an example for you to consider:

Imagine for a minute you are talking with your spouse. You two have been together for 10 years. You know everything about each other, and there are no secrets between you. You tell your spouse that you've met someone new and you really like them and you feel like this new connection could become a really deep, meaningful part of your life.

Your spouse's eyes well with tears and they ask you "How could you do this to me? I thought we loved each other! Now you want to run around with some other person? Am I not enough for you?" You tell them that of course they still mean a lot to you, you just want to be able to have more than one connection.

To this, they reply "You can't have two partners! That's not even possible. You must not want to be my spouse anymore. If you really care about me, you'll end things with this person."

Does that sound ridiculous? No?

Then how about this one:

Imagine for a minute you are talking with your best friend. You two have been best friends for 10 years. You know everything about each other, and there are no secrets between the two of you. You tell your best friend that you've met someone new. You really like this new person and you feel like this new friendship could become a really deep, meaningful part of your life.

Your best friend's eyes well with tears and they ask you "How could you do this to me? I thought we were best friends! Now you want to run around with some other friend? Am I not enough for you?" You tell them that of course they still mean a lot to you, you just want to be able to have more than one close friend.

To this, they reply "You can't have two close friends! That's not even possible. You must not want to be my friend anymore. If you really care about me, you'll end things with this friend."

I'm betting that many of you feel like the first example is more "reasonable" than the second, but they're identical except for the label applied to the relationship. In both cases, you have deep emotional connections to more than one person. The difference is one of these relationships is assumed to be romantic and the other is not.

How do you know if you have a lot of love to give? Well here are some signs:

- ♥ You keep falling in love with more people

- ♥ You find that loving someone new doesn't affect how much you love the people already in your life

- ♥ You find lots of people really interesting, attractive, or appealing

- ♥ You've had "emotional affairs" in the past

- ♥ You tend to have lots of deep meaningful connections rather than a few

For some partners, this reason to do non-monogamy can be very intimidating. After all, the scripts most of us learn about relationships tell us that if our partner falls in love with someone new it's because the love they felt for us isn't real (and maybe NEVER was). So going to your established partner to ask to share your heart with others can feel more intimidating than just wanting to share your body.

There are also some gender differences in the perceptions of this reason to be non-monogamous. In general, those socialized as women tend to struggle more with a partner wanting to be emotionally intimate with someone else than being physically intimate with someone else. For those socialized as men, this is often the opposite, with physical intimacy feeling more intimidating than emotional intimacy.

Reason #2 - Exploring Yourself

In the movie Playing By Heart, Sean Connery's character, Paul, says, "The wonderful thing about falling in love is you learn everything about that person and so quickly. And if it's true love, then you start to see yourself through their eyes. And it brings out the best in you. It's almost as if you're falling in love with yourself."

When we explore a new connection, be it a friendship, business, sexual, or romantic connection, we get a chance to see new aspects of ourselves. We stretch and grow and learn as we experience new people and see ourselves through their eyes. This helps us to expand ourselves in ways we might not otherwise be able to.

In order to function well in any relationship, most of us have to do a significant amount of emotional growth and expansion. We have to learn to identify our own emotions, talk about them, and manage them. We also have to learn how to hold and understand the emotions of others. Most of us have learned patterns of avoidance or reactivity (or both!) over our lives. While this can cause problems even in monogamous relationships, non-monogamy can bring into sharp relief the problems with the way we are approaching disagreements, conflicts, and challenges, because we have to work to meet our needs and the needs of multiple partners. In addition, we may also begin to experience new emotions - compersion chief among them - and that can be an unsettling experience.

Non-monogamy can also, through the added degrees of complexity, force growth in our relationship skills and communication. While it's not necessarily true that you have to be highly skilled at communication to do non-monogamy, it certainly does help! Frankly, if you don't get more skilled and efficient at communication when doing non-monogamy, you end up spending more time processing your relationships than actually having them.

For many of us, one of the greatest benefits of choosing non-monogamy has been the increase in skillfulness with how we navigate relationships. Better boundaries, clearer communication, and more ease in asking for what we want are just some of the ways we explore ourselves and who we are in partnership.

Finally, many folks enjoy the ways that non-monogamy helps them explore and expand themselves sexually. Plenty of people who are exploring non-monogamy may have never had the opportunity to have sexual experiences they've been curious about, whether because they got into a monogamous relationship when they were young or because they thought they just couldn't ever do it until they got older. Sexual expansion could include experiences with new people, multiple partners, exploring kinks, even experiences with folks of other genders. Non-monogamy can offer people a chance to expand their sexual horizons in ways they might not have anticipated.

Reason #3 - The Turn-On of Seeing Your Partner With Others

Some people try out non-monogamy because they are exhibitionists and/or voyeurs or think they might be. After all, in the monogamous world, we may almost never see other people having sex outside of porn. Secluding our sexual lives behind a closed door with one other person can feel . . . less exciting after a while.

There is nothing I love more than watching my partner in the middle of a blissful sexual encounter . . . with someone else. Seeing my partner experience pleasure brings me pleasure, too! I love seeing how they respond to so many different people and kinds of activities. And I love watching their interactions with others to get some ideas about how to make their toes curl the next time we're together!

When John and I started dating, he had never done non-monogamy before, but he was open to trying. At first, when I would have dates scheduled with others, he would struggle with some fears or insecurities. Then, one day John had the idea to have a threesome with his best friend Joe. John and Joe had done a bit of casual play before, but never in a properly negotiated way, so John invited Joe over to join us for an evening. While I had a pretty varied sex life before that point, I had never before that evening seen a man I cared about engaging sexually with another man. Seeing John and Joe kissing and stroking each other got me really turned on. Then when John went down on Joe, I nearly exploded from excitement. Watching John exploring and experiencing pleasure made things even better for me once I got personally involved!

When talking to people who have explored non-monogamy, many were surprised by how much easier it was to watch their partner with someone else than they thought it would be. While people exploring non-monogamy sometimes fear that they can't deal with watching their partner having sex with someone else, it's almost a cliche among non-monogamy communities that the people who were most afraid to see their partner with someone else become the most turned on by it! Watching someone you care about receive pleasure, seeing their body respond, and feeling second hand what you usually experience directly . . . well let's just say the reality changes many many minds.

Bad Reasons to Do Non-Monogamy

While there is no "right" reason to explore non-monogamy, there are reasons that tend to lead to problems. In general, non-monogamy is not going to "fix" a problem you're already having in relationships, unless that problem is that you keep wanting to date and/or have sex with other people. If you tend towards dishonesty or manipulation, you'll likely still do that in non-monogamy and have even MORE opportunities to fall into that pattern. If your current relationship is failing, it's unlikely that adding more people will somehow fix it. If you're bad at communication, having to communicate MORE deeply with MORE people about MORE topics . . . you can imagine how that might become a rapid downward spiral.

Here are some reasons for doing non-monogamy that lead to problems:

- ♥ Your current relationship is struggling, so you want to add more people to help it out

- ♥ You aren't good at honoring relationship agreements so you want to be able to do whatever you want

- ♥ You don't like paying attention to other people's feelings and needs

- ♥ You just want to have a ton of casual sex

- ♥ You're looking for people who are "easy" or who "give up" sex easily

- ♥ You feel like a monogamous relationship is "too much work"

- ♥ You think people of the gender(s) you date are incapable of commitment so you might as well not try

- ♥ You get bored with people easily

When you're assessing your own reasons for exploring non-monogamy, be honest with yourself. Are you hoping this will be like El Dorado, only instead of gold it'll be the magical city of pussy? Do you want to ride the cocktacular highway, shiny and chrome, into Valhalla? Are you hoping to find a way to never have to commit to anyone, ever? Ask yourself the tough questions about what is driving your decisions, because if you dive into non-monogamy from one of these backgrounds, you're likely to both a) struggle with non-monogamy and b) be very disappointed in what you find.

Relationship Structures

• • • • • •

There are as many forms of non-monogamy as there are people doing it. While this may seem like and exaggeration, each of us brings our own special flavor to relationships. What works well between any two people might be disaster for a different set of people. So what are all the different ways you can do this?

Here are some general categories and relationship structures you're likely to see:

💜 Monogamish

💜 Don't Ask Don't Tell

💜 Swinging

💜 Polyamory

💜 Relationship Anarchy

Each one is explained in detail below, in order from the structure closest to monogamy to least.

Monogamish

The term "monogamish" was first coined by Dan Savage to describe a style of relationship that is generally monogamous but which understands that there may be occasional outside sexual relationships. Generally those who are monogamish are emotionally monogamous and often appear socially monogamous. The occasional sexual encounters may be a rare indiscretion, or perhaps an experience in the context of play parties, clubs, or from other sources all together. Overall, folks in these configurations are generally mostly monogamous and are not looking to date other people.

Don't Ask Don't Tell

Sometimes, when opening an existing, previously monogamous relationship, folks want to be able to explore openness but feel uncomfortable knowing about what each other is doing. These folks might choose to do a relationship structure where they each have permission to explore, but where they keep the knowledge and information about those explorations from each other. Inspired by the now defunct military policy on homosexuality, people have dubbed this structure Don't Ask, Don't Tell (or DADT).

In some ways, DADT can offer an easy, gradual entry into non-monogamy. After all, the problem many of us struggle with early on is coping with our own emotions - fear, jealousy, and insecurity chief among them. Within DADT, we can - to some extent - shield ourselves for a while from these feelings.

However, these types of structures don't tend to work out well in the long run. After all, keeping secrets gets tiring. If your partner asks you to spend time together on a night you have a dalliance scheduled, do you tell them about the scheduling conflict? Do you have a code word? How much do you have to do to hide the evidence or realities of what's happening?

At best, DADT puts off the work of exploring the challenging emotions that come from non-monogamy. At worst, it leaves us with all the stressful emotional and logistical work of cheating.

Swinging

Swinging is a form of non-monogamy generally practiced by couples. In swinging, a couple agrees to have sexual contact with other couples or singles. Swingers can be "soft swap" (no PIV or PIA sex) or "full swap" (includes penetrative intercourse). Swingers may either play only as a couple (both of them together playing with a third person or another couple) or may play as individuals.

Swinging generally allows for primarily sexual connections and not for romantic connections. As such, swingers may think of their encounters more in terms of play than in terms of dating and may not consider other people "partners" even if they have played together for a while.

Swingers have a huge infrastructure online and in many cities. There are large swinger conventions all over the world and several websites dedicated to helping swingers find events and each other. Swing clubs are also often the first or primary sex inclusive play spaces found in communities, so in some places other types of events (e.g. BDSM nights) may be held at swinger clubs.

Polyamory

Polyamory literally means "many loves." The definition we'll work with here is "the practice of having multiple sexual and/or loving relationships at the same time with the knowledge and consent of all involved." This definition is purposefully broad because there are many ways to do polyamory. I've listed the most common below.

Polyfidelity

Polyfidelity is a form of polyamory where a group of people practice mutual exclusivity. This can be a triad, a quad, or more. These arrangements often practice sexual and emotional exclusivity.

Many straight couples who begin to open their relationships are often looking to form a polyfidelitous triad arrangement and are looking for a bisexual woman to be their "third." This is sometimes called "unicorn hunting" (see page 182), as the "hot bi babe" these couples are seeking is hard enough to find that they might as well be mythological creatures.

While unicorn hunting may not sound necessarily problematic, these couples have often very carefully defined what the relationship will be like . . . without any input or option of the third. As above with hierarchical polyamory, relationships tend to work best when they're able to find their own shape and form and when everyone in those relationships is empowered to make decisions. If, however, this structure is freely chosen by all involved, it can be perfectly healthy for those who choose it.

Hierarchical polyamory

Hierarchical polyamory is a style of polyamory with clearly differentiated levels of relationship. At the top of the hierarchy is one or more primary relationships. These relationships have the highest degree of emotional closeness and commitment, and often have the ability to set rules on what can or cannot happen in lower level relationships. Below primaries are secondary relationships. These relationships are generally less emotionally connected and less "serious" than primary relationships.

Secondaries may need to be approved by primary partners or may be subject to "veto" by a primary partner. Veto is where person A tells person B they must end their relationship with person C, even though A is not involved in the relationship between B and C. Hierarchical polyamory can also have tertiary relationships which tend to be more "friends with benefits" type arrangements.

For the purpose of this book, our definition of hierarchical relationships necessarily includes imbalances in power between the different levels of the hierarchy. That is, the primary partner gets some say over how secondary and lower level relationships function. Some people will call their most significant partner "primary" but not create unequal power structures in their relationship. In this book, I wouldn't label that as a hierarchy. For more information on this, you can check out the book More Than Two by Franklin Veaux and Eve Rickert or the specific post on this concept, "Can Polyamorous Hierarchies Be Ethical?" parts 1 and 2, all of which are in the resources section.

Often people new to polyamory choose hierarchy because it feels the safest. After all, the rules and structure give an illusion of control. If I have the power to approve any new person my partner dates, I can rule out the "dangerous ones." If someone feels like they're threatening the primary relationship, I can insist that my partner break up with them. Hierarchy is the closest thing to mainstream, monogamous relationships within the polyamory realm.

Ethically speaking, however, hierarchical polyamory has the most potential to stray into problematic scenarios. Franklin Veaux, Eve Rickert, and Joreth Innkeeper (all found in the resources section) all do excellent writing on this topic, exploring how hierarchical relationships can sometimes become unethical. What I'll say here is that most of the rules folks create in these situation are designed to protect them from their fears and insecurities. If we fear being replaced, we set up a rule that we think gives us the ability to stop it before it happens. But no rule is ever going to legislate away these problems.

If someone wants to cheat or leave you, they will, and no rule will stop them. It would behoove us then to figure out what our goals are from the rules we are setting and to think about whether rules can help us achieve those goals. As with rules, it is helpful to consider whether a hierarchical structure is creating situations that disempower all of us. When we try to control someone else, we directly take their power to make decisions from them. In non-monogamous relationships, however, we also disempower anyone else who they might be dating. And, often, end up making ourselves feel less empowered because we are trying to shrink someone else down, which tends to just make us feel small.

None of this is to say you cannot have priority structures in relationships. In fact, it would be nearly impossible to not have priorities. The difference comes in who gets to make the decisions about a relationship. If Alex is dating both Brad and Carly, then Alex and Carly should have equal power in their relationship. If Brad is able to tell Alex how to conduct their relationship with Carly then someone outside of the relationship has more say than those in it. If, for instance, Alex wants to see Carly twice a week and Carly wants to see Alex once a week, it makes sense they would see each other once a week. If Alex and Carly, though, want to see each other twice a week but Brad says they can only see each other once a week, that's a bit tougher to reconcile. The same way that we question people who tell their partners they can't have friends, hierarchy can easily stray into coercion and control.

Non-Hierarchical polyamory

Non-hierarchical polyamory is any practice of having multiple loving relationships without a codified hierarchy structure. Folks in these relationships may have people they see more often or with whom they are more committed than others, but they keep decision making power within each discreet relationship and do not "rank" their partners against each other. People practicing non-hierarchical polyamory may have any number of partners at differing levels of commitment or emotional investment.

Solo Poly

Solo poly is a form of polyamory that centers autonomy and self-determination over enmeshment and coupledom. Those who choose to be solo poly may not want to marry, combine finances, or cohabitate. Those who are solo poly may think of themselves as their own primary.

A common misconception about solo poly folks is that they do not want serious or committed relationships. While they do not want someone to impinge on their autonomy, solo poly folks do often want deep and meaningful relationships. This relationship style tends to be well suited to those for whom independence is highly important. Those who are particularly committed to examining societal constructs around relationships may be drawn to approaches like solo poly or relationship anarchy.

Relationship Anarchy

Relationship Anarchy (or RA) is a style of relationships that attempts to undo the societal distinctions created between romantic or sexual relationships and friendships. Those who practice relationship anarchy do not necessarily preference romantic or sexual relationships over those that are platonic, instead letting each connection find its own form. In addition, many in RA configurations do not believe in having any rules or agreements in their relationships, and operate instead from a place of boundaries only.

A person who practices relationship anarchy might consider a platonic friendship to be their highest priority relationship and also have a marriage with a cohabitating partner. In their dating and sexual relationships, they might focus on what behaviours they need from a partner in order to engage with them in various ways. They wouldn't ask a partner to change their behaviors or to agree to expectations of other relationships, and instead will make decisions about their own body and choices based on the information given to them by their partners.

Relationship anarchy can be hard to understand for those most recently coming from mainstream relationships. The name for it, including the polarizing word "anarchy," can be unsettling to some. Overall, the anarchy in RA refers to the lack of hierarchy or structure external to the relationships. People who practice RA may also participate in any of the other relationship structures as RA is often thought of as an approach rather than an actual structure in and of itself.

It's about ethics, not specific form

One of the biggest questions most people have when exploring or practicing non-monogamy is what structure their relationships should have. While I get where this focus comes from, the structure of your relationship is far less important than the ways in which you implement it. Let's look at some examples:

> *Example 1:* Jean and Ryder practice a strict hierarchy. They have agreed to not feel love for anyone else, have veto power over any new partners who they feel threaten their relationship, and set strict rules about what activities they can engage in with others. They have a date night curfew and require that they spend every night together. Neither of them is allowed to bring any other partners to the house.

> *Example 2:* Sam and Jo are relationship anarchists. They have no rules about each other's behavior and create their structure primarily or only from stating their own boundaries and having good

communication. Sam feels strongly that each person's feelings are their own responsibility, so when Jo is upset and disappointed that Sam cancels their date to spend time with a new partner, Leslie, for whom Sam has lots of New Relationship Energy (NRE), Sam tells Jo that Jo needs to be responsible for their own feelings.

Example 3: Jon and Betty are swingers and tend to only play together. They do this because they really enjoy playing together but are open to reconsidering if one of them meets someone they want to play with alone or who only wants to play with only one of them.

Example 4: Frank and George call each other primaries and call their other partners secondaries. However, they take great care to ensure that every person has equal power in their own relationships. They do not believe in veto and they are open to renegotiate any agreement that become problematic for the people it affects.

In the above examples, it can sometimes be hard to see whether what's happening is perpetuating coercion, control, and disempowerment because of all the ways in which the mainstream monogamy models teach us to practice disempowerment. What can be helpful is to substitute the terms of "friend" or "roommate" in place of "partner". Let's take another look at Jean and Ryder if they weren't romantic partners:

Example: Jean and Ryder are best friends who live together. They have agreed to not to be close friends with anyone else, have veto power over any new friendships that they feel threaten their relationship, and set strict rules about what activities they can engage in with others. They have a date night curfew and require that they spend every night in their shared home together. Neither of them is allowed to bring any other friends to the house.

When we look at this situation as a friendship, it seems like it's veering into abusive patterns. Can you imagine a friend who told you that you couldn't make new friends? Who said they had to have a say in who you were friends with? That would feel really controlling!

Sam, in the example with Jo, also seems to be struggling with practicing kindness and caring in their relationship. While relationship anarchy may not include rules, and while everyone is responsible for their own feelings, Sam seems to be exhibiting a lack of care about how their actions are affecting Jo. If your best friend cancelled plans with you, it would make sense if you were upset. If said friend then refused to care about that hurt, I doubt you would stay friends with them for very long.

In contrast, Jon and Betty seem to be working at valuing each other and empowering each other. Yes, they are swingers, a relationship style often called "less enlightened" than polyamory, but their relationship structure isn't dictating to them how they treat each other. They're open to re-negotiation based on what each person needs and they understand that sometimes things change over time.

Likewise, Frank and George use hierarchical language but don't seem to be enacting power imbalances in their relationships. They focus on making sure that everyone feels like they have a say in their own relationships, rather than thinking that they should be able to dictate what happens with metamours.

The monogamy mindset tells us that we don't have the right to full autonomy in romantic relationships. Ideas about the "ball and chain," expectations that you will change how you dress or act because of a relationship, or that your partner should be able to tell you who to be friends with, are all sadly common in this mindset. It teaches us to "sacrifice" for our partners and that we must "compromise" for the relationship to work. While I think everyone would agree that relationships have compromise in them, our monogamous programming can often make it hard to see when compromise has become control. Autonomy, on the other hand, is the ability and right to do what is best for you, to make your own decisions, informed by the wants and needs of your partner, but not dictated by them.

In the recent past there has been far more attention paid to psychological and emotional abuse in addition to physical abuse. Physical abuse is any kind of abusive action that affects the physical body. This includes actions like throwing things, hitting, and sexual assault. Psychological abuse involves our emotions and self-esteem. Tactics can include gaslighting (from the movie *Gaslight*, where you attempt to deny reality), insults, threats of harm to you or to themselves, isolation from friends and loved ones, and ignoring or excluding you.

Psychological abuse can be much harder to spot than physical abuse - there are no visible marks, the tools are subtle, and our basic psychology leads us to deny the signs for as long as possible. After all, most of us WANT to believe the best about our partners. We chose them, we are investing in them, so we want things to work. Most people also tend to believe that folks who do abusive things are "monsters," that they are easy to spot and easy to leave.

The reality is that abuse can be really really hard to identify, in large part because of the ways that the monogamous mindset tells us that our partners SHOULD be able to exert control over us. It's not uncommon for folks to say that they should be able to tell their wife, for instance, to not be close friends with other men, or to decide how much time they spend with friends, or tell their partner not to do vacations without their partners. This cultural programming makes it hard, in particular, because it blurs the line between influence and control.

In all relationships, it makes sense that the person we care about would be able to exert influence over us. If I'm talking to my best friend about where to live and they express a desire for us to live closer to each other, that preference, and my caring for them, may influence my decision. Influence basically adds weight to factors on one side of a decision scale. While it adds weight, influence does not override the decision making power structure - I'm still making a decision that is best for me, I just have more information about contextual factors than I did before. Control, on the other hand, would be my friend telling me that if I really cared about them I would live closer or that if I don't move closer to them it's because I don't love them. Control is designed to override the decision making power structure and force a decision in one direction.

Re-read the examples at the start of this section and see if you can identify who is using control and who is using influence. Things that often indicate control are rigidity, fear or insecurity, focus on scarcity, and centralization of power. Things that tend to indicate an influence-based system are distribution of power, flexibility, openness, and caring.

As you can see, at the end of the day it is much less about the technical structure of a relationship and much more about how the people in that relationship conduct themselves. Is their relationship one that is focused on exerting control or providing influence? Are they acting from places of caring and empowerment or fear and disempowerment?

Many problematic structures come from an attempt to legislate away a feeling. In the first example, Jean and Ryder seem like they're afraid of how opening their relationship up might destabilize their own relationship. They likely have worries about being replaced or about being neglected. These fears are very common and most of us completely understand where they come from. However, building a structure to avoid an outcome almost never works. Half of marriages end in divorce, 50-60% of people in monogamous relationships cheat - if a structure was going to solve these problems, you'd think monogamy would have figured it out over the last several thousand years.

The desire to create rules to avoid feelings makes sense intellectually - in some ways. However, in practice, when we avoid doing something because our brain tells us it's scary, we end up reinforcing that it was actually scary and we were afraid for a good reason. As a psychologist, I see this commonly, especially with PTSD. One of the most common symptoms of PTSD, and the symptom cluster hypothesized to prevent trauma symptoms from healing on their own, is avoidance. If you're in a bad car crash, your brain suddenly has new evidence that driving is dangerous. The next time you attempt to get in a car, your brain might tell you that if you do, this time you'll die. If you then decide to just not get in a car, your brain tells you "See! I knew it! I knew this was dangerous!" The only way to prove these thoughts wrong is to take a chance and get new evidence.

If you're worried that your partner will leave you for someone else if you let them fall in love, the only way your brain will ever learn something different is to see your partner love someone else and still love you. If you're worried that your partner is going to break your risk-aware sex agreements, the only 100% certain way to prevent that is to handcuff yourself to them and never sleep.

We cannot create structures to prevent challenging feelings. There is no way to guarantee that things will not change. So focus on creating structures that validate empowerment and that treat every person involved like full human beings.

Desire-based approach to relationship structures

• • • • • •

If you're like most people, you probably read through those different relationship styles and looked at what is most likely to help you avoid pain/fear/problems/heartache...and then started leaning strongly towards that option. This is a super common way that people pick their relationship structure - one focused on avoiding something we worry about, whether that's negative emotions or breakups or loss of status and control.

While this method is common, I propose a different way of thinking about this choice - one based on how you, as a person, experience desires. Because we live in a culture that tells us so strongly that pleasure is BAD - that it is the thing that will damn our eternal souls to hell and is a useless waste of our (precious monetize-able) time and energy - most of us aren't particularly in touch with what DOES bring us pleasure or what we DO desire. We are super aware of things that cause us pain or discomfort, but a life built on avoiding pain is bound to be less fulfilling than one spent focusing on pleasure and enjoyment.

So then how do you know what you do want? The Dimensions of Desire worksheet goes over several types of desires you might have in different areas related to sex, kink, and romance that play into our relationships. As you complete it, make sure to give yourself space to really sit with each of the items and see what your desire is. Just because you desire something doesn't mean you have to act on it, it's just important to be sure you're making a conscious choice.

What are the parts of desire?

Dominance/submission and/or top/bottom

Generally, a top is the one giving the action and the bottom is the one receiving the action (though this is not always true). Topping and bottoming can be done in a neutral, equal power space OR it can be done with added power dynamics. Those power dynamics are Dominance and submission. Desires for D/s and top/bottom tend to be somewhat related but do not have to be so the scale here is separated into 2 parts; pick your place on each.

Sadomasochism

Sadomasochism (or s/m) refers to people who enjoy giving/receiving intense sensation or pain. Sadists derive pleasure from giving intense sensation/pain to another. Masochists derive pleasure from receiving intense sensation/pain. Someone's s/m desires may be related to their D/s or top/bottom preferences but do not have to be. Some have no s/m desires at all even though they enjoy D/s or top/bottom play. If you don't have any s/m desires, you can place your marker off of the spectrum or just leave this one blank.

Strength/frequency of kink desire

Some people almost never want to engage in kink or only want to engage in kink in very particular circumstances. Others want to engage in kink all of the time, even outside of defined scenes. Some people have a low or absent desire for kink while others have a very strong desire for kink. While the frequency someone desires kink may be related to the strength of their desire, it doesn't have to be. For instance, someone could have a very strong desire for kink but only want to engage in it once in a while, so you can indicate each here separately if they're different for you.

Strength/frequency of sexual desire

Just as with kink above, sexual desire can be very strong or very weak and very frequent or very rare. For this spectrum, sexual desire includes desire for whatever sex looks like to you – masturbation, hand sex, oral sex, penetrative sex, phone sex, etc. If your spectrum looks different for sex with yourself than it does for sex with others, you can put an S for self and an O for others.

Sexual role identification

During sex, some people like to be the giver and some like to be the receiver. Maybe it's different for different kinds of sex, maybe it's different with different kinds of partners, or maybe it's pretty similar across the board. Feel free to indicate here how your sexual role desire plays out. You could use H for hand/manual, O for oral, V for vaginal, A for anal, M for masculine type lovers, F for feminine type lovers, or create your own system! (Just be sure you write a key down somewhere if you create your own system)

Desire for variety

Some people tend to have desire for only one person for a period of time. Some people have desire for a lot of new people. Likewise with the activities you engage in – some folks love to do the same thing over and over while others like to mix it up. Maybe for you there's a strong desire for variety of activities but low for partners – that's great too! You can use A for activities and P for partners (or whatever other symbols work for you)

Strength/frequency of romantic desire

Some people love sex but don't really want a deeply romantic relationship. Others want lots of love and intimacy and romance but aren't interested in sex. Furthermore, as with the kink and sexual desire spectra above, strength and frequency may not be identical. Mark on here where your desires are and feel free to break it into 2 parts if they aren't the same for you.

Desire for relationship structure

Some people love having a rigidly structure relationship. For instance, the slave in a 24/7 Master/slave dynamic may have agreed to give their Master the ability to make any number of decisions for the slave. Others hate rules and structures and may want a very free-form approach to relationships that is based in their full freedom and autonomy. There's no right answer here, so be honest and indicate what the right balance is for you.

What does my desire look like?

Kink D/s or top/bottom desire

Dominant ▭ Submissive

Top ▭ Bottom

Sadomasochism desire

Sadist ▭ Masochist

Strength/frequency of kink desire

None ▭ Colossal

Never ▭ Always

Strength/frequency of sexual desire

None ▭ Colossal

Never ▭ Always

Sexual role identification

Giver ▭ Receiver

Desire for variety: Partner

None ▭ Limitless

Desire for variety: Activity

None ▭ Limitless

Strength/frequency of romantic desire

None ▭ Limitless

Desire for relationship structure

Free-form ▭ Rigid

Now that you've filled it out, look at your answers and see what came up for you. For instance, when I complete this, I find that I have a huge need for autonomy and a low need for relationship structure. As such, a solo-poly or relationship anarchy approach might best fit my desire profile. I could choose to do monogamish or swinging or another high structure form, but it's likely I would have to do more work to feel good in that style than one that is built closer to how I want to operate.

Something else to note is that some of these desires may change over time. If you've never really done much in the world of non-monogamy, you may not have a good read on how much variety or independence you want. If you've always been in highly structured relationships, you may not know how you would feel about a less structured one. This is totally normal. I highly recommend that you return to this worksheet multiple times to see if/how things are changing for you.

One more note that I want to offer is that humans are sometimes terrible at predicting what they will want or how they will feel about something in the future. Many people think that they will feel insecure and upset about their partner having sex with, or falling in love with, someone else and then find that they actually feel compersion instead. The flip side can be true as well - some folks find that they have more fears and wobbles than they expected once things actually start happening. If you find your experience not lining up with what you predicted, that's not a good thing or a bad thing necessarily - it's just a thing.

Most of us will have this happen at least once during our non-monogamy journey, and some will find it happening far more frequently. Be kind to yourself and give yourself space and time to process any ways that your experience doesn't line up with your expectations. (See the sections on self-care (page 172) and Conscious Monogamy (page 193) for some ideas on what to do to take care of yourself.) Don't assume that it will ALWAYS be any given way or that you can't change and grow. At the same time, don't force yourself into something that just doesn't fit for you. If you are just a naturally monogamous person and you find that non-monogamy just doesn't fit for you, that's okay. Non-monogamy isn't better or more enlightened or cooler than monogamy, especially consciously practiced monogamy.

If you're embarking on a non-monogamy journey with one or more partners, sit down with them and look at your answers. How do your desires match up? Where are they different? What new things did you learn about yourself or them as you did this worksheet? What blind spots did you discover? This exercise can be a great conversation starter for both or all of you about how to get your needs met in your relationships, so give yourself the space and energy to really look at this with curiosity and kindness.

Terms for relationships

When you have relationships that are outside of the norm, sometimes it can be hard to know what to call them. After all, how do you define dating? What if you're in a serious relationship with a non-binary ("enby") person, you can't really call them your "boyfriend" or "girlfriend," so what label do you use?

I met Kary in an unusual way. I was at my good friend's house and my two friends were telling me that I had to meet their roommate. The roommate, Kary, was also a sex educator and involved some of the same communities. Just as the conversation was about to finish, Kary came out of their bedroom, naked, and gave me a big hug. They were one of the most attractive people I had ever seen and the more I got to know them, the more I fell for them. We began dating right away and fell for each other quickly.

There was only one minute problem - I didn't know what label to use with them. Kary was non-binary and genderqueer and didn't feel comfortable with terms like girlfriend or boyfriend. We had a few long chats brainstorming different terms until we landed on "sweetie."

A few months later, that term didn't seem to fit anymore, so we talked about it again and decided on paramour.

In the end, having the freedom to come up with our own relationship titles made us feel like we were making a relationship that was truly ours, one that fit our own idiosyncrasies and identities.

When the relationships you're involved in are outside of the "norm", it can sometimes be a challenge to know how to refer to the person you're seeing; especially if you're already involved in a relationship. How do you refer to your second or third partner? Here are some options that you can use to brainstorm the best terms for your partners:

- sweetie
- boo
- bae
- partner
- lover
- boy/girlfriend
- Paramour
- Honey
- Squeeze
- Goyfriend
- Spouse
- Datemate
- Siggo (significant other)
- Imzadi
- Beloved
- Smoosh
- Loveperson
- Bothfriend
- Genderfriend
- Sweetheart
- Cuddle buddy
- Girlfriend
- Feyfriend
- Enbyfriend
- S.O.
- Steady
- Soulmate
- Epox
- Wubbie
- Companion
- Boifriend
- Lovebug
- Punkin
- Plus one
- Lifemate
- Companion
- OOMA (object of my affection)
- LOML (love of my life)

It probably goes without saying that the idea of these terms is to find what works for you and your partner that helps you both feel connected to each other. There's no right or wrong here, only good fits and poor fits.

Opening from closed

While opening from a closed relationship is fairly common, creating a non-monogamous relationship from a pre-existing monogamous one is actually much more challenging than starting a relationship that has always been non-monogamous. I can hear the disbelief - "But Dr. Liz, wouldn't it be easier if you already had someone you loved and trusted to be there for you?"

What tends to happen when folks open a relationship that used to be closed is that there are lots of landmines to find and address. When you build the foundation of a monogamous relationship, you will almost certainly add in elements that are not compatible with the style of non-monogamy you choose. When you start a relationship non-monogamous, you tend to build it so that it can remain non-monogamous. You set your expectations and assumptions at a level that includes the realities of dating other people. When you start monogamous, you may end up tripping over assumptions you've made about what your partner does for you, what you mean to them, and what it is that defines your "specialness" in that relationship.

All this is to say that if you're opening up an existing relationship that was previously monogamous, you're going to have to be much more aware of what stumbling blocks might get in your way.

Common ones include:

♥ What constitutes cheating?

♥ What information needs to be shared and when?

♥ How can we be sure to respect the autonomy and personhood of all of our partners, not just each other?

♥ How can we negotiate changes to prior agreements and expectations?

♥ What are our firm boundaries? What is each of us unwilling to compromise on?

♥ How will we handle when one of us has more dating options than the other?

♥ How will we handle it if one of us likes non-monogamy and the other doesn't?

♥ How can we support each other's autonomy while continuing to stay connected to each other?

For help with this, check out the section on the Monogamy Mindset (page 125).

What are you committing to?

● ● ● ● ● ●

In the world of fairy-tale monogamy, the question of what you're committing to in a relationship is pretty straightforward - sexual fidelity, emotional connection, primacy. So what happens when you decide you don't want sexual fidelity, or that your deep, long lasting friendships are as emotionally important to you as your sexual and romantic partnerships?

One of the most common questions I get from folks newly exploring non-monogamy is "but if you're not monogamous, what does commitment mean?" While I think that this idea about commitment in relationships sells monogamy short, I get where it comes from. After all, when we watch movies or TV shows or read books, people are "committed" in a relationship when they decide to stop dating and sleeping with other people. Those two aspects - fidelity and commitment - are so intertwined in most of our societal consciousness that some people struggle to conceptualize them as indeed separate aspects.

So then, when you throw out the fairy tale script, how do you decide what commitment means for you?

Commitment means different things for different people. Joreth InnKeeper has put together a list of the commitments she makes in her relationships at her website (link in the Resources section). If you read over her commitments, you can see that in this model, commitment is about how we commit to act for ourselves, our partners, and our metamours.

When you're in a relationship, how do you aim to behave? How do you take care of yourself? What are you invested in doing for the sake of the partnership? How do you honor all the people involved in your relationships?

Some areas you might think about when exploring what you commit to in a relationship are:

Communication: How do you communicate? When? About what? With whom? What skills will you use? How will you respond when your style clashes with your partner's style? How often do you want communication from partners at different degrees of closeness or entwinement?

Consideration: How do you make decisions when the outcomes affect one or more of your partners? Who do you expect to consider your wants and needs and to what extent do you want sway over their final decisions? How do you reconcile things when what one person wants clashes with what the other person wants? Where is the line between influence and control or coercion for you? How do you want to behave in a break up? How do you want to be treated in a break up?

Time: How often do you like to see people? Do you want alone time or time with metamours or both? How does too much or too little time affect your relationships and how does that influence what you can commit to? What makes something "quality time" for you vs lower quality?

Understanding: How do you want to understand a partner? How do you want to think about them when things are hard? How do you want to help someone better understand you?

Metamours: What is important to you in metamour relationships? How do you want to think of your metamours and how do you want them to think of you (family/

friends/sister wives)? What are you committed to do to facilitate your relationships with your metamours?

Partner selection: How do you choose the people with whom you partner? How will you take care of yourself in the way you choose partners?

I've included a worksheet here where you can brainstorm and sketch out your own commitments for each of your relationships. You can either do that alone, with your partner, or some combination thereof. Don't worry about getting this "right" on the first try, instead treat it like a place for exploration and ideas, of which you can then negotiate the specifics.

What am I committing to?

Use this space to come up with some ideas about what your commitments might look like!

Communication:

Consideration:

Time:

Understanding:

Metamours:

Partner Selection:

Loving more than one person

If your style of non-monogamy is polyamorous or relationship anarchy, a very real issue you'll have to face is learning how to love more than one person. In this chapter, we're using "love" to refer less to the feelings, and more to the use of love as a verb - to those actions, behaviors, and decisions we make as a means of honoring and showing our loving feelings for someone. This usage of love is very similar to the kinds of commitments you might have come up with in the previous section.

Most of us are great at understanding love as a feeling. We feel warm fuzzies, want to spend more time with them, care about their desires, and seek greater intimacy. And yet, love as a feeling is not nearly as meaningful if we are not putting effort and mindfulness into how we tend to and nurture that love. After all, if I love someone dearly but I never talk to them or reach out to them, they likely are not aware of or feeling the love I have for them. Love is not just a noun, it is a verb. Each of us bears the responsibility of putting effort and attention into how we are loving each other as an active verb, not just how we feel about each other.

While the book has some religious connotations (and thus some anti-non-monogamy leanings), The Five Love Languages by Gary Chapman can give us a useful framework for understanding what loving looks like in action.

The five languages from the book are:

- 💜 Gifts: You feel loved when your partner gives you gifts; you show love by giving your partner gifts

- 💜 Acts of Service: You feel loved when your partner does things for you (e.g. chores, house maintenance); you show love by doing things for your partner

- 💜 Words of Affirmation: You feel loved when your partner talks about their feelings towards you; you show love by telling your partner what you love about them and how much you appreciate them

💜 Physical Touch: You feel loved when your partner touches you (not necessarily in a sexual way); you show love by touching your partner and creating physical connection

💜 Quality Time: You feel loved when your partner spends focused, intimate time with you; you show love by spending focused, intimate time with your partner

You can find a free quiz to see your love languages at 5lovelanguages.com/profile (note: they use binary gender identifiers and the online form requires your email address, but you can also open a PDF without providing your email).

Knowing your love languages gives you great information to help your partners win with you. These languages can also change over time, so even if you've done the test before, it can be worth retaking it. I recently re-took it and found out that my scores have changed!

My primary love language used to be just touch, but is now a tie between Physical Touch and Acts of Service at 9 points each. Next for me is Quality time at 7 points and Words of Affirmation at 5 points. Gifts? Well that's a 0. It's not that I don't like gifts, it's that if I could choose any other expression of love, I would likely choose it over a gift. The exception to this would be gifts from people with whom I have a long distance relationship, in particular gifts intended to replace the lack of physical touch.

With one of my partners, Carl, we were only able to see each other once every month or two. Because touch is so important to me, Carl bought me a bear (Daddy Bear) that I could snuggle with at night when I was missing him. When I was getting ready to go to Burning Man for the first time, I didn't want to take Daddy Bear and ruin him at the playa, so Carl bought me Mini Bear to be my travel companion. Every time I cuddled them, it reminded me of Carl's touch and helped me feel closer to him.

Acts of Service has become more important to me as my life has become more busy. Being a solo entrepreneur, I often struggle to find enough time to do the things that I need to do. Making sure laundry, and dishes, and cleaning, and errands are all getting done often feels overwhelming to me. So when someone does something nice for me to lighten my load, it helps me feel much more connected to them because it frees up more of my time and energy to spend on them.

Gifts for me are lovely, they make me have a little moment of connection and joy, but then I have to find places to put them. I also feel anxiety around gifts because I feel like I'm not particularly good at giving them. I want any gift I give to be PERFECT, to show thoughtfulness, to be something they will LOVE, and because this puts a lot of pressure on me, I often struggle with finding gifts for others, especially for calendar-bound occasions (birthdays, holidays).

When you know your partners' love languages, you know how you can most effectively show them love. For instance, if you're dating someone whose primary love language is Receiving Gifts, you can give them small thoughtful gifts to show you care. For Quality Time, you can schedule dates and put away your technology while you're with them.

One thing to be aware of is that all of us have languages we "hear" best or receive best and languages we "speak" or give best, and these languages are not always the same. For instance, I love receiving Acts of Service but I tend to primarily show love through words of affirmation and touch. If you're particularly partial to one language, or particularly low on one language, it can be more of a challenge to learn how to speak the language your partner can hear.

When you add in more partners, this becomes even more challenging. You have to keep track of how each partner gives and receives love, plan to meet those needs, and remember which gestures land best with which people. Therefore, it behooves you to have some strategy to keep track of what each person needs and appreciates and how you can meet those needs. Some folks like a spreadsheet, some folks like to draw pictures or charts. Use whatever system works best for you to remember how to show love to the people you care about.

Now I'm sure some of you are thinking "Why should I have to learn to show love differently? Can't they just learn to hear love the way I speak it?" And I get it. Having to adjust how we do things often feels cumbersome. Ideally, in a relationship you would find a balance of learning to hear how your partner speaks and speak how your partner hears. This act of meeting each other in the middle is about the platinum rule - do unto others as they would have you do unto them. While you could just stick with what you know and are best at, it's far kinder and more loving to learn how to accommodate your partner's needs. After all, just because I love getting lots of touch and hugs from partners, that doesn't mean that they want the same thing. In fact, for some partners, my bottomless desire for touch has felt overwhelming and smothering. We cannot practice the Golden Rule in a way that actually honors the realities and differences of our partners because they are not us. So sit down with your partners, go over your love language quizzes, and see how you can each better meet the other's needs.

Balancing the actions you perform for love is only one part of learning to love multiple people. Most of us have learned a scarcity model of romantic love - the more romantic love you give to one person, the less you have available to give to others. Monogamy in some ways rests on this framework - you must ONLY love one person because if you love others you are taking something away from them.

Capitalism, as a system, teaches us to view most things from a scarcity mindset. Many of us believe to our core that there is not enough time or money or love or resources to go around. And yet, for most everything but time, scarcity is not a reality. The mindset shift that helps you embrace your ability to share more love is moving to an abundance mindset. If you can learn to believe deeply that there is plenty of love, then loving one person no longer feels like it is taking away from the love you have for others.

Learning abundance is a real challenge. After all, capitalism reminds us daily of this artificial scarcity of all things! In addition, you have internet memes and cultural norms that reinforce the idea that you can only really love one person. The fairytale model of love, which is intimately connected with the relationship escalator, tells us that one day our prince (or princess or non-binary monarch) will come, we will love them fully, and never desire anyone else. We will live happily ever after. If we end up desiring someone else, or unhappy, then clearly this was not "the one" and we must start over to find the one. And it is an emphasis on ONE.

When you first start having multiple loving relationships, you can run into lots of hangups from the monogamy mindset. I go in depth into understanding monogamy mindset hangovers in its own section (page 125), but the most common one here tends to be a feeling that if you are falling for someone else, it must mean something about your existing relationship(s) or, vice versa, that if your partner is falling for someone else it must mean something about your relationship. This belief is insidious and can poison an otherwise healthy relationship. After all, if we feel like our partner is loving us less, we're likely to pull away in protection or to cling to them out of fear. We may end up choosing behaviors that nearly guarantee our feared outcome of our partner wanting to leave us. Or, if we are the one falling in love, we may begin preparing for the end or mired in shame and guilt about our fickle, restless hearts.

In reality, the growth of new love does not necessarily mean anything about your current love(s). Just as making a new friend doesn't mean you're less close to an old friend, or having another child doesn't mean you love your older child less, the love we feel for a new partner can just be a new love all its own. If you're noticing those scarcity beliefs coming up for you, sometimes acknowledging them and talking them over with a partner or friend can help you see whether those thoughts are actually in line with what you believe

---

Recently, I've been falling hard for my lover of a few months, Brad, who lives in Portland. He's a gleeful sadist and he hits all of my sexy, exciting buttons. We've also been working on being more open

and vulnerable with each other and about talking frankly about where we're at emotionally and what we have available for each other.

Towards the end of last year, Brad had just started seeing another woman, Jo. From everything he told me, Jo sounded awesome, and I was really happy he had someone local who he enjoyed spending time with.

After one of their dates, Brad was gushing about how he and Jo were doing. Usually, I'm all about compersion and reveling in my partner's happiness. This time, though, for some reason I felt like his excitement about her must be draining his excitement about me. The stories I was telling myself included: I'm not as pretty as her so he must want her more, he's not going to want to see me anymore, if he's falling for her he won't fall for me anymore. These thoughts felt really uncomfortable and brought up feelings of fear and insecurity in me. I told him I was having some wobbles (those uncomfortable, insecure feelings that bubble up sometimes) and filled him in on the stories my brain was telling me. Because he's practiced at non-monogamy, Brad was able to ask me what I needed from him and then provided all the reassurance and interaction I needed to help quiet the voices.

Even the most experienced of us can struggle sometimes with how we interact with multiple loves. So if you're finding this hard, don't worry, it's not just you! With practice though, and with choosing vulnerability, we can learn new ways to challenge and overcome the voices that tell us that love is finite. Important tips to overcome those stories are to notice them when they're happening, talk about them openly and frankly, and let your partner know what you need to help quiet them down. If your partner seems to be having wobbles, often helping them name their thoughts and feelings can help immensely. Further, showing up by offering and providing the support they need can ensure that you're able to navigate these challenges with as much ease as possible.

Just as juggling 7 balls is more complex than juggling 3 balls, the more loves you have the more complex it can be to ensure that they are all tended adequately. This brings up what some folks call "Poly-saturation," which is when you reach the point that you can no longer have new relationships. Every person's point of poly-saturation is different. For some folks, having 2 meaningful partners is all they can handle. For some it's 5. There's no right or wrong level here, just differences in personal skills and resources. After all, the more efficiently you can communicate and help your partner feel loved, the less time and energy you are spending on that relationship maintenance, and the more you have available for others.

People who are newer to non-monogamy often become poly-saturated with fewer partners than those who have been doing it for longer. Those with busy schedules or with children may also be poly-saturated at fewer partners than those with more free time or who don't have as many major responsibilities. Knowing how you function, and at what level you tend to become overwhelmed, is a vital skill to loving multiple people because while love may not be a limited resource, time is.

Gender Differences

Here's a story we've heard over and over in my communities - a straight, cisgender couple decides to open their relationship and explore non-monogamy at the behest and initiation of the man in the couple. He thinks that getting into non-monogamy will fulfill all of his dreams of frequent and varied sex. However, once they open up, he finds himself struggling to find people to play with. The woman in the couple, on the other hand, finds herself suddenly swarmed with offers from people of many genders. She has as many dates as she could want and can hardly swing a cat in a club or online dating app without hitting someone who's hitting on her.

We live in a culture that teaches us that "men" are the sexual aggressors and pursuers. We also live in a world where most women, trans, and non-binary folks have had negative experiences with men who are hitting on them. These factors tend to lead to some big gender differences for those exploring non-monogamy.

Cisgender men often struggle when they first enter the world of non-monogamy. Within consensual non-monogamy (CNM) communities, most folks who sleep with cis men choose their partners based on referrals and endorsements. As in the world of business, it truly is who you know. Cis men who have been in the communities longer have dated and interacted with more people and, therefore, have more word of mouth. It is an unfortunate reality that many, especially cisgender women, will not date cis men they don't already know about through their friends and communities.

So, if you're a cis man exploring CNM, expect that it may take a while before you start seeing the kind of attention that others get. Focus on being kind, respectful, and honest. Respect the needs and boundaries of everyone with whom you interact. Spend lots of time getting to know other people simply as people - especially of your preferred gender to date - and form genuine friendships and connections with them free from any pressure to become sexual.

The better a person you show yourself to be, the easier it will be for you to start building the reputation you need in order to get the dates you want. Also, as much as possible, try to prepare for and manage the feelings you may have if your partner is getting more offers than you are. These things are almost never equal, and it's neither your fault nor theirs that things happen the way they do. Do your best to support each other.

Cisgender women often face the opposite problem of cis men. When they join CNM communities, cis women are often swamped with requests for dates and sex. While this can feel flattering for some and at certain times, many cis women find themselves feeling overwhelmed by the offers. The feeling can be a mix between feeling like the prettiest girl at the ball and a piece of meat surrounded by scavengers.

If you're a cis woman, figure out what you need to take care of yourself in these situations. How do you screen potential connections? What's important to you? How do you care for yourself when you feel overwhelmed or burned out? Who can you talk to about these experiences and whose recommendations can you rely upon? If your partner is struggling with a dearth of options, it may be hard for them to understand any challenges you have with too many options. Try to have sympathy for them and find ways you can each support the other.

For those who are trans or outside the gender binary, different areas and different types on non-monogamy can be more or less welcoming. In my previous home of San Francisco, and current home of Portland, Oregon, much of the polyamory community is fully aware and supportive when it comes to trans and non-binary folks. In smaller areas, or in swinger communities, it may be more challenging to find as much support. We, unfortunately, live in a culture that sometimes paints trans and non-binary folks as dangerous or ill and CNM communities are made up of people who come from the same mainstream cultural messages. These messages, of course, are wrong, but we are all steeped in them, like it or not. If you're outside the cisgender binary, you may have more of a challenge finding folks. That's unfortunate, but sadly true, especially if you're not in a major metropolitan or liberal area. Your best bet is to find the queer CNM communities nearby, if possible.

Structuring Your Relationships

● ● ● ● ● ●

So you've found some folks you want to have relationships with. How do you figure out what those relationships look like in particular? By that I mean, what are the nitty gritty details here? After all, when you're operating on the mainstream monogamy script, the expectations and agreements are pretty straightforward (or at least we assume they are). But once you put that script aside, you need to figure out what's involved in your new screenplay. There's nothing quite like transitioning to non-monogamy to force you to identify all of the assumptions inherent in the ways you've previously done relationships.

How do you determine these details? What are the different components and approaches? In this chapter, I'll give you ideas on the different ways of approaching the definition phase of your relationships.

Boundaries

For the purpose of this book, we'll be distinguishing between boundaries, agreements, and rules. Franklin Veaux and Eve Rickert in More Than Two do a great job of discussing the differences between these.

Boundaries have to do with your own self - your body, mind, time, and heart. You can set boundaries about anything that is fully under your control, but not things that aren't. For instance, I can have a boundary that I use condoms for sex with all of my partners, but I cannot have a boundary that all of my partners use condoms with all of their partners. The latter could be an agreement or a rule depending on how it is structured.

Boundaries are essential to healthy relationships because the things we say no to give our yes its meaning. Don't believe me? Entertain this fantasy then: Tonight, you're going to go out with someone you find extremely attractive. Just before you begin playing with them, a fairy whispers in your ear that they cast a spell, so whatever you ask your date for, your date will say yes, whether they want it or not. What do you feel good about asking for knowing that they'll say yes, even if it's not real? I'm guessing most of you had a visceral response there because, in this situation, consent is impossible.

When we set boundaries we take care of ourselves and of the people around us. After all, who wants to do something with a partner who is merely enduring, not enjoying, what you do together? When we tell someone no, we free them to find someone else to play with who genuinely wants what they want, rather than creating a situation where we've spared their feelings temporarily but prevented them from the enthusiastic experience they would likely prefer.

A Note on Kindness vs Niceness

Throughout this book, I talk a lot about being kind towards others. I think it's important to say a quick word about the difference between kindness and niceness. Growing up, many of us were taught growing up how to be "nice." This goes doubly for those who were socialized as women and femmes - we are expected to be nice to everyone all the time. Niceness is about the veneer we place over our true feelings and experiences. Niceness is smiling when someone is hitting on you and you're uncomfortable, and pretending things don't bother you when they do. It's being friendly to someone's face then talking about them behind their back.

Kindness is a whole other creature. Sometimes the kindest thing you can do for someone isn't very nice. Setting a boundary is kindness, and so is telling someone that they're hurting you or that they aren't living up to their own values.

Kindness is about acting from a place of wanting to help everyone do their best and be the best they can. Kindness understands that we are all imperfect and that we often cannot see the ways in which we are hurting others. Kindness has a much higher bar to clear than niceness and takes far more courage and vulnerability.

I met Ed through the atheist meetup group I joined when I moved to Savannah, GA from Honolulu, HI. Ed was younger than me, but made it clear from our first meeting that he was interested in me. He was cute, and I still didn't know many people in Savannah, so when he indicated that he'd like to hook up, I figured it was worth a shot. Things started well enough. He certainly wasn't the most skilled lover I'd been with, but he was still pretty good. I was enjoying kissing and touching him and exploring him as a new lover.

Then, when it came time to have penetrative sex, Ed started complaining about using a condom. I'm sure you can guess the things he said - "I can't feel anything," "It just doesn't feel good," "Can't I just slide in for a minute?" I wasn't hearing it, and insisted he put one on.

After a little while of penetrative sex we took a quick break and he removed the condom. He kept pushing and pushing to not use a condom, and I found myself in my bedroom, alone, in a huge empty house, with not many local friends, with a man who could easily overpower me and who didn't want to use a condom. I was getting so tired of saying no and insisting on condoms. I kind of just wanted it over with. So I gave in. We finished having sex without a condom.

Afterward, I didn't feel good about it. I felt like it was a bad decision and like I had given into pressure from him and acquiesced rather than really consenting. I wouldn't label this as rape or sexual assault necessarily, but there had definitely been an element of wearing down my resistance that made the consent shaky. I had been nice, gone along with something to stop making a fuss, rather than standing up for myself.

The next time I saw him, I told him I wanted to talk with him about what happened last time. I told him that I felt like he had pressured me and that I didn't feel good about how things had gone. I told him that it was hard for me to even talk to him about it, and I was an older woman with a lot of life experience who tends to be pretty good at standing up for herself. I let him know that the kinds of things he did might make other folks feel uncomfortable too and that they might not be able to tell him about it the way that I was telling him about it. He looked so hurt and shocked and I could tell he was genuinely upset that I hadn't felt good about what had happened.

In that moment, giving him that feedback wasn't nice. He probably felt terrible hearing about how he had impacted me. However, it was KIND to let him know how his actions had affected me. If I had stayed silent and let it hurt me in isolation, he might have never heard from someone and kept on choosing behaviors that would hurt others.

In life in general, it is helpful to find the strength and courage to be kind. I firmly believe that kindness is the way to create real, lasting change and to solidify and build deep connections. While niceness keeps the peace in the short term, it leads to built up resentment that distances us from others. Real connection can only form when we are honest and real about who we are, what we need, and how things are affecting us. Vulnerability is the key to connection and closeness and it's also what is necessary for us to find ways to be truly kind.

Common boundaries and questions to ask yourself

While it's true that everyone has slightly different boundaries, there are some areas that most folks will end up having boundaries about. Many of these boundaries are things we assume everyone "knows" they should or shouldn't do, but assuming that others share your same understanding of interpersonal boundaries can lead to complications. For instance the amount of personal space you expect everyone to give varies largely depending on what country and geographic area you come from. Here are some areas you might want to think about when thinking about your own boundaries:

Sexual risk management: What kinds of sexual behaviors are you willing to engage in with people who make certain kinds of sexual risk decisions? What do you want or need to know about someone's sexual risk management protocols before you feel good about engaging with them sexually?

Touch: Who gets to touch you? Where? How? When? How do you make decisions about what kind of touch you're open to receive? How do you want to touch? Are there kinds of touch you don't want to give?

Time: How do you allocate your time? What kinds of talks or activities are you open for or not available for during certain times? Do people in a relationship with you ever get to assume they have a certain time with you or does everything need to be booked or something in between? How much time do you need alone? How much time do you need for self-care and recovery? What makes time spent with someone more or less quality for you and how much quality time do you need?

Money: How do you allocate your money? Who gets a say in the allocation of your money? Who can access your money and how much of it can they access?

Space: With whom do you share space? How much space do you need for yourself? How do you know when you need more space? How neat or clean do you need your space to be? What can people do to show respect for your space?

Language: Are there words you like people to use to refer to you? Are there any you don't want used with or around you? Are there words you won't use for others? How do you feel about sarcasm, teasing, and criticism?

Agreements

Agreements are an empowering way to make decisions for more than one person. In an agreement, everyone affected has the power to renegotiate when needed. Agreements and rules can often look very similar, so the key piece to differentiate them is who gets to renegotiate it. If anyone who is affected by it can ask for a renegotiation session with those who created it, then it's an agreement. If someone affected by it has to "take it or leave it," then it's a rule.

Example: Carson and Kennedy agree to spend Thanksgiving together every year. After several years together, Carson begins dating Monroe seriously. Monroe's family does a big Thanksgiving celebration that is very important to them so Monroe asks Carson to join them for Thanksgiving. Carson, Kennedy, and Monroe all meet together to talk about how to handle the conflict over Thanksgiving plans.

In an agreement, we recognize that things change. What people want and need changes over time as we grow and learn and meet new people. The agreement that fit us perfectly yesterday may feel confining tomorrow. In agreements we also recognize that everyone is a person with their own wants and needs, not just the couple or triad or whatever that initially created an agreement. We honor the autonomy and empowerment of all involved parties, not just those who were there first.

How to structure an agreement

When creating an agreement in a relationship, it's important to be precise and clear. Many people lack adequate clarity in the agreements they create, leading to misagreements (see page 269).

Here are some questions to consider when making relationship agreements:

💜 What is the goal of the agreement?

💜 What details are important in this agreement and which ones aren't?

💜 Are there any assumptions underlying this agreement that haven't been identified or outlined?

💜 What are the conditions under which this can or will be renegotiated?

💜 Is this agreement time bound or ongoing?

Common agreements:

💜 Barrier use in sex: it's common for folks to make agreements about what barriers they use for sex both within their relationship and with other partners

💜 Frequency of contact

💜 Frequency of dates

💜 How to handle holidays

💜 When to disclose about new dates/partners

💜 What activities to do together

💜 When to check in with each other about activities with others

Here's an example:

> *Jax and Chase are creating an agreement about their risk-aware sex practices. They agree on several important details. One is testing frequency, which they negotiate to be every 6 months for each of them, staggered 3 months from each other so that one of them is tested every 3 months. When it comes to barriers, they agree to be fluid bonded, but with other partners want to use condoms for penetrative sex by bio dicks or dildos, and barriers for oral or hand sex to be negotiated in each situation.*
>
> *Jax's goal for the agreement is to get clear communication and to minimize the risk of transmission of STIs. Chase's goal is to feel more emotionally safe about them engaging sexually with others. In talking about their goals, they identify that Chase has an assumption that "fluid bonding" implies greater emotional closeness and commitment and that if Jax wanted to be fluid bonded with someone else, it might make Chase feel really insecure and sad.*
>
> *Jax explains that they tend to have 1-3 fluid bonded partners and may have a different approach than Chase to decisions about sexual risk, one with fewer emotional associations. Chase asks Jax to have a conversation with them before becoming fluid bonded with other partners if possible so that they can get some reassurance about their fears.*

How to re-negotiate an agreement

The only constant in life is change, so it behooves us to prepare for change in our relationships! As we make agreements, it's helpful to create them with the assumption that they will need to be renegotiated and to plan for that process.

Often, people will put off asking to re-negotiate an agreement even when they feel like it's not working well for them. Why? Well, frankly, most people haven't had great experiences asking their partner to renegotiate an agreement. Many of us have been met with anger or a fight when we let a partner know that we wanted to renegotiate.

However, when we wait to renegotiate until it's already causing us strain or resentment, or until it feels urgent, it's much harder for us to have a productive conversation about it. After all, it's reasonable for our partner to need some time to adjust and understand the change. So it's important to check in regularly about all of our agreements and to let our partners know as soon as we think we may want to renegotiate an agreement.

Here are some tips:

- 💜 Start talking to your partner as soon as you think it might be time to re-negotiate an agreement

- 💜 Let them know what agreement you want to renegotiate

- 💜 Tell them, as objectively as possible, why you want to renegotiate

- 💜 Ask them what their reactions are and what support they would like from you

- 💜 Treat this as an opportunity to brainstorm solutions with your partner; this is a chance to take a new plate to the buffet, not you taking away their toys

- 💜 If one of your partners expresses some discomfort with your current agreements with a different partner and how they are affected by them, try to listen to their concerns and ask them what they need from you

- 💜 Whenever possible, try to have all affected people re-negotiate agreements together

Rules

Franklin Veaux and Eve Rickert do an excellent job of discussing the definitions of rules vs agreements vs boundaries in their book More Than Two. For the most part, the sections here build on their definitions so I strongly recommend you review those chapters from More Than Two.

Rules are anything agreed upon by two or more people that affects others who cannot renegotiate it.

Example: Frankie and Stevie are primary partners. They have agreed that they will not spend the holidays with anyone else. Frankie starts dating Jules. After three years together, Jules asks Frankie if they can spend a holiday together. Frankie tells Jules that it is not allowed because of the rules.

Rules generally come from a good place. Folks don't tend to create rules with the goal of hurting or disempowering others. On the contrary, most rules come from a place of wanting to protect and cherish the important parts of a relationship. When you really love someone, it can be tempting to set up a rule that you will keep each other first forever no matter what. Change is scary for most people, so we will often find ways to minimize what we view as risky or challenging changes in our lives.

As we discuss elsewhere, our culture teaches most of us that a certain degree of control and coercion is normal in relationships. When coming out of monogamy, many people will try to find ways to keep things as "normal" as possible, which can lead to recreating the same kinds of control-based systems that monogamy teaches us.

Here are some of the most common rules we see in non-monogamy:

- ♥ Rules around risk-aware/safer sex practices

- ♥ Rules around holidays

- ♥ Rules around particular sexual activities

- 💜 Rules about sleepovers

- 💜 Rules about shared beds

- 💜 Rules about feelings

- 💜 Rules enshrining priority

- 💜 Rules about amount of contact with others

- 💜 Rules about allocation of money

- 💜 Rules about travel

Rules in non-monogamy can seem like a great solution to many common struggles. But there are drawbacks.

Pros:

- 💜 Easy for those creating the rules

- 💜 Feel better in the short term

- 💜 Create a feeling of safety

- 💜 Can be a way to indicate commitment to a partner

Cons:

- 💜 Disempower those not involved

- 💜 Assume things will remain static

- 💜 Often make negative feelings more likely

Are you wondering how rules might create problems in relationships? Unfortunately (for me, fortunately for you), I have a story about it.

While living in Savannah, I met this dreamy guy, Trevor. We both went to the local atheist Meetup, and the first time I met him, I just wanted to tear his clothes off. One of our first conversations was a debate about feminism where I was justifying feminist positions to him (I know, I know, hindsight is 20/20). Within a couple of weeks, we were hooking up. I told Trevor that I was polyamorous and asked if he had ever done polyamory before. Trevor was intrigued and wanted to try it.

Early in our relationship, I went away for a weekend right as Trevor was getting together with a partner he'd been seeing to break things off. I came back from my trip, had unbarriered sex with Trevor, and afterwards asked him offhand how things had gone with his transition. That's when he told me he'd had sex with the now former partner. And that he hadn't used barriers with her either. I assumed that this was a rookie mistake, that because he was new to polyamory he had just not understood that he should update me with relevant risk information before we have sex. We reviewed our agreement and moved forward.

Fast forward a couple of months. When I got surgery on my shoulder, I hadn't seen Trevor for a while because my parents were in town while I was recovering. After they left, we got together and he was taking care of me for a few weeks. About 4 weeks after my surgery, he sat me down with the "we have to talk" face and told me he had been having sex with someone for a month. They hadn't been using barriers. She was married, monogamously as far as her husband knew. And, as I'm sure you can guess by now, Trevor and I had engaged in unbarriered sexual activity since he'd been having sex with her.

I lost it. I was so angry and felt so betrayed by him. Yet, for some reason, I decided not to end things. He seemed genuinely remorseful and asked how he could re-earn my trust. So I told him I would agree to try as long as he followed a whole new set of rules. These rules were more like a trap than anything else - he had to text me when he met up with her and when they parted, he couldn't have sex with her until she told her husband about her relationship and she met me, she couldn't go inside his house, she had to start talking to me.

If you had asked me at that time, I would have told you my goal was to increase transparency and bring things back into an ethical alignment. And I thought those rules would help us do that.

In reality, I was trying to keep him from hurting me again but in a way that was guaranteed to create more hurt. I was setting traps for him to fall into. Each time he failed to live up to a rule, I created new rules. I tried to legislate away my feelings of fear and anger and insecurity, and instead I ended up only making myself feel worse.

How did it end? Well, they're now engaged and I haven't spoken to Trevor in years.

How do you know when a rule is a good idea? Here are some guiding questions:

- 💜 Is there any way to get these needs met through boundaries or agreements?

- 💜 What's the stated goal of the rule? What are the unspoken, underlying goals?

- 💜 How will you handle it when the rule is broken?

- 💜 How can this be renegotiated?

- 💜 How will we know when this rule isn't needed anymore?

Communication

I'll admit, as a therapist I'm usually of the mindset that more communication is usually better. Why? Well, communication is how we help other people win with us. In a beautiful utopian paradise, all of my partners would know exactly what I want and need at all times. They would anticipate my every whim, possibly even before I was conscious of them.

In our real, non-utopian world, however, my partners cannot know what will work for me unless and until I tell them about it. In monogamy, folks often assume that their partners are on their same page; they think there must be some standardized rule book about how relationships work. While that's not even true in monogamy (just look at research on what people consider cheating!), it's especially untrue in non-monogamy. Out here, there is no script to follow. So, if we want our partners to give us what we need, we have to ask for it. And, in complementary fashion, we have to get good at receiving the communication from our partners too.

In this chapter, we'll talk about what you need to hone your communication skills and help your relationships flow more smoothly!

Receiving communication well

While most communication tools focus on how to GIVE good communication, far fewer discuss how to receive communication well. Aside from reflective listening, most folks don't learn how to receive communication, especially challenging communication. So here are some discreet tools to use when someone is talking with you about something hard.

Reflect, then speak

This one is my favorite tool when I'm noticing my emotions are flaring hard or I'm feeling particularly defensive. When I'm having trouble hearing and instead just waiting for a chance to challenge and disagree, I'll often turn to this tool to help me get back to being open and vulnerable.

How to do it:

Person 1 begins by talking about their thoughts/feelings/understanding about the topic while Person 2 listens. When Person 1 is done talking, Person 2 summarizes and reflects what they heard Person 1 say and then asks if they got it right and included everything. If they missed or misheard anything, Person 1 fills in or clarifies until they feel completely heard. Then, they switch roles and Person 2 says what they need to say while Person 1 summarizes and reflects until person 2 feels fully heard.

Why it works:

This tool is excellent at forcing you to build empathy and understanding. Since you don't get to jump in with your defenses until the other person feels heard and understood, it's much much harder for things to escalate or for you to act from a place of overwhelming emotions. Also, when people feel heard, they are more likely to work from places of compassion and kindness than when they feel like they have to fight to be heard. Knowing that you will be heard helps you wait to say what you have to say. That pause ensures that you're acting from what your partner is ACTUALLY saying and not just what your brain wants to fill in.

Reflect and clarify

One of the biggest causes of fights and conflicts is misunderstandings. Each of us has our own beliefs which filter how we receive the information from the world. Sometimes those filters lead us to misunderstand what someone is trying to tell us.

▌ How to do it:

When your partner is saying something that is bringing up challenging emotions in you, follow these steps

1. Reflect what you heard them say

2. Ask a clarifying question

It's important to monitor how you phrase your questions and what tone you use. It's easy for this tool to read as sarcastic even when you don't mean it that way. For instance, avoid extreme statements (anything involving always, never, have to, can't, must). When you're reflecting, try to focus on having warmth, openness, kindness, and curiosity in your voice rather than anger or defensiveness. A statement like "I'm hearing that you're upset with what I said. Was it my tone or the words I used or both?" can come across VERY differently when delivered sarcastically than when delivered from a space of understanding.

▌ Why it works:

It's much better to clarify something BEFORE you respond than to start a disagreement based on a way you misunderstood each other.

Hit Pause

When we're in the middle of a discussion, many of us feel pressure to respond to things as quickly as possible, even if it means our mouth is moving before our brain has figured out what we are going to say. Many of us aren't comfortable with silence of even a few seconds. We're so uncomfortable with silence that in training to become a therapist I was told to wait 7 seconds before speaking after asking a question in order to entice the clients to speak more. Seven seconds.

How to do it:

💜 If you notice a swirl of thoughts in your mind when it's your turn to talk, ask for a moment to think

💜 Take a few deep breaths

💜 Think about your possible responses and notice how your body reacts to each one. If you notice your body tensing or becoming more agitated, check to see if that response is real for you or if it's about meeting some outside standard

💜 Wait to speak until you have a fairly clear handle on what you're going to say

Why it works:

Sometimes our brain needs time to sort things out, especially if we've just heard something upsetting and/or surprising. Taking time to breathe, and not say anything until it's sorted, prevents you from saying things you'll later regret or that you don't actually mean.

Time Out

I know, you hear "time out" and you think of kids. But there's a reason that asking someone to walk away for a minute works well to address strong emotional reactions. Our limbic system, once activated, takes time to calm back down, even if the upsetting thing is no longer present. The amount of time for that recovery varies from 15-30 minutes, or enough time to walk away, make a nice cup of tea, and drink a bit of it.

How to do it:

💜 Before you ever use one, talk with your partner about time outs

💜 Agree on a code word or phrase you'll use to take a time out (e.g, I need a time out, Halt, Red, etc.)

- ♥ Agree on a hand or body signal you will use to signal a need for time out if words are hard

- ♥ Practice with each other when emotions aren't high so you can each get used to calling time out

- ♥ When you notice strong emotions coming up for you, evaluate if you're still able to have a productive conversation

- ♥ If you notice that the conversation seems to be escalating and/ or that you're having trouble listening well, it's probably time for a time out

- ♥ If you check in with yourself and notice your anger, sadness, fear, resentment, upset, or jealousy levels are at or above a 7/10, it's probably time for a time out

- ♥ Use your agreed upon phrase and/or gesture to call for a time out

- ♥ Tell your partner when you'll come back to finish the discussion (generally at least 20 minutes and no more than a few hours is best)

- ♥ When the time is up, return to the conversation (it can be helpful to start with the "Reflect, then speak" exercise)

Why it works:

When you give your body time to clear out adrenaline and your limbic system time to calm down, you're far more likely to be able to have a productive conversation.

Things that stop you from talking

We all generally go into our relationships with the best of intentions. We're going to show up, communicate, be vulnerable, be real! Then reality hits us and we find ourselves struggling to live up to the standards we want to meet. In particular, folks often find themselves getting worse at communication the deeper the partnership goes. After all, when things are casual you've got very little on the line if you find out something isn't a fit. If you're married and cohabitating and you worry that this conversation might be the beginning of the end? Those are some high stakes!

Numerous things can get in our way, especially when we're looking at struggles with communication. Here we'll focus on two specific issues: fear of their reaction to what you're saying, and shame and guilt.

Fear of their reaction

A major factor that often prevents clear, honest, adequate communication is operating from a fear of how someone will react to what we need to tell them.

John was pretty new to non-monogamy when we started dating, but he was excited to try. We agreed to be up front and open with each other about when we were seeing other people and to run things by each other first. The first time I had a date-type activity scheduled with someone else, John gave his okay as I planned it. But, come the morning of said date, John was inconsolable. He was crying, and afraid, and struggling with what he had already agreed to. After about an hour of listening to his fear and concerns, I told him that I thought he should journal about it and I left for my date. I assumed that this was just the result of him being new to this and that after he saw how excited I was to see him when I got back, he would feel better and we would move forward.

Things did get a bit better for a little while, but then it was time for me to go into the Army on active duty. We had agreed to continue dating long distance and to keep checking in with each other about developing new sexual or romantic connections. I encouraged him to get out there and date and even tried to set him up with folks I knew. Within the first week at my Officer's Basic, I had met someone I really wanted to hook up with, so I followed our agreement and texted him to ask permission to do more than make out with Ken. John texted back a no.

I don't think I had ever considered the real possibility of getting a no for one of these requests. I was surprised and caught off balance. Starting the next day, John and I were on video chat every day talking about my desire to hookup with Ken. And every day, John was crying inconsolably at the idea. After 4 days of an hour or more comforting him about my desire to do exactly what I had told him I would want to do, I finally snapped. I told him that I didn't understand why this was such a big issue now - I had told him who I was and what I needed, I had given him trial runs in safer contexts. I had even hooked up with his friend so that he could have an ideal situation. I vented my frustration and anger. It seemed like John heard me and within a day, he had decided he was ready for me to hook up with Ken.

I should have known that this was him acquiescing, not actually agreeing. While I thoroughly enjoyed the rest of my Officer's Basic, including enjoying trysts with a few people, I started hearing from mutual friends that John was not doing well. Though he had told me he agreed to everything I was doing, in private he was still crying and struggling. I eventually broke things off with him because what I wanted made him miserable and what he wanted made me miserable.

In the story above, both John and I did things that ended up discouraging good, clear communication. For my part, by snapping and venting my frustration with John I made him feel like he couldn't be honest with me about how hard non-monogamy was for him. For his part, he made me feel like I couldn't trust his "yes" or "no" because he had said yes to too many things he wasn't actually a yes to. He was saying yes because he wanted to be with me, not because he was actually okay with me seeing someone else, but because he knew "no" would have likely meant a breakup.

Furthermore, he'd made it hard for me to be open with him about what I needed because, while he was having these difficult reactions to my needs, he wasn't actively working on processing and moving through them. I couldn't take a long term situation where, every time I wanted to see someone else, it resulted in days of emotional processing and support. I needed him to just say no if this wasn't going to work for him.

When we approach communication from a place of trying to avoid a negative reaction from our partner, we will almost always end up making things worse than they started. Whenever you notice yourself feeling like you can't communicate clearly and openly with your partner, that's a huge red flag that needs to be addressed immediately.

Shame and Guilt

Shame and guilt are highly effective at silencing us when we most need to talk. Guilt is the feeling we get when we believe we have done something bad; shame is what we feel when we believe we are bad. And sometimes, when we have something to tell our partner, we begin to worry about what it might mean about us. Here's an example of how guilt and shame might show up.

Carl and I had been dating for a while when I first felt some pangs of jealousy come up. Well, I know NOW that they were pangs of jealousy, but at the time I was unwilling to consider that I could be feeling jealous. After all, I'm the therapist and educator who teaches people how to develop compersion and let go of their desires to control or coerce people! I'm supposed to be "better" at this than other people!

When I told Carl I was having some challenging feelings, I think I initially labeled them as frustration or sadness. He asked me a few questions about what I was noticing in my body, what my thoughts were, and what was bringing them up and then said to me "it sounds like you're jealous." I vehemently denied this. I couldn't possibly be jealous! But after he talked to me about it for a bit, I realized that he might be right.

So why hadn't I seen it that way? Why hadn't I been able to accept that jealousy might be what I was feeling? I was ashamed that I might be less than "perfect" at polyamory. The way I thought of myself was as someone who ONLY feels compersion, not jealousy. So to admit that I was jealous made me feel like I was doing something wrong.

Luckily, Carl was able to normalize my feelings and help me accept that I could have those feelings. Funnily enough, once he did, I felt much less discomfort and upset than I had initially. Acknowledging that I was jealous took a lot of the sting out of the emotion and helped me move on from it.

Most people at some point end up feeling or wanting something they think they "shouldn't" because of who they are or who they want to be. And if our brains were perfectly rational machines, maybe we wouldn't. However, humans are complicated, messy creatures and our hearts, our minds, and our fears sometimes don't quite line up. When we face that internal conflict, when we worry that what's true for us means something bad about us, we may find ourselves clamming up when we most need to be talking.

In general, if you notice yourself avoiding talking about something, that's the very topic you likely most need to be discussing. If you notice yourself hitting up against internal conflicts, try talking them out with a good friend or professional helper first. Someone on the outside may be able to help you get some more clarity before you bring the issue to your partner. And if you're still struggling, the Difficult Conversations worksheet (page 91) can be really helpful. Pay special attention when scanning the feelings chart to see if there are any feelings that you may be having trouble acknowledging.

Difficult Conversations

In an ideal world, our relationships would be easy peasy. Conflict would be a fiction, our partners would meet our needs effortlessly and without even asking, and we would find ourselves surrounded by fulfillment and joy. In the real world, we are most likely to get what we want and need when we ask for it. While that sounds so simple in writing, the act of asking for what we want can bring up loads of fear and uncertainty.

When we ask for what we want, we are vulnerable. Most folks in our culture aren't used to acting in a space of vulnerability. We socialize those assigned as men to "man up" and never talk about what hurts or saddens them. We socialize those assigned as women to take care of others and that advocating for themselves is "selfish." These messages lead folks of all genders to avoid bringing up important, challenging conversations until the needs are so pressing that they cannot be ignored anymore. What could have been a quick, relatively low challenge conversation, instead is only brought up once it's an emergency.

Asking for what we want, letting someone know something hurt us, transitioning relationships, these conversations bring up anxiety and fear in most of us. And yet, the longer we wait to have the conversation, the harder it will be. Problems snowball over time, they don't get smaller. And, while we may have a plethora of solution options available if we discuss something early on, the more it festers, the fewer the options that tend to be available to us in the end.

Personally, I've both messed up and succeeded with difficult conversations. I'll start with my less than stellar story:

Despite my current reputation, I haven't always been great at boundaries and tough conversations. Like a lot of people, I grew up in a family where there wasn't a lot of space for me using my no and making requests. Sometimes things would be fine, but other times things would blow up, so I learned to just "shelter in place" to avoid conflicts. That is, when I sense a conflict, I shut down, making myself and my feelings and needs as small as possible, and wait until the storm passes. When I'm noticing strong emotions from someone else, therefore, I find myself clamming up and just assuming that they would bulldoze me into giving them what they want regardless of my thoughts and feelings.

Fast forward to the relationship I had with the man I would marry. I built with him a relationship that was all about his needs and his wants. I worked so hard to make sure his needs were met and I kept telling myself that if I just did the right things, he would know and start meeting my needs. Did I ever tell him those needs? Ha! No. I just kept hoping and feeling sad and resentful and angry.

The thing is, I taught my ex that I didn't have any real wants or needs because I never asked for them. Once I started graduate school, I started recognizing that communication was key to getting what I needed from him. So I tried out this new idea... badly. Through passive aggressive means, I tried to hint to him what I wanted and needed. Or I would get frustrated and blow up at him. I didn't yet know how to let him know what I wanted or needed in the moment in a way he could hear it, so even if he would have potentially wanted to give those things to me, I was basically guaranteeing that I wouldn't get them anyway. I didn't know how to have a difficult conversation in a way that we could both walk away feeling great about it.

More recently, I've been working hard on practicing vulnerability and taking a chance that the people I love will give me what I want or need if I just ask for it. One of my recent relationships, with Carl, took this to a whole new level.

Early on in the relationship, I told Carl that I was working on choosing to be vulnerable and that I often found myself retreating behind my walls when things got hard. Because I clued him in early, he knew what to look for to see if I needed some help getting through tough conversations. He explicitly encouraged me to let him know what I wanted and needed so that we could talk about it in the open.

When I had something to talk about, I could let him know I was feeling nervous about bringing it up. He would listen attentively and reflect what I said. Then I could either volunteer what I needed from him or he would ask me questions about what I needed. The more I took the chance to ask for what I wanted, and the more it went well, the easier it became. I found that choosing vulnerability and courage, instead of making me feel weak, frustrated, or hurt, made me feel even stronger and more supported. In our relationship, it also let him feel comfortable knowing that if there was something I needed from him, he would hear it from me.

In this chapter, I'll give you a few different tools to help you approach difficult conversations. The elements I'll cover are: figuring out what you need to talk about, brainstorming solution options, coming up with the phrasing most likely to be successful, psyching yourself up for the conversation, developing a plan to receive challenging feedback, and self and relationship care after a tough conversation.

Part 1 - What are you talking about

While it may sound simple, sometimes figuring out what you need to talk about can be more complicated than you expected. For instance, the topic we think we want to talk about may be cover for a deeper problem that we haven't yet prepared ourselves to talk about.

Troy and I had been dating for 7 months when he moved across the country from Georgia to California to be closer to me. He moved into my house, sharing my same bedroom. I thought that I could be okay with this kind of arrangement, and assured myself that we'd gotten along great before when we'd spent long periods of time together. However, the longer we lived together, the more suffocated I felt. He was just ALWAYS THERE and I didn't know until we were living together just how much space I really needed.

Rather than talk about this, instead I started picking fights with him. I critiqued him for the smallest, most ridiculous things. One time, I even criticized him the whole way through making me a quesadilla. He started to get hurt and frustrated, for good reason, and I just couldn't figure out why I was so on edge and critical. I was slowly pushing him away to try to somehow get the space I was missing.

He, in turn, started clinging harder to me. He wanted more time, more attention, more quality of interaction. I just got worse and worse, and he got more and more needy. We were driving each other bananas.

Eventually, things came to a head and I asked him to move out in order to save the relationship. He needed time to find a new place to live, so I told him he could stay with me during that time. However, I was still feeling suffocated, and started pressuring him to move out even faster. He felt sad and confused, again for good reason, and I couldn't explain to him why I was struggling so much to stay true to my promise. Very shortly after he moved out, we broke up. Things had gotten too far into negatives for us to be able to recover.

In this relationship, I kept thinking that what was bothering me was the dishes, or where he put his clothes, or whether he helped out with laundry. However, none of these were the real issue. I could've talked for hours and hours about the minutiae (and did), and wouldn't have gotten any closer to solving the problem. I felt too guilty for having told him I would be okay with him moving in to take it back and ask him to move out. I felt like changing my mind would ruin our relationship, so I talked instead about everything else BUT my real problem.

When you're determining what you need to talk about, take some time to sit with your concerns. If you're noticing lots of little nitpicking elements, ask yourself if something else is below it. Really give yourself some time and space to examine whether the issue you're talking about is really the issue, or whether it's the cover for something much bigger.

Part 2 - Brainstorm solutions

Sometimes when we've noticed an issue, we think we already know exactly what we want from the other person. This might be fine - if I'm noticing that I get nervous when I haven't heard from a partner in a few days, a solution might be for them to text me at least once a day. However, sometimes the solution we think we want may not be the best solution for us, our partner, or our relationship.

It's easy when we notice a problem to latch onto what our brain tells us will fix it. I think this is where a lot of potentially problematic rules come from - our brain says "the problem will go away if you can make them not do x" and so you tell your partner not to do x. What happens here sometimes is that we have confused what we need with how we want that need to be met.

Our needs are totally valid. If your need is for lots of physical touch, that is totally okay. We will often do best in relationships, though, when we give our partners space in the process of figuring out how to meet those needs. Humans, in general, tend to do better with solutions that they feel they had a say in. If you think about it, which bosses have you most enjoyed working for - the ones who told you how to do every little thing or the ones who told you their large scale goal and let you suggest how to meet it?

Once you notice a problem, feel free to listen to the initial solutions your brain provides. If you want to have a great problem solving session, you may want to be sure that you don't become so attached to those specific solutions. Learning how to brainstorm, to create a space where the goal is to come up with as many ideas as possible BEFORE choosing which one to go with, can be a very helpful skill in preventing this kind of stuckness. Before you talk with your partner, try to come up with several possible solutions that could work for you, and then also give them room to brainstorm some solutions too. After all, your partner is more likely to feel heard and cared for if they get to come up with ideas, not just follow yours.

Part 3 - Find your phrasing

As a psychologist, I have seen over and over again how much of a difference the words we use can make in how someone receives us. If you've done something that doesn't work for someone, imagine how differently they might receive "That was shitty!" versus "Hey honey, I felt sad and hurt when you did that. Can we talk about this and figure out how to move forward?"

When we're upset, most of us are drawn to talk from our emotions. While this isn't necessarily bad, it's prone to come out less skillfully than we might otherwise prefer. If we're looking at the goal of this conversation as to find a solution with our partner, then it matters more, in some ways, how they will receive our communication than how emotionally satisfying it would feel to deliver it. When we talk to our partners with phrasing filled with accusations and insulting implications, we are likely to pull out defensiveness from them, leaving us in a fight instead of in a collaborative co-creation of solutions.

How do you honor what you're feeling while also sharing your message in a way your partner is more likely to receive?

"I" statements: As much as possible, focus on "I" statements instead of "you" statements. In a good "I" statement, we focus on what we observed, felt, and need rather than on attacking our partner.

Owning your feelings: While I don't necessarily agree that no one can EVER make you feel something, I do think that we do ourselves a disservice when we abdicate responsibility for our feelings. In fact, just naming a feeling can often help us feel less caught up in it and more able to process it in a healthy fashion. It's also helpful because once we know what we feel we can more easily figure out what we might need.

Owning your interpretations: Our brains are designed to make meaning of what we encounter in the world. As such, our brains will often fill in a backstory for why someone would do something. While that backstory could be accurate, it is more often about us than about the other person. When we take responsibility for the narrative we have ascribed to someone, we acknowledge that we don't necessarily know why they did something and give ourselves space to be wrong and them space to fill in the blanks.

Avoid extremes: Certain language patterns tend to come up in conflicts and end up being counterproductive. Words like always and never are often signs that we're making a generalization that is bound to be untrue. When we use these words, we can end up in a fight over whether they are actually always or never instead of talking about how to solve the problem we're having.

Look at these two examples and see which you might receive better if your partner said them to you:

Example 1: You left the dishes in the sink again. You do this all the time and it makes me so angry. You just don't even care about what I want.

Example 2: I noticed that the dishes are still dirty. When I'm told that a chore is going to get done and it doesn't, I feel frustrated and angry. The story I tell myself is that what I want doesn't matter. Can you help me understand what happened?

If you're like most people, hearing example 1 would likely trigger some defensiveness in you. You might talk about how you don't, in fact, always leave the dishes in the sink, or about how your partner didn't give you enough time, or that you had other things happening, or that they're making too big of a deal out of it.

Receiving example 2, however, is more likely to bring out our empathy and understanding, especially if delivered in a caring, vulnerable tone. Our partner in this example is letting us know about how something has hurt them, and if we care about our partner, we're likely to want to figure out a way that we can both be happier with this outcome.

In general, the Tough Conversations Worksheet (page 91) is designed to help you find the kindest, most caring language possible for talking about a conflict. But if you're struggling, remember those tips above and see whether you would react defensively to receiving something similar to what you want to say.

Part 4 - Receiving challenging feedback

If you have relationships, at some point you're going to mess up. More than that, you're probably going to mess up BIG. None of us are perfect, so no matter how hard we try, we are bound to have blind spots and challenges. When this happens, we're going to need to be able to receive the feedback that we messed up in a way that leads to growth and connection rather than to greater harm and heartache.

I've put this section on receiving challenging feedback right after the one on phrasing because these two concepts go hand in hand. If you're unable to receive even the most caring, empathetic feedback about something you've messed up, you're going to struggle to have a meaningful relationship. After all, your partner can't tell you you're always doing things right unless they're lying to you.

It's important to prepare yourself to receive challenging feedback before you START a tough conversation as much as it is before you RECEIVE a tough conversation. Why? Well, what if when you start the tough conversation it uncovers something you've been doing that's been contributing to the problem? Or what if your partner just cannot give you what you want to resolve the situation?

Preparing yourself to receive tough feedback involves 1) accepting that you may not get what you want 2) that you might be wrong and 3) that being wrong or not getting what you want isn't the end of the world. If you notice yourself having a strong emotional reaction to feedback, take a breath (or a time out if you need it) and try to figure out what you can do to move forward. Don't get stuck in trying to be "right" or "perfect." Instead, let yourself be flawed and think about how you can choose actions moving forward that align with your values and your best self.

Many of us struggle to receive challenging feedback. For much of my life, I was such a deep perfectionist that any criticism or critique was crushing. I just couldn't stand to face any evidence that I wasn't as perfect as I wished I could be, because the only other option was to be a shameful failure. So how did I avoid or respond to these critiques? Well sometimes I would lie to avoid them or to hide my guilt, sometimes I would convince myself that the person offering them was mean or wrong, and sometimes I would just collapse in on myself and spiral down into shame and sorrow.

None of those strategies are helpful ones in the long term. One of my big turning points around this came on my internship. When I started my internship, I was living in a new place, newly in the Army, and doing kinds of therapy and testing that I hadn't necessarily done before. I knew I was smart and could pick things up quickly, but I also knew that I just couldn't expect to already be great at everything I was doing. After all, I was surrounded by problems I had never faced before, in a setting I was new to, and in a new identity for myself.

For the first several months, I took lots of hits to my fragile self-image. I was getting criticism, most of it constructive, very often. I was running up against the edges of what I could just quickly pick up, and instead having to learn how to be in the struggle, and be okay with not being great at something immediately. I couldn't bluff my way out of this, I had to just learn slowly and be okay with not being perfect.

It was hard, and I mean really hard, to start letting go of those patterns. But the more I worked on it, the less anxiety, worry, and pain I experienced. The kinds of small critiques

that used to wreck me I could now accept and take in stride.
As I grew in that way, I started learning and progressing more
quickly because I was able to get out of my own way.

When you're planning a tough conversation, give yourself a few minutes to develop a strategy for coping with tough feedback that you might receive. How can you take care of yourself? How can you continue to show up with caring and empathy and vulnerability if you're feeling hurt or wanting to get defensive? If you need ideas, go back to the section on receiving communication to see if there are tools that might help.

Part 5 - Psyching yourself up

Starting a conversation is often the hardest part. If we think of relationships as having inertia, starting a tough conversation is the equivalent to applying a force to either start or stop motion. We're swimming against the current, and taking a risk that this conversation could lead to a big change. That change might be a good one, or it might be one that we don't want. However, we cannot just avoid these conversations forever.

If you're noticing that you're nervous or worried about starting a tough conversation, that is totally okay. There is nothing wrong with you if this is hard for you! Most of us struggle with asking for what we want or with telling our partner that something isn't working for us. I've had people in my classes find out that they've been using words with each other for over a decade that their partner didn't like - over 10 years with no conversation! However, hard isn't the same as impossible. Nor does it mean you can avoid it or opt out. Instead, you might find it helpful to figure out how to get yourself prepared emotionally to start these conversations.

Some strategies folks find helpful to get them ready for a tough conversation include:

💜 Planning out what you're going to say (like filling out the Tough Conversations worksheet, **page 91**)

- 💜 Having friends give you encouragement

- 💜 Practicing the conversation with a therapist or person you're close to

- 💜 Coming up with a mantra or phrase that you can repeat when you're feeling nervous

- 💜 Reminding yourself that your needs matter

Part 6 - Self and relationship care for Tough Conversations

Sometimes having a tough conversation can be hard on us, our partner, and our relationship. After all, we're changing the course of what's been happening and starting something new. This means that after a conversation, we may need to figure out how to best care for ourselves and our relationship.

Self Care: What is it that works best for you to recover from a tough conversation? Is it doing the laundry? Having a hangout with friends? Taking a bath? Getting in the shower? Cuddling? Hearing affirmations from your partner? Tune into what would feel good for you and take the chance to ask for it.

Relationship Care: Think about what you might want to feel close to your partner after a tough conversation. Then, think about what kinds of things they might want in order to feel close after the conversation. Are they someone who needs processing time alone? Will they want touch? Will it be helpful for you two to go do something together or will you need some recovery time apart? Will it help to book a date so you have something on the calendar or do you need breathing room?

Don't be afraid to ask your partner what might help them feel better when the conversation is over. There's no right or wrong answers, and you're not obligated to do something just because they ask. However, you might find that opening the door to the conversation helps you both feel more heard and more secure.

Prep sheet for tough conversations

Feelings
What are your feelings?

Sad						Mad						Scared					
guilty	ashamed	depressed	lonely	bored	tired	hurt	hostile	angry	selfish	hateful	critical	confused	rejected	helpless	submissive	insecure	anxious
remoreseful	stupid	inferior	isolated	apathetic	sleepy	distant	sarcastic	frustrated	jealous	irritated	skeptical	bewildered	discouraged	insignificant	inadequate	embarrassed	overwhelmed

Joyful						Powerful						Peaceful					
excited	sensuous	energetic	cheerful	creative	hopeful	aware	proud	respected	appreciated	important	faithful	content	thoughtful	intimate	loving	trusting	nurturing
daring	fascinating	stimulating	amused	playful	optimistic	surprised	successful	worthwhile	valuable	discerning	confident	relaxed	pensive	responsive	serene	secure	thankful

Prep sheet for tough conversations

Trigger/cause

What objectively happened that caused it? What would a video tape show?

Meaning

What is the story you're telling yourself about it? Why does your brain think this happened?

Compassion and curiosity

What is the kindest story you could tell about it? What questions could you ask your partner to find out what was going on for them?

What now

What do you want or need from them? To be heard? To understand? Some specific action? The more specific your request, the easier it is for them to give it to you.

Format for the conversation:

💜 Ask if it's a good time. If not, schedule a time

💜 Lead with vulnerability. A great way to do this is by talking about how you're feeling about having the conversation

💜 Own your feelings. Tell them the feelings you've been having from item (a)

💜 Tell them the objective situation and what the meaning was that you made of it. It can be helpful to preface your meaning by using a phrase like "the story I'm telling myself" or "my brain is telling me"

💜 Ask them a question or ask for what you need

Example:

"Hi honey, is this a good time to talk? I probably need 15-20 minutes. I'm feeling nervous about having this conversation because I'm worried that it'll upset you or cause a rift in our relationship. I'm feeling sad and hurt.

"When you said you didn't want to dominate me this weekend, after talking about how excited you were to dominate Regina, my brain told me that I did something to make you not want to top me. The story I've been telling myself is that I did something wrong or I'm not as pretty as she is. I doubt that's really what was going on, but I'm having trouble figuring out where it was coming from. Can you help me understand what led to this change?"

Risk

● ● ● ● ● ●

When folks first start exploring non-monogamy, they often worry about the risks. What about sexually transmitted infections? What if your partner leaves you? What if you lose friends? When even considering non-monogamy some people see red flags all over and tell themselves that it would be too risky for them to even consider.

The thing about humans as creatures is that we are biologically encouraged to over-perceive risk, especially in novel situations. Think about it this way: when encountering a new creature, what is most likely to keep you alive? Assuming the creature is friendly and harmless or assuming the creature is a threat? In our brains, we are deeply wired to assume something is risky until we're proven otherwise. However, this tendency also causes us to underestimate the riskiness of things we are frequently exposed to.

Here's some concrete examples:

💜 You are much more likely to die in a car crash than in an airplane, but most people feel more fear and perceive more riskiness in flying

💜 You're more likely to die very close to, or inside of, your home but people perceive more riskiness the farther they are from home

💜 You are more likely to be assaulted by someone you already know, but most of us perceive strangers as more risky

All of this is to say that humans as a species aren't generally accurate at assessing risk. What feels risky to us often isn't as risky as it feels, and what feels safe sometimes isn't. Our brain struggles to distinguish between discomfort (or lack of knowledge) and danger.

When we talk about risk as related to non-monogamy, this understanding of human brains is of the utmost importance. As you start something new, you are likely to see more risk than is realistically present. You are likely to have your brain throwing up warning signals all over the place, even if there isn't any real danger present. You are going to struggle to accurately assess your risks. So this chapter is intended to give you the objective information you need to make decisions about what risks you want to accept.

That's the other thing: there is no risk-free way to do non-monogamy. Just as there is no risk-free way to drive, or to do monogamy for that matter! When it comes to risk, the most any of us can do is attempt to manage and mitigate, not eliminate. The only risk-free way to live life would be in a climate-controlled bunker with enough food for a whole life, no sharp edges or corners, and no other people. Do you want that life? I know I don't. So your mission, then, is to decide which risks are worth taking in order to live a rich, fulfilling life.

When all we focus on is risks, we lose track of the other side of that coin: rewards. For a couple of years, I was a skydiver. Every time I stepped out of the door of an airplane, I was taking a risk. But that feeling of flying through the air, the freedom of floating through the sky, the beautiful views when under canopy, all of those were so worth the small risk involved. (An aside - did you know that hot air ballooning is more dangerous than skydiving? Yet another example of how we don't accurately estimate risk).

The greatest rewards we can find are often just outside of our comfort zone. When my marriage ended and I was stepping into non-monogamy, I was taking a huge risk, and I did have some big losses. I lost a lot of friends, I narrowed my dating pool, and I had to start writing my own script for how my life would look. Some of those risks, and resulting problems, were tough. I still struggle with how many folks won't date someone who's non-monogamous. However, I am much happier now that I'm living a life where I get to be myself and enjoy many wonderful loves in my life.

What are the risks involved in non-monogamy? They fall into three categories:

💜 Physical risk, bad things happening to our bodies

💜 Emotional risks, the big time feels, trouble and strife within and without our relationships

💜 Social risks, ways our friends, family, and community might react to our non-monogamy

In this chapter, I'm going to cover all three types of risks and what you can do to manage the amount of risk you're taking on.

Physical Risk

Most often, when I talk to folks about the risks they're worried about with non-monogamy, the ones they bring up first are related to STIs. STI stands for sexually transmitted infection, and covers a wide variety of type and severity of infections.

Our culture, you probably know, has a LOT of weirdness around sex. Sex is everywhere around us. It's used to sell just about anything, and yet having frank and open conversations about sex is frowned upon. Sex is dirty and wrong and gross but you should save it for the person you most love.

Due to our collective hangups around sex, most people have stronger fears about and aversions to infections they have decided are STIs than to other types of infections. In reality, the line between the common cold or mononucleosis and the herpes simplex virus (HSV) or chlamydia is kind of a murky one.

So how do we define an STI? Is it anything that can be transmitted through sexual contact? If so, why aren't colds, flu, and mono considered STIs since they're often transmitted through kissing and sharing saliva? If HPV can live literally anywhere on your body, and we can't test for it except on the cervix, then how do we know when it was sexually transmitted vs moved from another part of the body when wiping or masturbating?

If it seems like I'm saying that STIs are never a big deal, or that you shouldn't worry about them and just bareback everyone, that's not at all what I'm saying. What I am trying to do is shake off some of the shame and stigma you've likely internalized through years and years of living in a sex negative culture.

I think it's really important when we talk about these kinds of things that we are honest about the real implications most of the STIs have on people's real lives. For most people, most STIs aren't actually a big deal. If you're testing regularly, the likelihood that any STI other than HIV or Hepatitis will be life threatening for you is pretty close to zero. Herpes, which has some of the greatest social stigma, has almost no negative long term health consequences - it's painful and can be unsightly, but it's not DANGEROUS. When people talk about STIs they tend to think and act around them as though they are necessarily worse or more problematic than other infections.

It's no surprise that things associated with sex are given a worse rep in a culture that is hugely sex negative! For instance, the flu kills people every year and can be contracted all sorts of ways, but no one tells you you're dirty or shameful for getting the flu. Chicken pox can be deadly and can lead to shingles in adults, but no one shames folks for having had chicken pox.

Our culture is terrible at taking a clear, unbiased view of things related to sex. That includes consensual sexual behaviors and STIs. For those of us raised in or around in the 80s and 90s when AIDS was a death sentence, we have LOTS of internalized messages that say that unprotected sex is necessarily wrong and shameful. If we want to move beyond these hangups, we need to think about WHY we treat sexually transmitted infections differently than others and start figuring out how to undo those scripts.

In general, I'm of the opinion that everyone gets to do whatever they want with their own body. That includes deciding to not use any barriers for any reason they want. The part of my brain that wants to judge them for that decision is every bit as wrong as the parts of other people's brains who want to judge us for doing non-monogamy. What matters is that everyone is giving informed consent, not what conclusion they come to from there. The key to informed consent is that someone knows all the information pertinent to their decision before making it.

It's also important to note that testing gives us a snapshot of someone's situation, it doesn't necessarily tell us everything. Some STIs have dormancy windows of up to 6 weeks, so if someone had any sex between 6 weeks before their last test date and when they are having sex with you, you are accepting the risk that their status has changed. If you can't accept that risk, you will necessarily need to be much more restricted in who you play with and in what kinds of risk aware sex procedures you use. If you want some really in depth information about different STIs, More Than Two by Franklin Veaux and Eve Rickert has an extensive chapter on them with great information -- both for those diagnosed and for those whose partners are diagnosed.

This brings up another point - STI transmission isn't the only physical risk. Pregnancy, injury, and disability are also real risks associated with sex (well, pregnancy is only a risk if someone with sperm is playing with someone with eggs). So when you're thinking about how to assess your physical risk, don't leave those elements out.

How do you assess and manage this risk? There are several components:

1. Regular STI testing and health check ups
2. Good communication
3. Use of barriers
4. More communication

Testing

Regardless of how many people you're having sex with, it's never a bad idea to do regular STI testing. What does regular mean? Well, if you're not having very much sex or only engaging in lower risk activities (e.g. use of toys, hands), then once a year might be frequently enough for you. For other folks, getting tested every 3-6 months is probably a better fit. How many months exactly is right for you? Well that depends on your risk profile, health insurance, and access to care.

In an ideal world, those of us with multiple partners would get tested every 3 months. This gives you the greatest fidelity of your current status and also lets you address any issues early on. Not everyone can afford or access that kind of testing, so you can take some creative means of gaining more fidelity. For instance, if you have 2 partners with whom you don't use barriers, but each of you can only get tested once every 6 months, you can stagger your testing dates so that there's a new set of results for one of you every 2 months.

 When you go to get tested, be sure to ask what they are actually testing for. Most clinics won't test for HSV unless you press them on it. If you have a penis, you aren't getting tested for HPV. While the ideal testing scenario involves blood, urine, and swabs of the mucous membranes (throat, anus, vagina), many clinic won't offer swabs at all or without significant prompting.

Simply going to a clinic and saying "Give me the full panel" could mean you're getting testing for HIV, gonorrhea, chlamydia, and syphilis, or it could mean you're getting all of those, HSV 1 and 2 type specific, Hepatitis C, and screens for Bacterial Vaginosis (BV), trichomoniasis, and "water warts" (molloscum contagiosum). You won't know unless you ask, and you may struggle to get the tests you want even when you do ask.

 You also want to get regular health checkups for other issues. Hemorrhoids affect half the population or more and can cause pain and itching in the anal and perineum areas. Chronic pain, especially forms like fibromyalgia and pelvic pain disorders, can significantly impact how sex feels. Blood pressure issues can affect the functioning of erectile tissue, as can diabetes. Prostate health is very important to sexual functioning. So when you're monitoring your physical health, getting checked for more than just STIs is crucial.

Communication

That covers testing and check ups, but what about the communication? All the testing in the world isn't helpful if you can't talk about it. There are a couple of different models of easy ways to cover the best parts. Reid Mihalko has a safer sex elevator speech. Evelin Dacker has the STARS model. Both are pretty similar and you can find information on both in the Resources section. Here's how I would share my information with a potential partner:

Dr. Liz's Safer Sex Speech

❝❝ *I was last tested in June for HIV, HSV 1&2, syphilis,*
chlamydia, gonorrhea, and hepatitis C and was negative for everything
but HSV 1. I also got throat swabs for gonorrhea and chlamydia that
were negative. I have HSV 1 with a history of oral cold sores, but the
last was about 6 months ago. I was last tested for HPV in June and was
negative.

I currently have two penis having partners with whom I do not use
barriers for penetrative sex, and one vulva having partner with whom
I do not use barriers (and who also does not use barriers with one
of my penis having partners). With everyone else, I use condoms for
penetration by bio dicks or dildos. I often use gloves for hand sex, and
barriers for oral are negotiable depending upon my partner and their
risk factors and risk comfort.

Because of a latex sensitivity, I only use non-latex barriers. I don't
currently have any relationship agreements to be aware of, but I
generally tell my ongoing partners about the fun I have, so if you'd like
to be anonymous or send a special shout out, let me know. I really love
giving and receiving hand sex and both giving and receiving biting. I

don't like people who jump into a D/s dynamic without negotiating that with me beforehand. How about you?

A few things to notice here - this brief speech ends with an invitation for the person or people I'm talking with to join me in sharing their information. In addition, I talked about what I've been tested for, when, and the results as well as what might affect those results. I also talk about barrier use, relationship agreements, things I like, and things I don't like. This short little blurb gives a potential partner a lot of information about me and if they are able to give me similar information we can both make decisions about what we feel good about doing together.

Another thing to notice is that the speech isn't presumptive about any particular activities. I'm not necessarily saying "we're doing this," I'm just giving my partner(s) information they might need. The language also isn't judgmental. I'm not using terms like "clean" or "dirty," nor am I assuming some risk aware sex decisions are better than others.

One last note on language - in my speech, I talk about people with whom I don't use barriers rather than saying people with whom I'm fluid bonded. Why? Well technically unprotected mouth kissing is fluid bonding (after all, HSV and HPV can be transmitted orally). While many people may understand what you mean when you say fluid bonding, they may not, so clarity of language is important here.

Barriers

The third component of assessing and managing risk is use of barriers to prevent STI transmission. As we covered above, testing gives you a snapshot and a positive test result from someone else doesn't guarantee whether they will or will not transmit the STI to others. If you want to lower your risks, there are both physical and chemical/medication barriers you can elect to use when engaging with others.

Condoms

First, and most common, are condoms. Condoms can be used on bio dicks or toys to protect the covered area from coming into contact with other mucous membranes or skin areas. Most people think of condoms in conjunction with bio dicks or dildos, but you can also roll one down a wand vibrator, put it on a butt plug, or use it on just about anything you intend to insert into an area with exposed mucous membranes.

What does that include? Mouths, vaginas/vulvas, penises, and anuses the ones you're most likely to be playing with, but technically noses and urethras also count. You can use condoms as a barrier for any activity involving any of these areas. One caveat - a condom only protects the area it covers. So, if you're putting a bio dick or a toy into someone and an area not covered with the condom comes into contact with the areas around the mucous membrane (vulva, perineum, penis), STI transmission can still occur. This is most likely to be a risk for STIs like HSV and HPV which are transmitted through skin contact.

If you're using a toy that is made of a high quality, non-porous material such as stainless steel or platinum silicone, you can always sanitize the toy between uses by boiling, bleaching, or other methods, but it's still often safest to use a condom when sharing these toys with other bodies.

One more thing you can do with condoms is cut them into dental dams. We'll talk more about dental dams a bit later, but if all you have is a condom and you want a barrier to put over a vulva or an anus, a condom cut up the side and with the tip and base cut off can absolutely serve.

Condoms come in many varieties - different sizes and shapes, different colors and textures, different materials, and even ones that are designed for insertion in a vagina or anus instead of for rolling down a phallic object. There's no best kind of condom; much of this is about personal preference. You can often find variety packs of condoms through online retailers in order to try out different ones to see which ones work best for you.

If condoms are an important part of your sexual risk management protocol, you should probably have your own regardless of your gender or genitals. After all, the responsibility for meeting your risk aware sex protocols falls as much on you as anyone else. If you're scared about buying condoms, most online retailers put innocuous sounding names on your credit card statement and on their packaging.

Whenever you're using condoms, you want to be sure to check the expiration date on the packaging. Most condoms are good for 3-5 years, depending on the material and what kind of lubricant is used. Also inspect the packaging for any punctures or damage, as damage on the outside could mean damage on the inside. Heat can also damage condoms, so if you've had one in your back pocket for a while, or left one in the car, it's best to assume those aren't going to be effective. When opening condoms, be sure to squish the condom down in the package before you tear it open; this will help ensure you don't tear the condom.

Dental Dams

Dental dams are the second kind of barrier we'll talk about. While the name is unfortunately un-sexy, dental dams are generally used to provide a barrier between a mouth and another broad mucous membrane area - mouth, vulva, anus, perineum. Dams can be purchased separately as their own item, but often are thicker and more expensive than other options you can find for similar oral protections.

Cling film is a great, inexpensive alternative for purpose built dental dams. Some people have heard that you need non-microwavable cling wrap for dental dam purposes and frankly the science on this isn't 100% conclusive yet. Why? Microwave safe cling film has tiny pores that open at high temperatures to allow some steam to release so that your microwaved food doesn't explode. Pores opening would possibly contribute to potential compromise of the barrier, but these pores generally only open at temperatures FAR above the temperature of the human body. Finding cling film that isn't microwaveable can be nearly impossible, so while the research isn't 100% on whether you need non-microwave type cling wrap, you're probably going to be okay using the kind that can be microwaved.

Other alternatives for dental dams are cutting open a condom as described above or turning a glove into a dam. Here's a handy (hehe) illustration of how to cut a glove!

Turning a glove into a dam

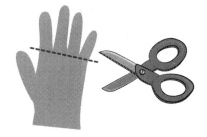

1. Using scissors, cut all the fingers (not the thumb) off of the glove

2. Cut up theside of the glove on the pinkie finger side, opening it

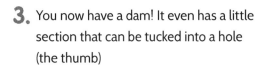

3. You now have a dam! It even has a little section that can be tucked into a hole (the thumb)

With any dental dam, you want to be sure that you cover all of the area you might possibly put your mouth on. This means you'll likely need a larger piece of barrier than you would initially think. Also, it helps to put a bit of lube on the side with the vulva/anus/perineum/whatever on it so that the barrier can move around a bit with your mouth. Finally, be sure to hold the barrier in place and check it frequently for any tears or slipping.

Gloves

The last kind of physical barrier I'll cover is gloves. But hands aren't mucous membranes! I know, however, hands can get really dirty and we use them for just about everything. Hands can also have small cuts on them which would expose them to any STIs, especially skin-borne ones like HSV and HPV. What we're primarily working on curbing with glove use is fluid transfer or cross-contamination.

If you touch my genitals and then touch your own with the same hand, and you didn't wash your hands in between, we just had a mucous membrane to mucous membrane interaction. Gloves are very inexpensive and can make having less risky sex much much easier. Plus, for play with anuses or for fisting, the smoother texture of a glove can make insertion easier and more comfortable.

With most gloves, you'll want to turn them inside out before use since the outside of most gloves tends to have a texture to allow for grip that can feel abrasive on delicate tissues. If you're playing with someone and using gloves and you want to touch another item or another person, just take off the glove and either grab it or grab a new one.

Medications

In terms of medications, there are a couple of different ones that can be helpful in stemming transmission of some STIs. If someone has HSV, they can take Valacyclovir or other similar medications to reduce their risk of outbreaks and their risk of asymptomatic viral shedding. Taking Valacyclovir reduces the risk of HSV transmission by 50% and using condoms reduces it by an additional 50%, so when you combine these with avoiding any contact during an active outbreak, the risk of transmission becomes vanishingly low.

For those of us who have sex with more than 3 people a month, current medical recommendations are that we consider starting Pre-Exposure Prophylaxis or PrEP. PrEP is a daily medication that significantly reduces the risk of HIV transmission. While this medication is most often recommended or known of in gay male populations, anyone can be on it, even if they don't have any HIV positive partners they know of. There are less than 5 cases of transmission of HIV to those on PrEP ever so the medication is highly effective.

More communication

Risk aware sex conversations aren't a one and done kind of thing. We need to keep checking back in with each other about what might have changed our risk profiles.

This can include new lovers, changes in barrier use with others, use of intravenous drugs, or needle sticks (such as in a healthcare setting).

In addition, we need to understand that the information we're getting from our partners may not be perfect. They may not know that they have acquired an STI, or they may have too much shame to communicate about an STI with us. While it would certainly suck to have someone not give us all of the information, that is a realistic risk we take every time we talk to someone about physical risk. If you can't trust that someone is honest, or don't know them well enough to know whether you can trust them, it may behoove you to make more conservative risk management decisions.

If you go to the online resources you'll find links to buy everything included here.

Safer Sex Kit

Your "safer sex kit" is the set of supplies you bring with you so that you can manage your physical risk when interacting with sexual partners. You should generally have your own supplies because otherwise you can't guarantee that a potential partner will have the supplies you'd like.

Here's some recommendations for what to put in your own safer sex kit:

- Condoms of different sizes, at least standard and large. Latex and non, or all non

- Lube: this can be in packets or bottles. Each has pros and cons.

- "Female" or internal condoms

- Gloves (preferably non-latex) of different sizes, at least small & medium; Venom and Black Dragon are excellent brands. (Turn inside out for use)

- "Dental dams" in a small kit, saran wrap in a large

- Nail clippers and nail file

💜 Bandaids

💜 Wipes - Travel baby wipes or toilet wipes to help clean up

Emotional Risk

As social creatures, rejection and heartbreak can feel fatal to people. And yet, when most of us talk about managing risk related to sex we don't talk about heartache nearly as much as HIV. Why is it that our thoughts on risk are so confined to "bugs" and exclude our feelings?

One of my favorite authors and thinkers is Brené Brown. She is a shame researcher whose books talk about how each of us can choose vulnerability and connection in a world where most of us fear shame. Unfortunately, most of us struggle with how to be vulnerable and real in a world that feels scary and threatening. Most of us have had a time, or many times, where our soft squishy insides got mangled by someone else, and the more times this happens the higher and harder we tend to make the walls protecting and hiding those soft squishy bits.

Paradoxically, we require and crave the kinds of connection that cannot happen when we stay behind these walls. So how do we balance the task of keeping ourselves from getting too knocked around and the desire to form deep, intimate connections with others?

Now I'm not saying that every sexual encounter needs to be a forever love. Goodness knows that I've got far more people I'm willing to have sex with than people I'm a good fit for dating. What I am saying is that being present with the actual person we're spending time with is an important task. Not just for helping them feel seen and appreciated (rather than objectified), but also for us to be able to enjoy greater sexual pleasure. The more disconnected we are from ourselves and our partners, the harder it is to have hot sex.

When we decide to be real with people, to show our true selves and to be vulnerable, we open ourselves up to several potential emotional risks. We could fall in love with this person, and they might or might not fall in love with us. We may get our hearts broken or break their heart. The connection we develop with someone else might affect our current relationships, in positive or negative ways, no matter how brief or "casual" the connection. We might find that our interests, in terms of sex, relationship, or both, aren't a good match for this new person, and any other variety of distinct risks. The reality is that choosing to relate to others opens us up to joy and despair and everything in between, and the more connections we're making, especially simultaneously, the more complex the variables and interconnections become.

One of the best tools for exploring and mitigating emotional risk is to ask yourself and your partners lots of questions about how their feelings tend to behave in connections with others. What has caused them jealousy before? What are their deal breakers? What makes things flow more smoothly? What kind of pre-care or after-care do they need and do you need? The more that we acknowledge and discuss our emotions and the situations/issues affecting them, the more likely we are to be able to mitigate the risk and prevent negative outcomes.

Social Risk

Anytime you step outside of the societal norms, you are taking a social risk. While it would be lovely to live in a world where everyone is encouraged to be themselves and is accepted as who they are, humans as social creatures tend to want to pull back anyone who steps out of line. These tendencies are particularly strong when it comes to challenging something that is perceived as foundational to society, such as monogamy.

When you are non-monogamous, you may find yourself ostracized or judged by others. People who used to be friends may view you with suspicion, family may judge or exclude you, and communities may treat you differently than they did before. While I wish I could tell you that you will definitely be okay, unfortunately we live in a time and a world with plenty of prejudices, and while the prejudice against non-monogamous folks is nowhere near as detrimental in terms of danger and overall effects as other structural prejudices like racism, it can still have lasting and deep negative effects.

When you're deciding to engage with someone, you may want to consider how that connection might affect you socially. One dimension along which you can make choices that affect social risk is how much you're "out." After all, if no one knows, you aren't likely to suffer any immediate consequences. However, being closeted isn't often a permanent solution, and can often create immense anxiety over being outed or exposed.

Social risks might involve what you do in public, what you post on the internet, what events/locations you go to, and who you choose to surround yourself with. They may also change if there are factors such as a divorce, child custody, or certain occupations (e.g. school teachers, politicians) involved in your decisions. Your social risks are also likely to be affected by where you live and work in terms of geography. The more liberal an area and the more common non-monogamy is there, the less likely you are to face particularly severe risks.

To consider the social risks, fill out the risk management worksheet. You may also want to take a look at the coming out worksheet (page 265) to help you decide about outness.

Managing Risk Worksheet

When most of us think about managing our risks in sexual relationships, we tend to focus mostly on STIs and pregnancy. But what if, instead, we took a big picture approach?

Managing Physical Risk

What are the physical risks here? This could include STIs, pregnancy, injury/disability, etc.

What measures are available to mitigate these risks?

What measures feel right for you and your partner to mitigate these risks?

How much risk are you willing to assume in exchange for the benefits you want? How does that affect your risk management decisions?

Managing Emotional Risk

What are the emotional risks here? This could include falling in love, heartbreak, affecting current relationships, mismatched interests, etc.

What measures are available to mitigate these risks?

What measures feel right for you and your partner to mitigate these risks?

What are the potential emotional benefits for you?

Managing Risk Worksheet

How much risk are you willing to assume in exchange for the benefits you want? How does that affect your risk management decisions?

Managing Social Risk

What are the social risks here? This could include judgment of friends/ family, expansion or contraction of social circle, outness, positions in communities, etc.

What measures are available to mitigate these risks?

What measures feel right for you and your partner to mitigate these risks?

What are the potential social benefits for you?

How much risk are you willing to assume in exchange for the benefits you want? How does that affect your risk management decisions?

Dating struggles

● ● ● ● ● ●

How we will react once either we or our partner starts dating can be highly unpredictable. Some people think they will have a hard time when their partner dates and then find they feel primarily excitement and happiness when it actually happens. On the flip side, some folks who expected to experience primarily compersion (happiness for a partner's happiness) instead find themselves struggling once their partner dates.

Dating one person at a time can be complicated, and adding in more folks increases the degrees of complication. So what sorts of problems tend to arise? Common struggles that come up when we (or our partners) date include handling new relationship energy (NRE), time management, and avoiding common pitfalls.

Handling NRE

New relationship energy, or NRE, is the term that folks use to describe those excited, giddy feelings you get when starting a new relationship. These feelings can last from six months to two years and are related to very real changes in neurotransmitter levels that, in essence, get you high on love. From an evolutionary standpoint, our bodies basically want us to make as many babies as possible. So when we meet someone whose body chemistry seems like it goes with our body chemistry, our body wants us to make rash, impulsive decisions that are driven towards reproduction. However, it's hard to know when we're in it how much of what we're feeling is NRE and how much will still be there when we finally get sober.

NRE is one of the best and worst parts of dating. On the upside, it feels awesome. With dopamine, serotonin, and oxytocin coursing through your brain, you feel happy and sparkly and shiny and excited. You're learning so much about a new someone and seeing the world, and yourself, through their eyes. The movie Playing By Heart described this phase as getting to see yourself through the other person and in a way falling in love with the you that they see. If you've had trouble in the past with people treating you poorly or being abusive (emotionally or physically) towards you, this rush of attention and reinforcement can be particularly powerful. Folks in the midst of NRE often find themselves being more confident, and thus more attractive to others, so you can find that the happy start of one relationship opens the doors to many other potential new relationships.

On the downside, though, you're literally intoxicated. You aren't thinking clearly. The limbic system is working in overdrive and that can impair your frontal lobe functioning. Since the frontal lobes are where impulse control, future planning, and complex decision making happen, this can lead to some decisions that feel awesome in the moment but end up in regret. People in the throes of NRE often break agreements, neglect existing relationships, or make promises they won't want to keep once the spell is broken.

If you're the partner of someone who has entered NRE, it can be a tough experience. You might feel neglected or unwanted or angry at a partner who is suddenly breaking plans and agreements. If you had previously been their "new shiny," having a partner find a "newer shinier" person might make you feel down and sad and rejected.

So how do we handle this biochemical hijack? How can we best set ourselves up for success? Let's take a look at it from both the perspective of the person in NRE and the person whose partner is in NRE with someone else.

When you have NRE

When thinking about how to handle NRE, the first step is awareness. What are your personal patterns in NRE? Think back to the beginning of your past relationships. What sorts of things did you do that were out of character or that created problems later? You can ask your current or past partners for input as well about what they notice when you're in NRE.

As I mentioned earlier, I identify strongly as solo poly. My version of solo poly includes that I don't know if I'll ever want to get married again and that cohabitation would have to be very carefully negotiated and definitely involve me having my very own room that is only mine.

The thing is, when I'm high on NRE my brain makes me want to make all kinds of promises that I end up regretting once the wave has passed. In my relationship with Troy (the same person I talk about in the boundaries and changing levels chapters), I was so intoxicated that we talked about marriage and kids and living together. I told him that I definitely wanted to be his wife, definitely wanted to share a bedroom, and wanted to have kids with him. I told him that I was so certain of these things that he could move across the country from Georgia to California and that things would be magic once we lived together.

In that relationship, I learned a really hard lesson - the things I want to say and promise during NRE aren't real once the energy fades. Right around eight months into our relationship, my brain stopped pumping out those cuddly feel good neurotransmitters and I was suddenly sober in a situation that didn't suit me. I had built an entire theoretical future with Troy, I had promised him things, that now sounded to me like a prison. I had to have many hard talks with him about what had changed for me.

Obviously, and with good reason, Troy felt deceived. He had been given assurances, promises, guarantees and now I was rescinding them. I tried to explain to him that I still loved him, I just couldn't do things the way we had talked about, but that transition was too much without a significant full break.

Now, when I start any new connection and start feeling the NRE building inside of me, I have a conversation with my partner where I talk about my NRE patterns. I let them know that in the past I've made promises while high that I later regretted and so I ask that we don't work towards any life-changing decisions until we've been together 6-8 months (the typical course of my NRE). Further, I talk to them about creating times and spaces where we can talk about the fantasies our NRE brains are feeding us from a stance of how lovely the fantasies are without developing attachment to them becoming real outcomes. This approach has gotten me some weird looks but has also saved me, and the folks I've dated, plenty of pain.

Once you know your patterns, then you can develop a strategy to address them. Common patterns include:

Positive/feel good elements

- 💜 Discussing major life changes
- 💜 Making long term plans
- 💜 Wanting lots of touch
- 💜 Sharing special places/activities/media
- 💜 Talking with them far more than you usually would
- 💜 Smiling more often

- 💜 Increased libido

- 💜 Make yourself SUPER available, maybe more available than you can be long term (time, space, emotional intimacy)

- 💜 Performing acts of service beyond what you might usually do

Negative/feel bad elements

- 💜 Making promises you won't be able to keep

- 💜 Neglecting established partners

- 💜 Spending more time than you really have available

- 💜 Spending more money than you have available

- 💜 Not sleeping/working out/other self care because you're spending the time and energy on the new relationship

- 💜 Falling into mononormative/mainstream dating scripts

- 💜 Neglecting friendships

- 💜 Trouble focusing at work

- 💜 Risk taking behaviors (e.g. unbarriered sex)

- 💜 Pushing the person away

- 💜 Avoidance/running

- 💜 Fear (of vulnerability, or of doing things you'll regret)

- 💜 Insecurity and fear of losing the person

What if you don't know your patterns? Think back to the last time you were smitten over someone. What did you do? How did you feel? Do you have any friends who could tell you what they saw? Does your partner remember?

No that you've identified your patterns, think about what signs or signals you can look for as an early warning that you're starting down the NRE path. The earlier you can catch that you're getting swept away, the easier it is to enjoy the feelings without creating collateral damage.

In general, things to keep in mind when you are the one with NRE is that this rush of chemicals is temporary, but the impacts of your actions may not be. Remember to continue setting aside time to nurture yourself and your relationships with others. Let your established partners know that you're heading into NRE and give them permission to let you know if you're doing something that hurts them.

Tell the person you're in NRE with what your personal NRE patterns are and ask them about their patterns. Figure out, as much as you can, what pitfalls your patterns might lead the two of you towards. Talk to each other about how long NRE tends to last for each of you (again, that can be anything from 6 months to 2 years) and don't make any huge, life changing decisions until you know you're sober.

Find a friend or a few friends who can be your reality check buddies. Whenever you're feeling like exploding with all the NRE stories, talk to those friends about them. Let them help you figure out what you should treat as a fantasy, what you should tell partners about, and what is an indication of real changes and needs.

One last point here - sometimes you can be both high and right about the need for a big change. When my emotionally abusive relationship was on its last legs, someone let me know that I was attractive to them and that they liked me. I had been for so long told that I wasn't attractive and made to feel unwanted that this attention felt like the first breath of air after I had been drowning. I fell hard for this person and that NRE gave me the strength I needed to bring about the end of my abusive relationship.

However, once the NRE faded, the new person was . . . not what I thought they were. We broke up within a few months. While the NRE made it hard for me to see the realities of what didn't work between the new person and I, it also helped me see more clearly how miserable I had been and how big a change I needed in my life. Even a broken clock is right twice a day, and sometimes NRE cuts through the bullshit that's been clouding our vision.

When someone you're in a relationship with has NRE

We've all been there - our partner used to see us as the newest shiniest person in their life, then they meet someone new and all of a sudden we're chopped liver. They aren't talking to us much, they might cancel dates, and all they talk about is their new person. This. Sucks. Even if your partner isn't being particularly rude, feeling the heat of their attention transferring to someone else can be disheartening. So what do you do when your partner has some strong NRE for someone else?

First of all, take some time to take care of yourself. Have you filled out the worksheet on self-care while your sweetie dates? If not, do that now. What are the things you can do to take care of yourself when you're feeling left out, left behind, or less wanted? How can you show yourself some good love? You want to do this first because you're likely to be able to have much more productive conversations if you're relatively centered and if you've taken some time to care for your own needs.

Next, find something to focus on other than what you're not getting. Maybe that's a new dance class, a fun TV show, a new hobby, time with friends, a great book, or a new dating friend for you! Whatever form it takes, the more you can find and build your own joy, the easier it is to ride out the waves of your partner's NRE.

Third, figure out who your support people are. Who are the folks who can hear your concerns and complaints while keeping you balanced and grounded? We all have those friends who will jump right on the "fuck that guy!" train - those aren't the friends we're talking about here. Instead, you would likely benefit most from identifying which of your friends can hear you with kindness and compassion and help you keep things in perspective. After all, I'm sure that you've gotten stuck in the NRE hole once or twice yourself, right? Having friends who can love and support you and give you a solid reality check is essential for riding out a partner's NRE.

If none of these are helping you and your partner's NRE choices are still bugging you, take some time to figure out what you want and need from your partner and what they've done that upset or hurt you. Luckily, we've got a handy worksheet (page 91) to help you find the words for a tough conversation.

Now that you've sketched out what you need to say, ask your partner for a chat. Let them know about how much time you think you'll need and make sure you can both find a time that seems like it will work. Remember that you are going to have missteps too one day, so the more kindness and compassion you bring to bear in a conversation, the better things are likely to be for you when your partner needs to have a tough conversation with you about things you've done. Remind yourself that you care about this person and that they aren't themselves because of biochemistry right now.

When you sit down to chat, try to focus on what it is you need from them. It's easy when we're hurt to want to dump all of that pain onto them. While I'll never tell you that you can't do something, dumping your hurt onto someone doesn't often lead to a productive conversation and positive outcome. If what you want is to strengthen your relationship, a big crying, screaming fight isn't likely to do it.

Be honest with your partner. Let them know you're hurting and what is leading to the hurt. Then listen to them and try, as best you can, to understand their perspective too. Usually when someone is doing things from NRE, they aren't doing them with the intention of hurting you, they just aren't thinking of the consequences of their actions.

Finally, come up with a plan, the two of you together, for how you can move forward from here. Is there a code word you can say to them when the NRE is making them act like a jerk? Is there a commitment to a certain amount of time or attention that will help you? Knowing your love languages can be particularly helpful here as someone whose language is touch might not be happy with a plan that's focused on gifts. What can you both realistically stick with to help your relationship grow and thrive while they explore this new thing? How can you support your partner as they try to make it through their NRE with as little damage as possible all around?

If this conversation goes well, you'll likely emerge from it as a stronger partnership. However, if your partner can't hear your concerns or offer to make changes that will help you feel better during the NRE rush, it might be worth considering what that means for you in this relationship. Check out the chapters on boundaries and changing levels for more guidance about what your next steps might be.

Time management

Human capacity for love is limitless. Don't believe me? Look at a picture of a cute animal or a baby! Emotions are not finite, we can always love more and love deeper. Time, on the other hand, IS finite, and often becomes one of the biggest stumbling blocks in non-monogamy.

Every person has 168 hours in a week. If we take out 40 of those for work (yeah, right!), 56 for sleep, 7 for personal hygiene, 5 for transportation to and from work, we're suddenly down to only 60 possible hours free. We haven't eaten any meals, done any cleaning or laundry, had any alone time, participated in any hobbies, or socialized with friends. As you can see, time gets scarce easily.

One of the best skills to develop as a human, but in particular as a non-monogamous person, is time management. Time management involves several components: tracking, balance and prioritization, scheduling, and problem solving.

Tracking

One of the most common mistakes in time management is to try to keep everything in your head. Human brains simply aren't good at keeping track of lots of little appointments and commitments. When your life is fairly simple, it's easier to keep track. Once you're juggling dates and work and hobbies and friends, though, it becomes much much more challenging. Therefore, it's important to have a system that works for you to keep track of your scheduling and commitments.

In this day and age, there are plenty of great options for tracking your commitments. If you're a paper and pencil person, there are great planner and calendar options. A variety of sizes, shapes, and layouts are available. In paper and pencil planners you can also use colored pens or highlighters, stickers, sticky notes, and other items to track different partners or activities.

If you prefer digital, there are also plenty of digital options. Digital versions have some advantages over analog counterparts. In digital calendars, you can often send an invite to the other people participating, ensuring that everyone sees the same events available. You can color code and can access them on your computer and mobile devices, therefore accessing them without carrying around anything extra.

> **Whichever you choose, the most important tips for tracking are:**
>
> 💜 Check the calendar before you schedule anything (dates, hobbies, activities)
>
> 💜 As soon as you agree to something, put it in your calendar
>
> 💜 Check what's coming up for you regularly (weekly, monthly, etc.)

Balance and prioritization

One of the hardest parts of time management is deciding what to say "yes" to and what to say "no" to. As much as we may want to, we cannot say "yes" to everything, or even to everything we would like to say "yes" to. Part of the reality of adult life is that we have to make tough decisions about how we will allocate our energy and time. So how do we make these tough decisions? How do we know what to give our time to?

Folks end up with different ways of making these decisions. One method is to evaluate what you would regret most. Another is to check in with your own values and see which actions align most with your actions. Overall, I think the easiest system to use is one focused on balance.

In business, one of the common aphorisms is to pay yourself first - in other words, make sure that your salary is covered as a first priority, otherwise you might not get one. This same idea applies to time management. Most of us do a really good job of finding time for others and a less good job of finding time for ourselves. However, if you don't set aside enough time for yourself, you're likely to feel burnt out or resentful. So when scheduling, be sure you've set aside time for your own needs - alone time, hobbies, fitness, food, hygiene, and whatever else.

Second, be sure to block out some unscheduled time. Why? Well, life is unpredictable, and sometimes you get sick or your tire is flat or something amazing comes up. If you fully schedule yourself, you have to cancel plans to deal with these disruptions. Once you've blocked out time for you and some blank space, then you can start filling in your other commitments.

Key tips for balance and prioritization include:

♥ Pay yourself first! Schedule in the time you need to take care of yourself

♥ Leave plenty of "white space," or unscheduled time, so that you can be flexible and have time for unexpected events

♥ When you look over your calendar, pay attention to the balance between alone time, dates, hobbies, social time, and self-care time

Scheduling

How do you know which parts of your time to give to which activities? Every person does better at certain things at different times of days. Some folks do best with morning fitness, while others do better in the afternoon. It's important to understand how you function best. For me, if I've had a long day and lots of clients, I'm not going to have much energy left over for a date. I also know that if I don't make myself get up and work out in the morning, I won't end up doing it in the evening unless it's a class I've paid for or I'm meeting other people.

When doing scheduling, keep in mind how your emotional and physical energy ebbs and flows. Don't fall into the trap of squeezing things into the space that happens to be available, instead focus on finding ways to work with your own rhythms.

Tips for scheduling:

♥ Spend a few weeks paying attention to what times of days and which days of the week work best for different types of events

♥ Take note of what commitments were scheduled at times that didn't work for you

💜 Continue adjusting your scheduling to meet your own needs

Problem Solving

Finally, and perhaps most importantly, how do you come up with creative solutions when time is running short? We will all end up feeling at some point like we're overbooked or don't have time for all the things we want to do. How you solve this problem is likely strongly influenced by your style of non-monogamy and your needs as an individual.

Ideas for problem solving:

💜 Can you combine any activities?

💜 Can you spend time with multiple people at once?

💜 Are you a "fuck yes" to everything on your calendar?

💜 Are you saying "yes" to things that you're not a real "yes" to?

💜 If you had to get rid of half of the things on your calendar, what would you cut?

💜 Is this a temporary problem (e.g. you have more work deadlines this month) or a longer term one? If it's temporary, can some things wait? If permanent, what in your life might need to flex?

💜 What needs are you getting met? Which ones aren't?

Common Problems in Non-Monogamy

● ● ● ● ● ●

Monogamy mindset hangovers

"Be Mine". This phrase, splattered all over Valentine's candy and cards, expresses clearly and succinctly the ways in which the monogamy mindset teaches us problematic ideas about relationships. Does someone actually belong to you when you date them?

Even in Dominant/submissive relationships, the power dynamic is one that was agreed upon and can be exited at any time - we are not keeping real slaves here. And yet, as we move through our non-monogamous lives, most of us have to spend a fair amount of energy and effort unlearning problematic monogamy mindset lessons about how love and dating are supposed to go.

Here are some of the common relationship mindsets, instilled in us by society, that people struggle with when starting in non-monogamy.

Scarcity

In the monogamy, fairy tale model, we end up with The One. The One is our soulmate, the only person who could be right for us. They are our perfect match, and if we let them go, we will never find anyone who is as good for us as they were. Therefore, once we find our One, we have to hold onto them at any cost, because losing them means losing love, possibly forever.

The scarcity mindset in dating often goes hand in hand with the sunk cost fallacy. The sunk cost fallacy says that is it bad to lose something we have invested time, money, energy, or emotions into, regardless of whether that something is still actually doing anything for you. Humans are highly loss averse creatures, so we tend to prefer NOT losing something over potentially gaining something, even if we don't even like what we would lose.

Scarcity tells us that we only have so many chances at love, and that if we've put time and energy into a relationship we need to MAKE it work. It tells us that every minute our partner spends with someone else is a minute we lose, that any happiness our partner gets from others is at our expense. Is that true? Not really.

Let's start with time, since time is a genuinely scarce resource (we all only have 24 hours in a day). At face value, it would seem like our partner spending time with someone else is de facto robbing us of that time. Let's look more closely at it though - how much quality time can you reasonably spend with another person? If you've been deeply connecting with each other for 8 straight hours, can you really do 8 more? If time scarcity is such a big deal, why don't we encourage our partners to quit their jobs and never have friendships? Have you ever noticed that "absence makes the heart grow fonder?"

Even those resources that are truly scarce are rarely as scarce as we perceive them to be. After all, even if you spent 24/7 locked in a house with your partner, I'm willing to bet you'd end up sleeping or spending time locked in the bathroom. None of us actually wants ALL of our time to go to our partner, so neither should they want to give ALL of their time to us.

When we talk about something like love, what the scarcity model teaches us and what we see in reality diverge even more. Loving someone does not drain some finite pool of love that we each have to give. Just like loving one parent doesn't mean you love the other less, loving multiple dating partners doesn't diminish the amount of love you have available. When we feel scared as we watch our partner fall in love with someone else, our loss aversion center in our brain is telling us that this new love is somehow stealing from our established love. But is that actually true?

Part of unlearning scarcity is similar to skydiving - at some point, you have to just step out the door and trust your gear to work. Is it dangerous? Maybe. Will you have heartbreaks? Almost certainly! And yet, if you focus only on your potential pain you will miss out on vast amounts of potential pleasure. Seeing your partner fall in love with someone else for the first time doesn't have to mean the end of your relationship, but it's more likely to end your relationship if you make them miserable for feeling happy.

The strange thing about scarcity is that the more we believe it's true, the more we make it happen. If I believe that no one will date me, I'm going to be skeptical about anyone who says they want to. I'm going to be bitter and sad and angry, and I'm not going to put myself out there. As the old adage goes, "Whether you believe you can or you believe you can't, you're right." In dating, scarcity tends to rise to the level we expect it to.

When I got married to David, I thought for sure he was way too good for me. Why would this amazing dancer, so sexy and so desired by everyone around me, be choosing ME? I was just a young dancer, new to these dances, still in college. And yet he did! He wanted to kiss me and date me and we even fell in love. By the time he asked me to marry him, our relationship already had LOTS of problems.

We fought a lot. I felt like he didn't really respect my wishes or desires. He didn't help out around the house and often expected me to do things like cook and clean even though I was working more hours than he was. But I still believed that I wasn't good enough for him, that if I pushed too hard the universe (and David) would realize that this was a mistake and I would lose this huge prize I hadn't actually won. So I figured that if we got married, things would be less stressful, and we would have a better relationship.

At my engagement party, I remember telling a mutual friend that I wasn't sure about this whole thing. That I wasn't that happy and that I didn't know if I could be monogamous. She told me I was just having cold feet and that it was clear how much we loved each other. So, being in the thrall of the monogamy mindset and the scarcity model, I went ahead and got married. We had a huge fight the night of our wedding. And the fights continued for the rest of our time together. Over and over I asked myself if I should leave, but I kept thinking "What if this is the best I get?" So I stayed. I stayed when he eroded my self-esteem, and I stayed when I felt misery seeping out of my pores.

Eventually, I started standing up for myself. And, well, let's just say that there wasn't space in the relationship for me and my needs. So, when it ended, I was relieved in a lot of ways - I was free of this particular kind of misery I had been drowning in. In other ways, though, I was scared - what if this WAS the best I would ever get? What if no one wanted to date a 26 year-old divorcee? What if I never had love again?

My fears, on that front at least, were quickly squashed as I found a bevy of available suitors vying for my time and attention. In my marriage, I had come to believe that I couldn't do any better and that no one would want me, but the reverse was actually true. Lots of people wanted me, and plenty of them were better for me than my ex-husband. Each time I've had a major breakup I've heard scarcity whisper in my ear "But what if this was the best you could get?" and each time I've found that voice was completely wrong.

When we let our relationships and our lives be dictated by our fears, we close ourselves into smaller and smaller spaces. So is it scary to step out of the door into the open air? YES! There is nothing quite so terrifying as the unknown. But your happiness will not be found in making yourself smaller. So take the time to ask yourself whether your fears are based in reality or based in the story you've been told about how scarce love is.

Control/coercion

All of us live in a culture that normalizes coercion and control, and that fails to teach us consent. Don't believe me? Have you ever had a friend call you to invite you to a social event and you've said something like "I don't know, I'm not sure I can make it," only for your friend to respond with "encouragement" designed to "help" you say yes? Has your friend ever encouraged you to come out for "just one drink" or "just for 5 minutes?"

I get it, your friend would tell me that they could sense that you WANTED to come but felt like you couldn't. They sensed ambivalence so they dove in to help tip the scales towards the side that just happened to line up with their preferences. However, how is this different from insisting on "just one kiss" or "just a hand job" when someone has said no?

We are BAD at real consent in our culture. We all believe that we have the right, or sometimes even the obligation, to sway our friends to what we think they will enjoy or appreciate. We don't do well with receiving a "no" as a full and complete response. As I'm sure you can imagine, this ends up with serious consequences when we apply it to the dating world.

Being raised in a culture of control and coercion means that we have to all be much more aware of what we are doing and why. Once you start paying attention, you may find that you're pushing against people's "no" in lots of different ways and in lots of different contexts. That doesn't necessarily mean you're a bad person, it means you were raised in a culture that's bad at consent. You have to make the choice to start doing something different, and that means respecting any and all "no"s, even ones that are "soft" or less direct.

What does that sound like? Phrases like "I'm busy," "I'm not sure," "I need to check my calendar," or even ones like "I'm not sure I can find a ride" or "I don't think I can afford it" all mean "no." Phrases like "maybe" or "I'll think about it" or "let me get back to you" are often also a soft "no."

When you receive a no from someone, practice receiving it with gratitude. Okay, I know, you think I've lost it - why should I be thankful that someone told me no? Let me ask you this - have you ever been out with someone who told you yes, but you could tell they were a no? Didn't you wish they had just told you no instead? Our no is a way of showing love for ourselves and for others. We take care of ourselves by saying no when we mean it, freeing ourselves up to find something we're a yes to. For others, we free them up to find someone who is as big of a yes to that activity as they are. No one wants a reluctant partner!

When we thank people for their no, we tell them that we appreciate them taking care of themselves and giving us a chance to find someone excited about what we're offering. It takes some practice to make this mindset shift, but it's HUGE once you get there. If you want help with this, check out a Cuddle Party in your area - cuddle parties are great places to explore giving and receiving no.

On the flip side, in this culture of control and coercion, we often lose sight of our own internal yes and no. We may find ourselves saying yes to things we aren't a yes to, or saying no to things we want but think we don't deserve.

One of the first steps in reclaiming our genuine yes and no is to practice giving a loving no. For most of us, a real "no" is far harder to give than a real "yes," but we end up giving so many yeses that we don't really mean that we don't have space for the things we WANT to say yes to.

A loving no is a way of saying no that is firm and assertive while being kind and caring. Many of us fear that there is only a compliant yes or a harsh no, but this doesn't have to be the case. We can be as loving and kind and positive with our no as we are with our yes. Our no also isn't just one level - we can have no's that are more kind to no's that are extremely firm, none of which HAVE to be harsh unless we want them to be. For instance, if I'm coming up with loving no's for someone who has come up to me at a bar to talk to me, but whom I'm not interested in, I could have lots of ways of saying no. If they push past lower ones, I could move to more firm ones. For instance, here are some possible escalating levels of no:

1. (Smiling) Thanks for saying hi! Hope you have a great night. (Turn away)

2. (Smiling) It was nice to meet you, and I hope you meet someone great tonight (turn away)

3. (Smiling) I'm flattered that you came over here, and I'm not interested. I hope you have a great night! (Turn away)

4. (Smiling, but less so) I'm not interested, and I know it's hard to hear that. I hope you find someone else who is! (Turn away)

5. (With kindness in my voice but not smiling) I'm concerned that it seems like you're having trouble accepting that I'm not interested. I know that it hurts to get turned down, and I really do hope you find someone else; I'm not going to be the person for you tonight. Now please let me get back to my night. (Turn away)

6. Involve the bartender, ask them to bring in security or the police.

For those of us socialized as women, the latter levels of no may feel very intimidating or impolite. We are socialized to be nice, even to our own detriment. We are told to be afraid, and often we need to be cautious as women are assaulted and murdered for saying no. If you get the feeling that someone might be dangerous, getting security involved, or calling in friends for support and backup, might be your best option.

However, if your only fear is that you might be "rude" to use the higher levels of no, I want you to consider this question: Why is it that you don't get to be firm with someone who is being rude to you? By the time I have escalated to a "rude" level of no, I've generally already told the person no 4-5 times. They are clearly not hearing me. I've been as kind as I can to someone who is unwilling to respect my no. If someone insists on being pushy and aggressive, it is totally okay for you to be very firm in response.

Something that can be helpful for these fears is coming up with a "no mantra," a phrase or saying that you use to remind yourself that you get to say no.

Some no mantras might be:

- 💜 My no is a gift
- 💜 Those who don't respect my no don't deserve my yes
- 💜 I am the only person who can determine what I am a yes to
- 💜 By saying no, I free myself up to say yes to things that I want

Fill out the Loving No worksheet to build your own levels of no and your own no mantras, then take it with you (on your phone, or as a piece of paper) to help you find and keep your no.

Build Your Loving "No"

Your "No" Has Levels.

♥ What is your kindest, most loving and caring no?

● What might be a "no" that's still kind, but a bit more firm?

■ What's moving to more firmness from there?

▲ What are some other "nos" that are firmer still?

❗ What is your final, most strong "no"?

What's Your "No" Mantra?

What are some statements you could tell yourself to remind yourself about the importance of your "no"?

1

2

3

4

Possessiveness

Around Valentine's Day, the whole of the US is covered in signs declaring "Be Mine." What does it mean to "be mine" for someone? If you spend much time on the internet you'll find dozens of memes and articles blithely regurgitating the messages underlying "be mine." Sayings like "Your happiness is right here" or "If you think my husband is cute you want to fight me" are pervasive and reveal the possessiveness and ownership mentality that the monogamy mindset teaches us. In the monogamy model, our partner is responsible for making us happy. Therefore, we are often told we can "encourage" them to do things for us that will make us happy, even if that's not what our partner wants to do. We are also told that our partner should have to ask us about what they do with their time and their body, especially when it comes to sex and dating.

As you can imagine, this kind of possessiveness doesn't work very well in non-monogamy. In fact, this is what often underlies potentially problematic behaviors like vetoes or the one penis policy. Possessiveness is also what often drives people who want to limit how much their partner dates or who their partner dates or how their partner engages sexually.

A lot of possessiveness is about our own fears and insecurities. If we worry that we cannot meet our own needs, or that our partner will not help us meet them without pressure, then we may begin acting out of those fears rather than from our values. After all, I doubt many of us would agree with the statement "It's okay to control my partner if it's about something I really really want." Most of us have values that align with freedom and choice and autonomy, we just may not act from those values all the time.

How do you let go of possessiveness? First, you have to take a good look at what messages you've learned about when it's okay to exert control over your partner. A lot of this comes from scarcity mindset behaviors, so go back to that section and evaluate whether scarcity is playing out for you.

Second, ask yourself these questions:

- ♥ Would it be okay for me to make these demands of a friend? Why is it okay with a partner?

- ♥ Who really "owns" my partner? Who "owns" me?

- ♥ What am I afraid will happen if I don't "force" my partner to do this?

- ♥ Can I trust my partner to consider my wants and needs without my needing to exert control?

Jealousy as a sign of caring

How many times in a show or movie does a character (usually a woman) see their partner (usually a man) suddenly act jealous about them and then say "Wow, you really DO care!"? Unfortunately, part of what we're fed in the standard relationship model is an idea that someone getting jealous about what we're doing means that they care about us more than someone who doesn't get jealous. But does jealousy actually mean they care?

Jealousy can come from a lot of different sources. I dive more deeply into jealousy in general in the section dedicated to jealousy (page 158), but for here let's put it this way - people who aren't feeling or acting jealous aren't necessarily less committed and don't care less. In fact, a lot of the models we see about how folks enact their jealousy reinforces toxic ideas about controlling and potentially abusive behaviors in relationships. Someone telling you to stop being friends with people because they're jealous isn't a way to show love, it's a way to isolate someone from sources of support.

Some questions to ask yourself include:

- ♥ What does my partner being jealous mean to me?

- ♥ How do I receive caring from a partner? What actions show me that a partner cares about me?

> 💜 How do I distinguish between behavior that is controlling and behavior that is caring?

Specialness

One of the biggest struggles folks often face when coming out of monogamy is figuring out what makes them "special" to their partner when exclusivity isn't available. In monogamy, we get to be the only person our partner does a whole host of things with - sex, cuddling, kissing, cohabitation, having children, parenting, and romantic love. Therefore, most of us learn that what makes us special is being their "one and only." So in non-monogamy, if I'm not the "one and only" of anything, how can I possibly feel special?

This aspect of the monogamy mindset can get really deep into us and be hard to explore and change. After all, isn't it okay to want to be special somehow? None of us wants to feel replaceable or to blend into the crowd of our partners' other partners. While it's normal to want to feel special or unique, I think that most of us have been taught to confuse exclusivity with specialness. What makes you special, is not the thing you get that no one else does. What makes you special is the things you are that no one else is.

When we define ourselves solely by a special label or activity, we put ourselves on shaky ground. After all, if your partner then changes their mind and wants to use that label or do that activity with someone else, you aren't special anymore. And, if current statistics about things like infidelity and divorce are any indicator, the likelihood of a partner changing their mind is probably higher than we want to admit.

If, instead, we define our uniqueness by qualities we have, all on our own, no one can ever take that away from us. This uniqueness goes beyond simply having rare qualities - for instance, I know that I'm not like any of my partner's other partners because no one is quite like me. How many Army veteran sex therapists who used to skydive and like to knit are there in the world? But even then, even if they found another person with all of those qualities, would that person actually be just like me?

Finding our own solid, internal sense of specialness is about knowing, deep down, that no one is actually like us. It's also about trusting that our partner isn't dating us just because they wanted a partner with x quality. For instance, I'm tall and curvy. My newest partner likes dating curvy women, but my curviness isn't the ONLY reason he's dating me. The connection that we have may have been inspired by his attraction to my curviness, but who I am and why he loves me both go much deeper than that.

Some questions to ask yourself:

- 💜 What makes me unique as a person?

- 💜 What makes me a great partner?

- 💜 How can I remind myself of what makes me special?

- 💜 What tends to make me question my specialness the most?

- 💜 What do I need when I'm worried that I'm not special?

Sociocultural issues with non-monogamous communities

Unfortunately, non-monogamy is not a utopia. Since all of us in these relationships were raised in cultures with their own flaws, it makes sense that our communities would often mirror those flaws. Since we live in a culture that structurally perpetuates the kyriarchy, it follows that non-monogamy would also struggle with issues relating to racism, classism, sexism, homophobia, transphobia, and ableism. None of us grow up in a vacuum, and when we are surrounded by biases and structures of privilege and oppression, we have to actively work against them in order to build more equal worlds.

In this section, we'll cover briefly some of the ways that structural system of privilege show up in non-monogamy communities, some thoughts on addressing them, and other folks you can read for even more in depth information.

Racism

If you look at almost any article about non-monogamy, the folks featured are white. This is true of stock photos AND of the people chosen to represent non-monogamy publicly. While there have been a few non-white folks featured in some recent articles (I.e. Kevin and Antoinette Patterson, William Winters), to those on the outside, non-monogamy looks like a thing for white people.

On the inside, this trend unfortunately holds. I've been to multiple events where there were only a handful of non-white people in attendance. At most conferences about non-monogamy, most of the presenters, attendees, and conference organizers are also white; the only exceptions I've found are conferences run by and specifically centering people of color (POC). Walking into a sea of white faces is unlikely to make black, indigenous, and people of color (BIPOC) feel like they belong. But the problem runs even deeper - non-white folks face endless micro-aggressions and fetishization by the folks in the community. How many experiences of people boiling someone down to their racialized features would it take before they leave and never return? Not very many.

Since I'm white, I asked Kevin Patterson, author of the book Love's Not Colorblind, to send me a couple of paragraphs to add in here. Here's what he had to say:

> **❝ It's funny because I wrote a whole book about how race** intersects with polyamory, filled it with personal stories, and there's still a ton of things I left out. There are so many times now where I wish I had had my own book as a resource when I ran into an awkward situation. My first time going to an event hosted by the biggest group in my local community started with a racial microaggression. I was less than ten minutes in before somebody said something they thought was okay until they read the look on my face.
>
> At a conference where I was one of less than ten people of color, an older gentleman asked me what I was there to present. I explained that I was there to give a workshop on the racial dynamics of polyamory. In an almost entirely white event, hosted within an almost entirely

white community, this man told me that he didn't need to attend my workshop because he had just started dating a black woman within the last two months. I was too tired to explain that his use of a black woman as a shield was exactly the kind of thing that I spoke about in the workshop. For every one of these situations that I remember and cringe about, there's a dozen more that I've forgotten. Most run together for me, honestly. But I still showed up because I wanted to engage and because I'm never quiet about the racial elephant in the room. By that same token though, for every one of me that still makes themselves visible in these spaces...there are dozens more that just never return.

As Kevin implies, most of the folks who are doing the things that make BIPOC feel unwelcome would almost certainly swear they "aren't racist." They just love dark skin! They just wanted to touch the hair! They've just heard their dicks are bigger! They just thought those folks would be submissive! These people would tell you, emphatically, that their intent was not to hurt or upset anyone. And yet, even when you tell them these things weren't okay, they'll often scoff and say you're making too big a deal out of something or that they just can't convince people of color to participate or that they don't know how to find BIPOC to invite.

The most important things to cover here are that 1) your intent matters less than your impact and 2) we need to listen to BIPOC when they tell us something isn't okay. Luckily, Kevin's book, Love's Not Color Blind, is full of stories that address how all of us can be better about the racial issues in non-monogamy. I strongly recommend everyone read this book, especially those of you thinking "I don't really need to read that."

Classism

When we look at the costs involved in going to a swinger club or a sex party or a dungeon space, and then think about the cost of the sex toys and safer sex supplies, and the cost of dinners and drinks out on dates, it's easy to see how non-monogamy could feel unattainable for those who don't have a ton of spare money. While non-monogamy can in some ways lead to opportunities for savings in the long run, (shared housing, more breadwinners per child), in the short run it's often expensive.

Just as a BIPOC person walking into an all white space might feel unwelcome, showing up to a house party in an old Honda Civic when everyone else is in new luxury cars can have the same effect. Do we really want non-monogamy to be a thing only the rich can do? Do we want to normalize that you have to make a certain salary in order to be welcomed? Most of us have lots of internalized beliefs that those with more money are better, smarter, nicer, prettier, or otherwise more deserving. After all, as Ronald Wright said, "Socialism never took root in America because the poor see themselves not as an exploited proletariat but as temporarily embarrassed millionaires." We all believe that we'll be the next people to get rich and that our finances will then finally match our beliefs about who we are.

As you move through non-monogamous communities, take note of whether and how they make space for those with less disposable income. Are there volunteer shifts? Do they have a donation based door charge? Do they offer scholarships or income based payment? How do they make sure that everyone can have a good time, regardless of their income?

Sexism

Because we've got a special section on issues addressing trans and non-binary folks, this section and the next one will talk predominantly about cis folks.

"Slut" is how we punish women for saying yes. "Bitch" is how we punish women for saying no.

While in some ways women have more power in non-monogamy communities than in mainstream dating communities (e.g. easier time finding dates, cheaper rates at sex clubs), in others ways sexism is still prevalent. For instance, clubs offer lower prices to women with the thought that having sexy women around will lead the men to spend more money.

Men's voices are often privileged over women's, with the leaders of many of the biggest communities being men. Many of the most well paid speakers and teachers in the non-monogamy and sex-positive worlds are also men, even though there are far more women doing the work. In some sub-communities, men still treat women like their property, asking each other for permission to sleep with each other's partners rather than talking directly with the women. In addition, many people still view sex between two women as less "real" than sex that involves a penis. Women also tend to face more slut shaming than men do, often couched in the language of sexual risk.

The next time you are in a non-monogamy community, look around you and see who the leaders and teachers are. Who is most respected? Who is doing the work? Who gets paid for their work and who doesn't? How do people talk about women or treat them when they have a lot of sex? Who holds decision making power in sexual encounters? Who gives oral sex and who receives it?

Homophobia

While women having sex with other women is normalized in many non-monogamy communities, men interacting sexually with men may not be. This double standard probably comes from sexism - women having sex with each other isn't real, men having sex with other men is an abomination. After all, it's the presence of a penis that makes or breaks the realness of sex! (Ugh)

In addition, while women are expected to be bi, lesbians and gay folks may struggle to find a welcoming place in more heteronormative pockets of non-monogamy. When everyone arrives in male-female couples, then asks you where your partner is, you can feel invisible.

When you interact with other folks, notice what assumptions you're bringing with you to these interactions. Are you assuming everyone has sex with people of certain genders? Do you assume some people are couples based on their genders? If you're someone who has strong negative reactions to people having sex with folks of their same gender, take some time to think about why that upsets you so much. What is it about someone else's queerness that's impacting you?

Cissexism

How many times have you seen a gendered dress code for a party? How many spaces have you been to that have a Men's bathroom and a Women's bathroom? The non-monogamous world is often guilt of erasing and ignoring trans and non-binary (enby) folks. There are more than two genders and, no matter how much you think you can, you can't actually guess anyone's gender by looking at them.

Folks who identify as trans often face the same kinds of alternating exclusion and fetishization as BIPOC and disabled people. They also face an onslaught of microaggressions in the form of misgendering, dismissal, invasive questioning, and focus on their genitals as the true sign of their gender. It's just as inappropriate to ask "But what are you really, like biologically?" as it is to ask "But where are you REALLY from?" Trans and non-binary folks aren't freak show spectacles to objectify and degrade. They are whole humans with their own story and experience and desires. Being trans or non-binary also isn't necessarily related to your sexual orientation. Trans and enby folks can be straight, gay, bi, pan, ace, or any other identification.

If you look around your community and don't think there are any trans/enby folks in it, 1) there probably are and 2) they probably don't feel safe enough to be out. Start by addressing the "little" things like bathrooms, dress codes, pricing, and language used in fliers. See if you can find a trans/enby teacher to come to your community and teach a class, preferably NOT on trans/enby issues. Work to set up a night that is just for trans/enby folks so that they can have a space of their own.

Ableism

In our society, having impairments is thought of as a Bad Thing. We don't have good structures to support those whose bodies don't function the way we think they should. Simultaneously, we infantilize and objectify those who are disabled by using them as inspiration - the message is, if this poor creature can do something, what's wrong with you? In this book, I will used the word disabled in the way that the social model of disability does. In this model the idea is that people have impairments, but it is society that disables them. After all, for someone who uses a wheelchair, it is the absence of a ramp that impacts their ability to do things, not their utilization of a chair.

When it comes to non-monogamy while disabled, the same problems of exclusion and fetishization exist. For those with visible disabilities, people often define them by their disability and decide whether or not to have sex with them based on their feelings about those disabilities. For those with invisible disabilities, they are often told they aren't "really" disabled or, if they have mental health conditions, they may hear over and over again "don't stick your dick in crazy."

Shortly before I deployed to Afghanistan, my left shoulder started doing something . . . funky. I could hear popping and crackling when I moved it certain ways. As someone whose body has always done some weird stuff, I just figured this was my body doing its weird thing. Yes it hurt, and yes sometimes the pain was really bad, but I grew up figure skating, I could take pain.

While on deployment, my NCO (non-commissioned officer, the high ranking enlisted person working as my psych tech) heard my shoulder do its snap, crackle, pop routine and was horrified. He started urging me to see the doc on post. Being a stubborn person, I refused for a good few months.

On one particularly bad day, he insisted that I go, so I went to the aid station. When I showed the medic what I meant about my shoulder, his face said it all - this is NOT normal. The PA came in and said he had heard the popping sound (properly called crepitus) from 10-15 feet away. I was diagnosed with scapulothoracic bursitis, or "snapping scapula." The first line of treatment was to rest it and see if it resolved, with the option to get steroid injections in a month or so if it hadn't. A month passed, and it was the same.

Before the diagnosis, I had been doing high intensity interval training workouts, going to CrossFit classes, and working on getting a pull-up. Now, I couldn't use my left arm. When the Physical Therapist came through my post, he gave me some exercises to do to help with my shoulder and with my migraines. I started doing them regularly. Still no improvement.

I got my first steroid injection a couple of months before the end of my deployment. For a day or two, it felt great. But the pain and popping and discomfort soon returned. A month after the first injection, I got my second injection with much the same results. I returned to Hawaii for three months before moving to Georgia and was told to get physical therapy and a consult with orthopedics after my move.

Once in Georgia, I did a full course of physical therapy with no improvement and was referred to orthopedics. Luckily, I was assigned to one of the same doctors I had seen in Afghanistan. He told me he thought I was a good candidate for surgery and we scheduled it for June of 2014. I would be significantly impaired for about three weeks, so I made care plans with my parents and my then partner.

The surgery was a bursectomy, removing the inflamed bursa that were causing the problem. While inside, they found a ridge on my scapula that they thought might be causing the problem so they did a scapuloplasty as well. For the next month, things felt great. The popping and pain were gone! Well, the surgical pain was there, but it seemed like I was going to be better. Right around the 1 month mark, though, everything returned. I went in for my check up and was told that this was permanent - I now had a disability.

I was separated from the military due to disability. Between my migraines, shoulder issue, and other problems that had developed during my service, I was rated 80% disabled through the military system. These days, I work on controlling my chronic pain with massage, posture awareness, acupuncture (sometimes), medications as needed, and focusing on controlling my stress and activity. I still have pain every day, but it's pretty low level so I can cope with it. However, I have to be very careful of how I use my left arm, so every partner I have sex with gets a quick FYI that some positions don't work well for me because of my disability.

The reactions I get when I tell folks I'm disabled can be interesting. I've had some people tell me I'm not "really" disabled, just "Army disabled." I think they mean this as a compliment, but that's not how it feels.

I've had others who get very timid and scared when I tell them I have a disability, even if I tell them that I'm great at letting people know what I need for my body and that if I haven't said anything it's because I'm fine. I've had others say, "Well yeah, but it's not a bad disability, so that's good, right?" and others ask if it's genetic, you know, in case of kids.

When everything around you tells you that disability is a Bad Thing, it's easy to make those with disabilities feel like outsiders. The irony here is that all of us are at best temporarily abled. Our fragile human bodies rarely make it from birth to death without impairment but we often don't see how our society ables those without impairments until we ourselves have one. You don't notice how awful stairs are until you're on crutches, or how challenging a manual transmission car is until you have a sprained ankle. But while these frustrations are temporary, those who are disabled are facing challenges everyday.

When it comes to sex, we often think that disabled folks can't have sex, can't have "real sex," or are incapable of making their own decisions about sex. On online dating sites, folks with disabilities are often asked how they can have sex as one of the first questions from someone. Can you imagine how objectifying that feels?

Coming to terms with my disability has been a challenging journey, but I'm much better for it. For instance, I don't just endure uncomfortable positions, I either move myself or let someone know I need to move. I speak up for my body's needs much more assertively than I did before. And how a potential partner reacts to the news that I have a disability tells me lots of valuable information about them. If a partner seems uncomfortable or dismissive, that's probably not someone I want to be with.

On the other hand, if they ask me what I need for accommodations or how that affects my life, that's a person more likely to be a good fit.

If you have a disability, particularly a visible disability, you probably already know that dating is likely to be harder for you. Ableism teaches people that disabled people either aren't sexual or aren't sexy. It says that abled partners are obviously more desirable and a better choice because disability is a Bad Thing. Ableism also makes folks think that it's okay to ask really personal questions about our bodies and their functions. It can feel exhausting trying to educate people or help them be less bad at treating disabled people like people.

When you move through the non-monogamy community, notice how accessible your community is to those who are disabled. Are the spaces and events wheelchair accessible? Are there quiet, still spaces for people who become overwhelmed by noise and crowds? If a partner lets you know that they're disabled, remember that they're still a whole human. Ask them questions about what they want or need from you and let them be the expert of their needs and experience.

Some great folks to listen to and read on sex and disability are Andrew Gurza of the Disability After Dark podcast, Robin Wilson-Benson of SexAbled, Bethany Stevens, Claire Eh, and Ryan (@TrojanViper on Twitter).

Monogamous/heterosexual passing privilege

Folks who look like "normal" couples often have an easier time in the non-monogamy world than those who don't. For heteronormative couples who look like "regular people," and others who can be easily closeted or who "pass", their lives may be far easier than those who are not closeted or who choose relationship styles less close to the mainstream norm. When closeted folks do non-monogamy, they also to some degree force their partners into the closet with them, requiring new stories about how they know each other and what their relationship is to each other.

Sometimes, the choice to "pass" is necessary for reasons explored in the social risk section. There's never a right or wrong answer about whether any individual person should be out, especially in a time like now where there is no protection in the law for folks who are non-monogamous. On the flip side of the coin, protections and understanding are likely to take longer if fewer people are out. And, when you're passing, you're opening yourself to being exposed in ways you may not choose, so there's not really a safe haven here.

In general, it's helpful to think about how your decisions to "pass" are affecting yourself, your partners, and the non-monogamy community as a whole. Weighing these variables is complicated and can be challenging. As I've talked about throughout the book, humans in general are prone to being pretty risk averse, so you may have a tendency to over perceive risks and under perceive benefits. Talk it over with folks who have made choices to be out and those who have chosen to pass and try to see where you fall on that spectrum.

Couple (and other) privilege

A lot of folks have strong reactions to discussions of privilege, so let's start with talking about what privilege means in general. When someone talks about "privilege" as it relates to social justice or societal dynamics, what they are talking about is unearned benefits bestowed by society upon some folks and not others. Privilege doesn't mean that your life is automatically easy. It simply means there are certain kinds of difficulties you are less likely to face.

For instance, if you are white, it is unlikely that you will be discriminated against because of your race when it comes to things like employment or housing. If you're a man, it's unlikely you'll be treated worse because of your gender when it comes to things like salary or hiring. If you're cisgender (that is, your internal understanding of your own gender agrees with the gender they assigned you at birth), you're unlikely to have the same kinds of troubles accessing services and healthcare and bathrooms as someone who isn't cisgender.

The blog Privilege 201 describes the two ways the term privilege is used in discussions of social justice currently. The first, privilege_1, refers to these larger societal systems that confer benefits to some folks, without their having to seek them. Because society is structured to line up in those ways, the folks benefitting from societal privilege, or privilege_1, often don't see the ways in which privilege is making things easy for them. To them, this is how the world is for everyone because their privilege ensures they do not face the obstacles that are put up for others.

The second kind of privilege, privilege_2, is the one being referenced when someone says "check your privilege." Privilege_2 is the individual ways that we enact or exercise our societal privilege in our interpersonal interactions. For instance, this could include centering your own feelings when you're told that something you said was racist or claiming that the experiences of oppressed groups aren't really happening because you've never personally seen or experienced them.

Because privilege_1 is invisible, those who have it often don't recognize how it is influencing their thoughts, actions, and beliefs. A great example of this is Marie Antoinette wondering why the peasants couldn't just eat brioche if they were out of bread. In her world, she couldn't imagine NOT having an abundance of food continually available so her words, often translated as "let them eat cake," came off as insensitive and cruel.

When you have a lot of privilege_1 and aren't aware of it, it's likely that you'll end up doing or saying things that hurt people who don't have that same privilege. While you may not intend to act like Marie Antoinette, you may have found yourself doing so in form if not degree.

When someone talks about privilege, then, they are likely talking about the societal structures (privilege_1) and the ways in which those benefiting from those structures end up hurting those without (privilege_2).

Within non-monogamy, many communities are struggling to be more aware of how privilege_1 and privilege_2 are creating space that tend to be largely white, cisgender, upper middle class, thin, and heteronormative. If you look at most mainstream articles about non-monogamy, the folks featured are likely to be conventionally attractive white people living in relatively heteronormative structures who have plenty of money to have big houses. While this is the most media prominent face of non-monogamy, it isn't the whole story, but does reflect ways in which our cultural dynamics are recreated even in our subculture.

Some obvious ways that privilege_1 shows up in non-monogamy relate to race, as discussed more previously. People who aren't white are often tokenized or fetishized in non-monogamous communities or excluded from them. If all of the leaders of a community or almost all of the attendees at events are white, it's worth considering how that might make it much harder for people who aren't white to participate.

A second way we see privilege show up in communities is in the way those who stick closest to heteronormative scripts are often more welcome. For instance, it's fairly common and widely acceptable for women to be bisexual in non-monogamous communities, but it can be very challenging for men who are bisexual to find the same acceptance.

In addition, when discussing STI risk and prevention, people often focus on the practices people have when interacting with bio dicks than they do with vulvas. Few people expect two vulva havers to use barrier protection with each other, but someone having unprotected contact (especially penetrative sex) with a penis is considered shocking. People who do more traditional male/female coupling also often feel more welcomed and accepted than those who do less traditional structures.

On the whole, one area of privilege that tends to show up more in non-monogamy circles than elsewhere is couple privilege. Couple privilege refers to the ways in which society offers benefits to those who seem to be in heteronormative, monogamous looking arrangements.

Some examples of how couple privilege can show up:

💜 People who are married are considered more "mature" than those who aren't

💜 Many sex spaces will allow couples but not singles, especially not single men

💜 Viewing longer term, more mainstream looking relationships as more "real" than those that aren't

- ❤ Valuing the preservation of a pre-existing relationship over the evolving wants/needs of those involved

- ❤ Tax breaks for married folks

- ❤ Couple discounts

- ❤ Creating a relationship structure for a "third" or unicorn to fit into

Unicorn hunting

Hardly a week goes by in any online polyamory group without a couple who is newly opening their relationship coming in to say they are looking for a "third to complete their relationship." They're pretty much always looking for a hot bisexual woman who will agree to love them both equally, have sex with both of them, and accept the space in their lives that they have built for her. She obviously won't date or have sex with other people, will help them with child rearing, and will always "respect" their relationship as primary.

Now many of you may be reading that description and thinking "well what's so bad about that?" Let's take a different look at it.

> **Example:** *Jake and Leslie are married and want to start having kids someday soon. They have recently decided to open their marriage. As a part of that process, they had several long, in depth conversations about what this would look like. In particular, they talked about the kind of person they want to bring into their relationship and what their expectations are for that person. They also spent time deciding what that person can and cannot do. For instance, they need the person to have sex with both of them, love them both equally, and not date other people. Once they have a child, they want this person to help with childcare. She will however respect their relationship and understand that she cannot have her own children since they are the primary couple. Having fully formed this relationship idea, they go out looking for someone who will agree to all of their pre-decided terms.*

Don't see it yet? Let's try another one.

> **Example:** *Sarah and Joan are roommates who have decided to have a third roommate move in. As a part of that process, they had several long, in depth conversations about what this would look like. In particular, they talked about the kind of person they want to bring into their house and what their expectations are for that person. They also spent time deciding what that person can and cannot do. For instance, they need the person to have interact equally with both of them, like them both equally, and not be friends with other people. Once they have a pet, they want this person to help with pet care. She will however respect their relationship and understand that she cannot have her own pets since they are the primary roommates. Having fully formed this idea, they go out looking for someone who will agree to all of their pre-decided terms.*

In both of these examples, there have been big, important discussions about something that will affect someone, only that person doesn't get to be involved. Couple privilege is a big part of the system that teaches folks that it's okay to create a very particular confined box for another person and expect them to fit themselves into it. Can you imagine moving into a house where you get no say in the house rules? Where your roommates expect you to bow down to their preferences and not listen to yours?

Why should a romantic relationship be any different?

Couple privilege often makes life much harder for folks who aren't able or don't want to be in "traditional" relationships. After all, if someone isn't going to think of you as a "mature" adult until you're married and own a house, and you don't actually want marriage or cohabitation, you can feel left out of success and maturity.

Now like all other forms of privilege, folks don't necessarily ask to be given this privilege and having it doesn't necessarily mean you're a jerk. However, understanding that you have certain kinds of privilege requires you to be more mindful of how that privilege is affecting the things you're doing and thinking and how those choices may be affecting others. You can benefit from couple privilege and never treat other people like a living sex toy; the key is to make sure that your choices are informed by the ways that privilege is going to show up in your dynamics.

Letting Go of Judgment

As we've talked about in this book, there are almost as many ways to do non-monogamy as there are people doing it. However, it's fairly common within the world of non-monogamy for people to get, well, judgy about people who do it differently than they do.

> *Example: Dhruv and Satya are very involved in tantra and took spiritual names as a part of their practice. They also have chosen polyamory as a part of their spiritual path. Sometimes, they tell other people that polyamory is the most evolved path and that they are sad for the people who haven't been able to let go of their "attachments" enough to practice it. One night, they are at dinner with Amanda and Ken who are swingers. Amanda and Ken think that swinging is the only safe way to do non-monogamy because they have seen so many breakups in polyamory. Over the course of dinner, Satya and Amanda get into an argument after Satya says that swinging is too focused on sex and Amanda points out that Satya has plenty of sex in her polyamorous situation. Everyone walks away from the dinner feeling like they were misunderstood and the other people were wrong.*

There is no one "right" way to do non-monogamy. However, the human brain tends to do poorly with holding nuance - we want a clear good, a clear bad, an easy right and an obvious wrong. This tends to be particularly true for those who are under high amounts of stress or who have histories of trauma - the traumatized brain is particularly drawn to all-or-nothing, black-and-white thinking. Being on the edges of society often involves a certain degree of constant stress, with looming possible consequences of outing, losing friends and family, or even losing employment or child custody, so unfortunately our communities which should be some of the most supportive and accepting are often the most quick to judgment and shame.

In reality, all of us stepping outside of society's predefined scripts for what relationships should look like means we are all different players on a similar team: we all want the freedom to love how we want and to have sex in the ways that feel good to us. When we focus our energy on tearing each other down, we end up like crabs in a barrel. It is much easier and feels more powerful to choose the route of tearing down others to elevate ourselves, and yet I'm sure most of us wouldn't consider being judgmental to be a quality of our best selves.

As with many of the conflicts we describe in this book, it is easiest to stay judgmental about others when we come from a place ruled by the narratives we have created in our own minds. It is much harder to stay this way when we focus on coming from a place of compassion and curiosity.

Our judgments in these situations are often about our need to defend our own decisions to ourselves, and defense by negative comparison is often easier for us than by having to outline the individual merits. It is harder for instance to say that polyamory is a legitimate relationship structure on its own because of how well it works for those who practice it than it is to say polyamory is about love unlike those swingers who are all about sex.

This is a good time to bring up respectability politics. This concept, first written about by Evelyn Brooks Higginbotham in 2001 in her book, Righteous Discontent, about the black women's movement in the Baptist Church, looks at how each movement towards greater empowerment and recognition often into a cycle of trying to minimize or undermine any cultural or moral practices that mainstream culture does or would not respect. In feminism, this often looks like trying to find ways for people who aren't cis men to be successful in cis man created and privileging structures rather than changing the structures. Examples would be arguing for a woman's right to choose what to do with her body, but claiming sex workers are undermining feminism. Or, stating that trans women aren't "real" women because they weren't born as women. In queer communities, respectability politics often looks like emphasizing stable, monogamous relationship models over others. In short, respectability politics seeks to gain acceptance by saying "Look! We're like you!" rather than saying "Look! We're also people!"

Since mainstream culture valorizes love over sex, and more monogamous, marriage-and-kids looking relationships over other forms, respectability politics in the non-monogamy world often looks like shaming casual sex or those who have a lot of sex. Often, when someone is doing a different form of non-monogamy than we are, it can be tempting to point to the elements of that structure that either our personal "in group" dislikes or to those elements that mainstream culture would shame. So if you're solo poly, you might bemoan the way that swingers "treat their partners like sex toys" or how people in hierarchical poly aren't as "enlightened" as you are.

Our judgments are almost always more about ourselves, our own fears and shame, than they are about other people. So when you find yourself putting on your judgy pants, take a step back and see where that's coming from for you. If you're having any thoughts along the lines of "they're giving us a bad name" or "they're not as enlightened/open minded/evolved," those beliefs are almost certainly more about your need to feel okay and less about what they are doing.

Now this isn't to say that there aren't some harmful ways to do non-monogamy. As I talk about throughout this book, there are some approaches to non-monogamy that disempower others or that create unethical uses of power, coercion, or control. So how do you walk the line between acknowledging and pointing out problematic behaviors and not going to places of judgment for differences?

Brené Brown writes clearly in her books that shame is NOT an effective tool to use for behavioral change. As she writes, one of the best questions you can ask someone to get a feeling for their own relationship to shame is how they feel about the statement "Everyone is doing the best they can with the tools they have." People who are mired in systems of shame and perfectionism will often vehemently disagree with this statement. "No!" they will say, "Some people are NOT doing their best. They are doing it wrong on purpose!" or "No! I am having these troubles because I didn't do the best I could and this is my fault."

Shame is what tells us we are wrong or bad and deserve the bad things that happen to us. It is what lets us feel like those who are struggling must have done something to deserve it. Shame is often related to the just world belief, that good things happen to good people and bad things happen to bad people. And while it makes sense that parents and schools and religious institutions would want to teach us that good things come to us when we're good and bad things will happen if we're bad, this belief bears little resemblance to the real world. Most of us are not "good" people or "bad people," we are flawed, complex beings struggling to do the best we can in a complicated, messy world.

Another important concept to bring up here is that most of us learned about how to deal with people who do "bad" things using a carceral mindset. The carceral mindset comes from the system of carceral justice that most of us are raised in - if someone breaks the law/rules, they are a bad person and need to be punished for it. If they do very bad things, they are disposable and we should get rid of them, either through jailing or execution or shunning. The carceral system appeals to our desire to have clear lines between good and bad, innocent and guilty, and yet who among us has never broken the law? I know, you're saying "But Liz, that was different. I was a kid! It wasn't a big law! Those laws are dumb!" And that's the thing - our world is not so clear as the carceral system needs it to be.

The carceral approach also offers us only two options whenever we think someone might have done something "bad" - punish or acquit. If we like the person, we are likely to want to acquit, even if they did the "bad" thing. This is why so many communities have trouble dealing with sexual assault, harassment, and boundary pushing behavior. When your only options are shunning or doing nothing, you're going to want to see a lot of evidence of really bad things before you choose anything other than nothing.

When you see someone doing non-monogamy "badly," it can be very tempting to jump in with shaming, judgment, or social consequences (banning, talking about them online) to "fix" them or "punish" them. And yet, none of us would want folks from the mainstream, monogamous world to apply those things to us. Instead, we must work to find the places of compassion, kindness, caring, curiosity, accountability, and growth if we are to create a community that can help everyone in it be better with each other.

What does this look like? Well, I'm going to talk about this much more in the "when you see messed up stuff" section. In general, when you see or hear about someone doing something "wrong," take a step back and ask yourself - is this something harmful or is it something different? Are the choices this person is making hurting others? Are they mistreating others? Are they spreading dangerous misinformation? If you cannot locate any actual harm, it might be worth asking yourself whether what they are doing is actually "wrong." If it is creating harm, then it's even more important to take a step back and get a clear look at what is happening. What specifically are they doing that is wrong? What are the precise behaviors or beliefs that are causing harm? What is the nature of the harm they are causing? Use the Responding to Messed Up Stuff worksheet (page 246) to help you clarify what the specific harm is.

Next, you'll need to think about what it is you want to do about the harm. Do you have enough of a relationship with these folks to talk to them directly about it? Is there a community leader who might need to be involved? Is this something that you personally have to be involved in calling out or correcting or is there someone who is a better fit to handle it?

If you are the person who chooses to be involved in talking about it, and are not the person being directly harmed (we'll get to this in a bit), the next step is to take some time to try to understand and empathize with the other folks. What might be driving these choices? How can you find some caring and compassion for them? Can you see them as full, complex humans and not define them by this behavior? How might they best receive feedback? What kinds of factors might be influencing the choices they are making? How might they react to what you're going to tell them? How might they feel in this conversation? What kinds of support or help might they need to handle this conversation and to effectively make change?

After this, it's time to consider all of the different options you can think of for how they can make amends and demonstrate accountability for causing harm. It's important here to do some preliminary brainstorming, even though when you have the conversation you're going to give them a chance to brainstorm as well, because it's so easy to get mired into one or two options. When you brainstorm, be sure to come up with some "solutions" that you would never actually choose as this can help loosen up your thought processes. For instance, if the harm the person caused was mistreatment of one of their partners, you could have them put in a pillory in the public square and pummeled with rotting produce as someone yelled "Shame!" over and over. You need to spend a good chunk of time letting your brain come up with options because it'll want to stop after one or two, especially your most preferred options, but the bigger your response buffet is, the more likely it is to have a dish everyone can agree on.

The next to last step is to move forward with the conversation. With as much kindness and caring as you can muster, let the person know what they did and what the harm was. Let them have their initial reaction - most of us feel upset and defensive and hurt when we are called out about something. Show them understanding, and let them know that you want to find a solution together. Ask them what different solutions they can come up with, help them brainstorm with you. Let them know what you think accountability and change might look like and see if you can find common ground. Then come up with a plan for what happens moving forward.

The last step is to implement the plan and check in on how it's going. Is the person honoring their commitments? Do things need to change? How are they responding?

The last thing we'll cover here is how these steps might be different if you are the person being harmed by someone's bad non-monogamy. It is much harder to do the above process when you are the one directly harmed. When someone has hurt us, it is harder for us to find empathy and caring. So if you were harmed, it might be worth enlisting the help of others for the process. In general, it may still be helpful to go through the steps of identifying the what the harm was and where it came from, but you may not be the best person to then work with them through the process of accountability and change.

When we are harmed, it is also quite easy to fall back into patterns of thinking of and treating people like they are disposable. When someone has harmed you,

you do not EVER have to let them back into your life. You don't have to forgive them, you don't have to be their friend. However, as tempting as it may be to view this person as disposable because of the harm you experienced, it's important to make the distinction between "I don't want to have this person in my life" and "this person doesn't deserve to have a life." In "Why It's Painful and Scary to Talk About Transformative Justice and Why It's Time," Andy I talks about finding the solutions that honor both your rage and your compassion.

Jealousy, Insecurity, and Dating, OH MY!

"Don't you get jealous?" "How can you trust them?" "What if they date someone younger/prettier/etc.?" "What do you do when they're out with someone else?"

Any book on non-monogamy will cover these kinds of questions because these are the ones us non-monogamous folks frequently hear from those outside our communities. For this book, I've lumped these three areas together because of how they're interconnected. Jealousy, after all, is often triggered by our partner dating and may stem from our own insecurities. Sometimes the struggles with have with our partner dating are related to our insecurities and may trigger emotions such as sadness and fear and anxiety.

So, because they often play together in our brains and lives, I'm going to address these topics here together. We'll start with the green-eyed monster, then move into the things that make us feel shaky about ourselves, and then cover how to deal with your partner dating and be good to your partner(s) when you date.

Jealousy

Probably the most common thing I hear from monogamous folks when I talk about being polyamorous is "Oh I could never do that, I would just be so jealous!" Honestly, I never know quite what to say there because the correlation between the two parts of that statement makes no sense to me.

Here, let me zoom out to help you see it -

- ♥ I could never let my partner have friends, I would be so jealous!

- ♥ I could never let my partner travel for work, I would miss them!

- ♥ I could never date someone, I would be so sad if we broke up!

- ♥ I could never stay with someone for decades, it would hurt so much when they died!

- ♥ I could never be serious with someone, I would be so angry if they hurt me!

Do you see now why I just don't get these statements? For some reason, our culture has decided that jealousy is the one emotion that we never ever have to question or move past.

It's also the one emotion that has the ability to shut down potential decisions not with its presence, but with its potential to happen. These folks aren't talking about the reality they faced of experiencing their partner finding joy with others, they're hypothesizing that they would struggle and therefore ruling out the possibility entirely.

Does jealousy happen in non-monogamy? All the time. Just like joy, sadness, grief, excitement, anger, fulfillment, all the other emotions we feel in relationships. You're not bad at non-monogamy if you feel jealousy. Jealousy, like all emotions, simply gives us information; we have to decide what we then DO with that information.

Before we dive much more deeply into this discussion of jealousy, let's distinguish between jealousy and envy. Jealousy is "I want the thing you have and I don't want you to have it." Envy is "I want the thing you have and you can also have it." Envy tends to be a bit easier to cope with and overcome than jealousy.

Jealousy in our culture tends to cover many other feelings. The most common ones are insecurity, anger, disappointment, fear, resentment, and loneliness. When we feel like our partnership is at risk, we are much more likely to be upset by choices our partners make with other folks. When we don't feel good about ourselves, we are more likely to believe that others are "better" than us and will obviously lure away our partners.

If we've been trying to get a partner to do something with us and they never have and then they do it with someone else, we may feel angry and frustrated and disappointed and just lump these feelings into jealousy instead. When we're already upset with a partner, everything they do will build on that resentment and irritation and may push these feelings out of us as jealousy instead, particularly if we feel like we can't be honest about our resentments. Jealousy can be particularly strong when we feel like our partner is getting all the dates or sex or attention and we aren't getting it.

So what do you do about jealousy? As with most feelings, first just let yourself notice it. Notice how it feels in your body, notice the thoughts it brings up in your brain and what it tells you is the "truth." Pay attention to what the jealousy tells you to do. Write all of these things down or talk about them with a trusted friend, because until they're out in the open they're going to be hard to look at to see what's real and what's reaction.

Once you've identified the story that the jealousy is telling you and the actions it wants you to take, try doing a few deep breaths to calm down your body. Focus on slowing down your breath, breathing deep into your diaphragm/belly, and listen to your heart rate slow. Breathe for about 5 minutes. Now look back at what you wrote and ask yourself, if I was coming at this situation from a place of curiosity and compassion, how might I think differently about it? What are the questions I need to ask my partner? What is it that I want or need that I'm not getting right now? Try to find ways to phrase these in the most neutral way you can and remind yourself that you're putting in this effort because you (at least theoretically) love your partner.

Then schedule a time to discuss it with your partner. Using our tough conversation guide, let them know what you felt, what the story was that your brain told you, and ask them for what you need. Your request here could be reassurance, it could be specific actions, it could be a date night, whatever you think will be helpful. Then ask your partner for their feedback and what of your requests they feel good about.

Remember - they get to have their own feelings here too and they may not be able to do exactly the behaviors you want. Instead of focusing on specific details, instead come to the space of creatively collaborating on solutions.

Common Jealousy Triggers

While there's nothing that is guaranteed to trigger jealousy, here are some common situations or experiences that can bring up jealous feelings when your partner does them:

- ♥ Dating someone you perceive to be more attractive than you are

- ♥ Dating someone significantly younger or older than you

- ♥ Dating someone with more money

- ♥ Expressing NRE

- ♥ Desiring a deeper connection with a newer partner

- ♥ Wanting to do special activities with the partner

- ♥ Using a special pet name with someone else

Compersion

An emotion people who do non-monogamy often talk about is compersion, or joy in your partner's joy. While this is often called the opposite of jealousy, I think that they often coexist about the same situation. Compersion, like jealousy, is easier or more common for some folks than for others. While I feel compersion quickly and easily and frequently, many people struggle to ever really feel it. There's no right or wrong here. Being good at compersion does not make you more enlightened or better at non-monogamy.

Compersion can be learned. One of the most common questions folks tend to have is how to get rid of jealousy, but unlearning jealousy is often more challenging that learning how to have compersion.

When dealing with feelings, we can often think about feelings, thoughts, and behaviors as all being interrelated. After all, if we feel sad, we're likely to do sad behaviors (crying, staying in, low energy) and think sad thoughts. If we have sad thoughts playing in our head (no one likes me, I'm all alone), we're likely to do sad behaviors and feel sad feelings. Likewise, if we do sad behaviors, it's likely we'll have sad thoughts and sad feelings. This basic theory is what underlies cognitive behavioral theory.

When what we want to change is feelings, it's often easiest to work first on changing the thoughts and behaviors instead. For compersion, we can focus on some of the thoughts and behaviors that exemplify this feeling.

Compersion thoughts:

- My partner's happiness increases my happiness

- Love grows the more we share it

- My partner's excitement is infectious

- The more my partner is fed by their life, the more they have available to give to me

- My partner is choosing to continue building with me every time they spend time with me

- Everyone dating my partner is on the same team

- All of us share in improving my partner's life

Compersion behaviors

- Congratulating your partner on their positive experiences

- Expressing interest in the positive qualities of their partners

- Encouraging them to spend time with people who make them happy

♥ Developing positive metamour relationships

Insecurities

I don't think I know of any actual human being who has managed to make it to their adult life free of insecurities. At their base level, our insecurities come from the ways in which we fear we are wrong. We learn our insecurities from all sorts of places - the things people teased us about when we were younger, the messages we get from media, the ways our parents criticize us, the things we've been told by friends/partners.

Insecurities are like bug bites. They call out to us for our attention, telling us to please scratch at them. Yet when we do, we find ourselves even more itchy. The more we listen to what the insecurity tells us to do, the worse it gets until we're left with an open, tender wound.

In some ways, we can think of insecurities as the way our brain tries to protect us from rejection. We think to ourselves, if I can just change this thing then I'll never be rejected again. So we force ourselves into the shapes we think someone will love, fearing the whole time that they'll see we were never that shape to begin with.

It is normal to have insecurities. What we must be aware of and conscious about is what we choose to DO about those insecurities. After all, if we give into the ways they want us to act, often we end up damaging our relationships. If my insecurity tells me I am "too much" for someone, I won't voice my wants and needs, instead trying to just not have them. That cannot lead to success in the long term.

Some common areas around which insecurities arise in non-monogamy are

I'm not enough

Many of us, especially those still overcoming the monogamy hangover, have insecurities about not being enough for our partner. After all, if we were amazing, they would only want us! Or they wouldn't want anyone else nearly as much as they want us. Even if we know this isn't how we operate in our own relationships, sometimes this insecurity can be hard to overcome. Our monogamous programming tells us that it is our job to be everything for our partner - lover, friend, counselor, financial support, logistics specialist, hobby buddy, workout buddy, co-parent, caregiver, external memory, cheerleader. When we feel like we aren't able to be all of those things, we can worry that our "failing" will lead our partner to leave us.

If you're noticing a "not enough" insecurity coming up, ask your partner(s) to let you know what they love and cherish about you. Listen to what they say, really listen, without challenging or "yeah, but"-ing their statements. Ask them questions to explain things further if you don't understand what they're saying. Then thank them. If this comes up for you a lot, you can have them write it down or do a voice or video recording for you so that you can reference it as needed.

I'm too much

On the other side of the coin, some of us worry that we are too much - too loud, too needy, too emotional, too excited, too energetic, too lusty. It's almost as though the box that mainstream culture constructed for people to fit into isn't actually a great fit for a lot of us! Particularly for those socialized as women, we can worry that if we aren't "easy" or "chill" we will be discarded by our partners once they find someone who's less "much."

A lot of these insecurities are fed by cultural messages about "crazy" women, "domineering" bitches, or "nagging" wives. These messages place all the responsibility for conflict on the the person who cares more, a dangerous symptom of the cultural trend towards "chill" that leads to a goal of NOT caring deeply.

If you notice an insecurity about being too much, check in with yourself about where you learned what "too much" means. As with the above example (and all of the following), you can always check in with your partner about how they perceive you. Finally, take some time to see which of your behaviors are in line with who you are. Practice taking up some space in a way that is unapologetic. You may not be everyone's flavor, but plenty of people love folks who are "too much."

Size/shape

All of us are bombarded constantly by images of how people are supposed to look. Women are supposed to be thin, with good butts and boobs, and have small waists, clear skin, and long hair. Men should be tall, muscular, lean, with broad shoulders narrowing in a v to their hips. The average woman in the US now wears between a size 16 and 18, while in media a person size 8 or higher is generally "plus size." Many models are thin enough that they don't have menstrual cycles. The average man wouldn't be able to function well at the low body fat and high muscle mass portrayed in media and would need to practically live at the gym with a private chef.

As for trans and non-binary folks? Trans folks in media are usually portrayed as either comically ugly or as easily "passing." Non-binary folks are rarely portrayed in any way other than as the butt of a joke. As you can see, for most of us we are surrounded by messages telling us we're not the right shape or size or look.

It is common when our partner starts dating someone who we think is more attractive than we perceive ourselves to be to notice some insecurities coming up. After all, if my partner could be with someone who's that attractive, why would they keep me around?

Just remember that no matter how much we're told there's only one way for sexy to look, that's a lie. People of all shapes and sizes are hot and your partner wouldn't be with you if they weren't attracted to you. What you can do here is stand in front of your partner and ask them to tell you all the things they like about your body. You may be surprised which areas they point out as plusses that you may have assumed were minuses.

Another idea is to spend time in the mirror practicing giving yourself compliments. Most of us when we look in the mirror see the things we want to change. Focus instead on finding the beauty of what already is. If you have the resources, hiring a photographer for some sexy shots can sometimes help us see ourselves in a new light.

Finally, figure out what helps you feel extra hot and do it when you're feeling down. Maybe it's a special outfit, or some makeup, or the right cologne, or a straight razor shave at the barber shop. Whatever it is, knowing how to bring back your own internal sense of hotness can help you get through your insecurities.

Age

Just as we live in a sizeist culture, we also live in an ageist culture. Youth is revered and idolized and aging is denied and avoided at all costs. Cosmetic procedures, lying about your age - these are the symptoms of a culture that says that older is worse. In addition, sometimes a younger age can be derided in certain circles. Those not old enough are spoken of as immature or dumb or uninteresting.

While significant age gaps can have some very real impacts and drawbacks, we often see messages that encourage older cis men to find young women, older women to find younger men, and so on and so forth. It makes sense then that people may have insecurities related to their age.

If age-related insecurities come up for you, see if you can analyze where you learned the message that your age is less attractive than another person's. Think of the folks you know and ask yourself how much their age plays into how much you care about them or how attractive you find them - I'm willing to bet that age is barely a factor!

Share your worries with your partner and let them tell you whether they're founded in reality. Finally, spend some time thinking about how much weight you would want to give to the opinion of someone who would rule someone out based on their age. Is that someone whose opinion you need?

High sexual desire

You might think that in non-monogamy a high degree of sexual desire would be generally appreciated, but most of us have trouble getting past cultural norms about "insatiable" lust. Even within non-monogamy communities, those who enjoy lots of sexual variety and activity are often slut shamed and criticized.

What counts as a high desire for sex also tends to be very relative - when I'm chatting with a super slutty friend of mine, who often tells people to assume he's slept with 10x as many people as they would consider "a lot," my desire level seems pretty normal. But when I'm chatting with my friend who's asexual I feel like a fiend. There's no objectively right frequency or variety of sex to desire, but that doesn't stop our brains from telling us that what we're experiencing is wrong.

When insecurities about being too horny or slutty come up, sit down and think about whether your sexual desire has actually caused you to harm anyone or yourself. If it hasn't, how did you learn it was wrong?

A great metaphor here is food - some people like to eat once a day, some people like to eat three times, some people like 5-8 small meals. Is it wrong to eat so many meals? The right number of "meals" is the number that feels right for you, not the number that feels right for anyone else. Try to think of times your high desire has been a benefit for you. Ask your partners what they appreciate about your high level of desire.

Lower sexual desire

As above, so here there are two sides to the insecurity - what if your worry instead is that you don't have enough desire? We have labels for these folks too, ones like "frigid" and "impotent." After all, if you don't want ENOUGH sex that's even worse! There must be something broken about you! The struggle for asexuals to get recognition and acceptance, even by sex-positive therapists, shows how common it is for our culture to disbelieve that anyone could not want sex at our predetermined level. Sometimes, we have low desire because of stress or sadness or lack of sleep or medical issues; does that mean we should just lie back and "think of England"?

Returning to our food metaphor, it doesn't make sense to make yourself eat 5 times a day if your body only wants to eat 3. When you notice insecurities about low sexual desire, ask yourself how much sex it is that you "should" want and where you learned that from.

If you haven't read Come As You Are by Emily Nagoski, this would be a great time to take a look at how your brakes and gas are functioning. Also, check in with your partners - are they actually dissatisfied? Or is this about your own fears about how they will feel?

Sexual openness

All the time I hear friends and clients talk about insecurities that come up when a metamour is open to trying things sexually that they aren't. Whether it's something kinky, anal, group stuff, or deep throating, nothing makes us feel less than quite like knowing that someone else is saying yes where we said no.

Our complex cultural norms around sexuality simultaneously shame those who refuse to do what their partner wants AND those who agree to less normative sexual activities. While the saying may be "lady in the street, freak in the sheets," frankly you're likely to catch flack for either extreme. And relationally, knowing that your partner is getting something you cannot or will not give can feel particularly poignant.

When these insecurities come up for you, do what you can to redirect your focus to the enjoyment you get from the things you enjoy with your partner. Is your sex life still fun and enjoyable? Are you both satisfied with it? Not everyone needs to be an aerial dancer who can nail every pose in the kama sutra (though if you are, props to you). Talk with your partner about what they enjoy about your sexual connection. If you're feeling like experimenting because of these insecurities, make sure that you're saying yes for your own benefit at least as much as your partner's and be sure to set up a framework (like an experiment date) that enables you to change your mind if it's not working for you.

Same gender

This insecurity is best exemplified by the one penis policy. If you only have sex with people with vulvas, the penis having partner gets to be special forever. For many people, knowing that your partner is engaging with folks of your same gender feels different than when they engage with folks of other genders. Often, this is because folks of our same gender feel like more direct competition than those of other genders. After all, folks of other genders literally have things we do not and cannot have.

Much of this insecurity is also based in the scarcity models that lead to the "bro code" and "girl code" and that tell us to fight others of our own gender for the best partners and/or that people of our gender are always trying to "steal" our partner.

Noticing this insecurity coming up for you? Ask yourself whether the only thing special about you is your gender and/or your genitals. Very very few people choose who to date based only or predominantly on gender. After all, there are as many as a few billion people with your gender, but only one you. What does your partner like about you as a human? What do they get from your relationship that has nothing to do with your gender? Also, ponder where the messages are coming from that tell you that other partners of your own gender are more dangerous than those of other genders. Are those messages in line with your values and beliefs?

Specialness

Many people have a desire to feel "special" in some way with their partner. That specialness can be about specific activities, pet names, relationship types, or really any other aspect of your relationships. Coming from a scarcity, monogamy rooted mindset, if you're not the most special then you're nothing, so it makes sense that we want some concrete means of determining what makes us special. Yet our specialness to our partner is not, or at least should not, be just about a sexual position or a specific restaurant. After all, we as humans are far more than just one shared activity.

In particular, people can notice this insecurity coming up when the emotional connection deepens in a new relationship. If you and your partner have mostly had fairly casual, less emotionally involved connections with other people, then a deepening emotional relationship between your partner and your metamour may feel particularly threatening. If you define your relationship with your partner in comparison to others, you are destined to feel drawn to police and minimize and bring down their other relationships.

The More Than Two blog has a great post by Franklin Veaux called "Building Up, Not Tearing Down" that talks about how, when we feel like a new relationship is taking attention/time/etc. from us, we often aim to tear it back down to size. Instead, we may benefit more from working on building up our own existing relationship and focusing on getting our needs met there.

If insecurities around specialness come up for you, ask yourself what you believe it is that makes your relationship with your partner special. Also, think about where you learned that specialness comes from. Are those messages and stories in line with how you want to be now? Talk with your partner about what they value in your connection and what they love about you. Their answers may surprise you! If you find it hard to trust that your partner is going to stick with you even while they love someone else, it might be worth examining your beliefs around your own worthiness for love. Sometimes, this work is best done in a coaching or therapy context that gives you space to talk about how you learned you were or weren't special and were or weren't safe in your connections.

Income and finances

Sometimes, knowing that another partner has different financial means than we do can bring up insecurities in us. Particularly when our metamour's financial status more closely matches that of our shared partner, we can feel like they must better understand our partner or that they will be able to give them experiences we cannot match. This insecurity is often more common among cisgender men, but folks of all genders can find themselves falling into it. Our culture tells men in particular that their worth is wrapped up in what they can earn, in how they function as a breadwinner, so a partner meeting someone with more money can feel like they're meeting someone "better" than you.

If these insecurities about finances and income come up for you, take some time to think about who first told you that your money determined your worth and whether that's something you want to believe. Then, ask your partner how they feel about your financial situation. Are they finding it incompatible with theirs? Or is that something you're reading into on your own? Finally, remember that in capitalism, we are encouraged to define our worth by our productivity and compensation rather than by caring or kindness or love. Do you want to let the capitalist machine grind you down to the hours you work and the dollars in your bank account?

The goal here is not to eliminate insecurities altogether. That's not possible to start with, as even people with Narcissistic Personality Disorder tend to have rich, thriving insecurities. Instead, the goal is to find a way to sit with your insecurities, see them, and then ask yourself what you want to do about them.

I want to add one final note: your insecurities are not your enemy nor are they a bug or flaw. Our insecurities give us information about the ways we think about ourselves and about what we think others see in us. Most of our insecurities grew as tools to keep us safe in other contexts. When we try to beat them down or judge ourselves for having them, we tend to feed them even more. Instead, see if you can find a place of compassion and caring for the parts of you that are insecure. Show yourself the kind of love that you want to receive. See each of those dark places inside of you and fill them up with loving instead of shame. Only then can you hope to build a life where your insecurities can begin to let you take back control.

Self Care While Your Sweetie Dates

Sometimes when your sweetie is out with someone else, it can feel really really hard. Especially if you're having a dating rut, or if you're feeling down or insecure lately, there can be few things as challenging as sitting at home while the person you care about is off having (you imagine) the most fun ever possible with someone else. So how can you be sure you don't just fall into a spiral of self-hatred or resentment? Here are some different strategies you might try out and some space to brainstorm specific options for you!

Distraction

Keeping your brain busy focusing on something other than how much you miss your sweetie is a good way to help the time pass more quickly. Distraction could involve TV, video games, reading, exercise, puzzles, or anything else you find helps you keep your brain occupied. What might work for you?

Creativity

Sometimes the best cure for feeling bad is to make something! Engage your creativity with crafts, music, dance, and art. What kinds of creative activities could you turn to?

Self-soothing

If you can't have someone else to help you feel better, you could try out ways to help yourself feel better! Meditation, relaxation, a hot bath, cuddling up in a warm blanket, putting on your makeup, or other activities that soothe you are great options. Which ones are your favorites?

Self Care While Your Sweetie Dates

Reassurance

When your brain is being a jerk, sometimes it won't listen to you. So, find ways to have reassurance from your partner even when they're out and busy! Maybe a note from them, a recording of them saying they care about you, a date planned in the future, or some items left in the house can help that mean brain listen to reason! What kinds of reassurance might help you out?

Keep busy

If you're someone whose brain tends to spiral and get into loops, keeping yourself busy with other activities can be a great option! Do that deep cleaning of your house that you've been meaning to, knock out that project you've been putting off, get to those nagging house repairs, anything to keep your hands (and brain) on something else. How could you keep yourself busy?

Plan fun/pleasure

It's hard to stay in a sad loop when you're out having a great time! Plan some pleasurable and/or fun activities for yourself while your partner is off with someone else. Party with friends, schedule a date of your own, go see that movie you've been missing, masturbate for hours, or go to that concert! What does diving into fun and pleasure look like for you?

Supporting an insecure partner

Most of the section on insecurity up to this point has been about how to examine and work through the insecurities you have for yourself, but what do you do when it's a partner who is struggling with insecurities? Just as it's impossible for any one of us to completely rid ourselves of all insecurities, we are destined to find ourselves in relationships with imperfect, messy humans who have insecurities of their own. Even if we do our best to be good partners, we may find ourselves bumping up against those insecurities. So how can you support someone when their insecurities are flaring up?

Supporting an insecure partner is a delicate balance between offering them the kinds of love, compassion, kindness, and support that they need on one side and being mindful of and maintaining your boundaries and autonomy on the other. Why do I emphasize the latter and not just the former? Well, unfortunately when someone we care about is hurting, it can be easy for us to end up making agreements and concessions that move us past our own boundaries into a territory we then end up not feeling good about.

Remember John from earlier? When John and I started dating, he was new to polyamory. I promised to help him transition and made sure he had space and time to chat with me whenever I scheduled a date with someone else. However, no matter how much processing we did in the days leading up to a date, the day of a date always found John crying and inconsolable, worried that I would leave him or that he wasn't enough for me. I asked him what I could do to help, but his solution tended to be for me to stay home from my date. I understood why he wanted this, but something in me told me that I would resent him if I gave it to him. So I gave him reassurance, suggested some coping strategies, and went on my date.

I hoped that over time he would see that he had no reason to be insecure - I always came back from dates to our shared home with kisses and love and excitement and showed him how happy I was to be with him. But, no matter how many times I tried it, the day of each date still found him inconsolable and insisting the only helpful option would be for me to cancel my date. Eventually, he stopped asking for me to change, not because he was feeling better, but because he knew I wouldn't cancel my dates. So instead he cried to our mutual friends while telling me everything was fine.

I wanted so much to support him, to give him what he needed to be happy about my dates with other people. On the other hand, I didn't want to set a precedent that I would cancel my dates because he was upset. I was afraid that doing that would lead not just to resentment, but also to more and more emotional outbursts by John. I was afraid of having his feelings limiting me out of polyamory.

Sometimes, someone's insecurities tell them that the solution is to tear down the relationship that is scaring them. However, agreeing to shrink your world to meet your partner's comfort is unlikely to be a successful strategy in the long run. Instead, it often leads to resentment and to sneaky, dishonest behavior. So, when making decisions about how to best support your partner, be sure to check in with yourself about whether you're really a true "yes" to the solutions they're suggesting before you agree to them.

Strategies you might be able to use to help out an insecure partner can include:

- 💜 Offering verbal reassurance: If they're able to tell you what their brain is saying to them, you can offer to let them know what you really think and how their brain is wrong about them

- 💜 Offering to build up your connection: Instead of looking at what you can remove from a new connection, what can you add to your current connection? Is it a nice date? A weekend away? Ask your partner for help in determining what will help this relationship feel better for them without taking something away from other relationships

♥ Speak their love language: If they like touch, give them touch while they share about their insecurities. If they speak gifts, send them small things or hide notes around their place. If they like acts of service, put in some work or plan to after a new date. For quality time, schedule a nice chunk of time to keep you two connected. And for words of affirmation, record something for them or send them a physical letter with your thoughts of caring and kindness.

Post-Date Decompression Worksheet

Feelings

What are the emotions you're feeling right now?

Sad						Mad						Scared					
guilty	ashamed	depressed	lonely	bored	tired	hurt	hostile	angry	selfish	hateful	critical	confused	rejected	helpless	submissive	insecure	anxious
remoreseful	stupid	inferior	isolated	apathetic	sleepy	distant	sarcastic	frustrated	jealous	irritated	skeptical	bewildered	discouraged	insignificant	inadequate	embarrassed	overwhelmed

Joyful						Powerful						Peaceful					
excited	sensuous	energetic	cheerful	creative	hopeful	aware	proud	respected	appreciated	important	faithful	content	thoughtful	intimate	loving	trusting	nurturing
daring	fascinating	stimulating	amused	playful	optimistic	surprised	successful	worthwhile	valuable	discerning	confident	relaxed	pensive	responsive	serene	secure	thankful

What are you noticing in your body?

Who can you talk to when you need to gush about a really fantastic date?

Who can you talk to about a challenging date?

Post-Date Decompression Worksheet

How much does each of your partners enjoy hearing about your dates with other people?

How do each of your partners feel when you come home still buzzing with date energy?

If your partner struggles with you being "high" from a date, what are 3-5 steps you could take to help yourself come back to normal after a date?

(You can also cross-reference the Coping Skills worksheet for ideas.)

What physical measures does each of your partners want you to take before seeing them after a date? (e.g. shower, change the sheets, put away dishes, etc.)

What are 3-5 things you can do to reconnect or "drop back in" with your other partner(s) after a date?

Don't do
these things

● ● ● ● ● ●

Most of this book I'm focusing on what to do. How to build good skills and show up as your best self. But I wanted to also cover some common stuff that folks do that leads to issues. This is the "Please don't do this" chapter.

Don't Be A Douchebag

A theme you'll see throughout this book is that each person is responsible for their own feelings. This statement is totally true and it has one caveat - don't be a douchebag. Unfortunately, when some people hear that they're in an environment where everyone is responsible for their own feelings, those people become jerks. For instance, I've seen folks cancel a date on short notice with no apology and with a careless attitude who then tell the person they cancelled on to "deal with their own emotions" about their thoughtlessness. Just because each person is responsible for their own feelings does NOT mean that you have carte blanche to act with heartlessness.

So how do you find the balance? Well ask yourself this core question - am I acting from a place of kindness? Kindness is different from being nice. Someone who is nice will smile and lie to your face. They won't tell you the things you need to hear, only what you want to hear. Someone who is kind will tell you when you're messing up in a way that is about your growth and that comes from caring for you.

If at any point you find yourself not caring about how your actions will impact the people with whom you're in relationship, that might be a sign that it's time for reevaluation. Are you upset with this person and taking it out on them? Are you disconnecting from them? What is it that makes you no longer care about their feelings? We can all become less thoughtful than would be ideal when we are tired or overwhelmed-- are you in need of some self care? Usually when we're seeing someone it's because we care about them and want to share happiness with them, so be on the lookout for times you're not acting in that way.

How do you know if you're being a douche? The easiest answer is to ask your partners. Some folks will do a regularly scheduled "state of the union" talk so that they can check in about anything that has been bothering them. Having regularly scheduled talks can make people feel more empowered to voice their concerns and can ensure that problems are quickly identified before they fester into bigger problems.

These ideas relate to folks who are being careless from an unintentional place. There are some folks who are just jerks for other reasons. If you find that you generally don't care about how your actions will affect others, that can be a sign of something more significant. Folks who have histories of hurting others often don't know that they've hurt others. In fact, they sometimes think that the other people had it coming or deserved what happened. If these patterns sound like you, it might be worth looking into some more serious professional help to look at how your patterns might be influencing your ability to have healthy, caring relationships.

Cowboying/cowgirling/cowpersoning

Imagine you've been doing non-monogamy for a while and you meet someone for a date. They initially say they're cool with non-monogamy, but you notice they're not really dating anyone else. After a few weeks or months, they ask you why you still want non-monogamy and imply that you should want to be monogamous for them.

When a monogamous person goes into a non-monogamy community with the desire to "lasso" someone out for themselves, that person is called a cowboy/cowgirl/cowperson. As far as I can tell, their thought process is that the non-monogamy community is where the hot people are who do fun sex things and obviously they are so uniquely awesome that no one would choose non-monogamy when the cowperson offered monogamy. The Netflix series She's Gotta Have It provides ample examples of this dynamic. All of Nola's partners expect her to break up with everyone else and be monogamous with them, despite her frequent statements that she's happy with dating multiple people.

Why is this a problem? Well, cow-folks are generally deceiving their partners into thinking that they do want non-monogamy when they don't. It's a manipulative and coercive means of "tricking" someone into doing things your own way. It doesn't honor the wants or needs of the non-monogamous partner and, in fact, intends to steam roll them into complying with the desires of the cowperson.

What should you do instead? Be up front about what you are or aren't looking for. If you want monogamy, say it. If you want to do swinging, say it. If you want a strict hierarchy . . . you get the idea. If you feel like you need to use deception in order to get a relationship with someone, you probably need to do some more work on understanding and accepting yourself before you get into dating. Be honest! People can't fall in love with a person who doesn't exist.

Harem collecting

I am the LAST person who would judge people for developing lots of relationships and sleeping with lots of people. After all, I'm a proud slut and I like having a wide variety of lovers all over the world. However, some folks like to collect lovers in a way that becomes problematic. Most often, harem collectors are people who grab onto multiple partners and expect them to each be mostly exclusive with the collector. The collector is always free to find new partners, but they become upset or angry when their partners want to do the same. Even when the collector doesn't have enough time for their current partners, they keep finding new ones to add to their collection.

Why is this a problem? This model is often borne of insecurity and selfishness. In addition, the collector treats partners like collectible dolls, not humans. This relationship structure, like most problematic ones I talk about, is based in treating one person's needs like they trump those of others.

What should you do instead? Relationships don't have to be "equal." That is, you don't have to date the same number of people, but they should be equitable. Everyone should have the same freedom and power in a relationship. If you notice that you have a lot of "double standards" or that you want to be able to do things that you don't want your partner to do, it's worth examining where that comes from and whether it serves you. If your relationships are built on this lack of equity, it's unlikely they will be successful long term. It is likely worth putting in the effort to build the skills you need to enable greater freedom in your partners.

Unicorn hunting

I know, I already talked about unicorn hunting as an artifact of couple privilege. However, I wanted to talk a bit more about it here and how it becomes a problem in general.

There is nothing wrong with triads, or with closed triads. There is nothing necessarily wrong with a couple who prefer to do things with other folks together. However, those who are new to non-monogamy often enter without questioning or deconstructing their monogamy learned ideas about how relationships work. The handiest shorthand I've heard for unicorn hunting (and it is especially true for couples in strict hierarchies) is "There will be many long, heartfelt, in depth conversations about your relationship; you won't be a part of any of them."

In unicorn hunting, a (generally) cisgender, heteronormative couple seeks to find an attractive bisexual woman to "complete" their relationship. They have almost always come up with a detailed plan for how this relationship will work, what she will do, what she will want, how she will be with them. Almost always, these relationships treat finding a new partner like shopping for a sex toy. They've come up with the specifics, they just need to find the one that matches.

Unicorn hunting is called that because unicorns are fictional creatures - your chance of finding your unicorn is the same as you running across an equine creature with a horn coming out of its head. Maxine, a writer about non-monogamy, covers the statistical reasons this rarely works out in her post "Polyamory and Statistics, or 'Why haven't we found our third yet?'" The odds of finding a bisexual woman who is attracted to both of you and to whom both of you are attracted, who is single, and who wants your style of relationship are so close to zero as to be basically impossible.

Why is this a problem? Whenever a relationship has important decisions being made without the involvement of people who are affected by that decision, it has the potential to go poorly. If you and your partner decided between the two of you what the third person would be doing, you've left a key decision maker out of those decisions. Humans aren't puzzle pieces that you can just put into place where you feel like it. Basically, this style treats the needs of some people as more important and valid than those of other people.

What should you do instead? Well, if you want to have a triad, all of the people who would be in it should have an equal say in how that relationship works. Also, keep in mind that it's not likely you'll find someone who wants to date both of you equally, love both of you equally, or have sex with both of you equally, so think about how you'll handle situations where the person wants something different from each of you. Finally, think about what is leading you to feel unwilling to operate as individuals within a relationship rather than as a single unit. Usually, when we subsume our identity to something larger we end up opening ourselves to abusive patterns, whether as the perpetrator or the recipient. So take a lot of time to evaluate this decision and where it's coming from.

Slut shaming

You might think that everyone in non-monogamy realms is over the temptation to use slut shaming, but you'd sadly be wrong. Slut shaming is an umbrella term that commonly refers to behaviors involving making people feel badly for the sex they choose to have. This can include the number of partners, the kind of sex, their choices about barriers, or who they're having sex with. In this wide world of non-monogamy, there is bound to be a large variety of opinions and approaches. Just because someone does something different from you, that doesn't mean they are WRONG.

Slut shaming often looks like expressing horror about someone verbally, talking about them behind their back, discouraging others from having sex with them, or concern trolling (where you express a shaming judgment as a concern for someone's health or wellbeing).

Why is this a problem? Shaming is almost always more about us than about other people. It is not okay for you to judge what others decide to do with other consenting adults. You can choose to not have sex with them personally, but it is not up to you to decide what everyone else should do with their own bodies.

What should you do instead? Work really hard on unlearning the societal scripts that tell you that people who have more sex are "dirty" or "wrong." When you find yourself feeling judgmental, ask yourself WHY that's coming up from you. Are you envious of what they do? Do you make different choices but wish you didn't? Are you operating from internalized ideas about how to control others' sexual expression for "their own good" or the "good of society?" Remind yourself that every person gets to do whatever they want with their body and that their decisions about risk or about different sexual behaviors don't actually have to be the same as yours.

One Twue Way

In any community, there is always at least one asshole who has decided that the way they do things is the only right way, or the One Twue Way. They valorize a specific set of decisions and deride others as wrong or less evolved or ignorant.

This problem tends to be what I sometimes call an "Intermediate" problem. When someone is a beginner, they know that they don't know anything and are eager to learn. When people are advanced at something, they understand how deep the nuances are and how much they need to continually work at improving. Intermediate folks though know just enough to think they know everything. They're not actually as great as they think they are, but they also tend to be bad at receiving constructive criticism or feedback. They're caught up in their pride and spilling their hubris all over others.

In the world of non-monogamy, the only "right" way is any way that respects the consent and empowerment of everyone involved. That could look any number of different ways and could involve any number of structures. So if someone offers to teach you the "right" way to do things and implies it happens to be the way they do things, be skeptical.

Why is this a problem? This one is all about self-aggrandizement. The person doing it wants to be special and knowledgeable and important, so they will set the terms of the debate to center their own limited view.

What should you do instead? Honor that non-monogamy can look a huge variety of ways for a huge variety of people. When you notice yourself judging others or feeling pulled to place yourself in an expert role, evaluate where that's coming from and whether it's actually helpful. Do some research and listen to people who do things differently and try to understand them as much as you can. Remember to take ownership for your views instead of stating them as universal.

Punishing people for who they date

This one is often related to slut shaming. I'll start with a personal story:

Over the course of one very fun weekend at a kink event, I ended up making several new friends and meeting several new lovers. Those included Brad, two of his partners at that time (Syd and Sonia), and Claire. I met Claire first when I showed up to her special gang bang which had been organized by a friend of mine. I made sure to do some in depth negotiation since joining that kind of sexual situation can have lots of landmines, and Claire commented on how much she appreciated my communication and negotiation skills. Over the course of the weekend, I spent some time interacting with all of them (and others, of course) and I walked away with serious crushes on Syd, Sonia, and Claire and a passing, low level interest in Brad. When Claire announced a big birthday sexy weekend, I made plans to return to Portland for it in December.

They all lived in Portland, so I didn't see any of them again for a while. Shortly after the kink event, Claire started dating Brad. At the end of September, Brad came out to SF for work and asked if I knew of any fun sexy parties happening while he was in town. We agreed to go see an all male strip revue together and to go to a sexy after party for the show.

Going into the dinner, I don't know if either of us was certain whether it was a date. But he was witty and funny and delightfully sadistic so the dinner quickly turned flirty. By the time the show was over, we were deeply lusting for each other and our interaction at the play party was electric, resulting in weeks of comments from others about how hot our play had been. We saw each other a bit more during that trip and deepened our erotic connection, but we both acknowledged we weren't in a great place to start a romantic relationship.

Brad was coming out to SF for a large kink event in November, along with Sonia. Shortly before the event, Brad's relationship with Claire blew up. Claire messaged me to tell me why they had broken up and to say that Brad was no longer invited to her party but that she still wanted me there. I agreed and she was still excited to have me there. Two days before the kink event, Sonia and Brad ended up breaking up as well. Their breakup was more amicable and Sonia continued to express excitement that I would be seeing her at Claire's birthday event.

A week or two later, Claire messaged me again, this time to say that she didn't feel comfortable engaging with me sexually in any way because she didn't trust Brad's risk aware sex protocols. I honored her boundary, but internally wondered if something else was happening since the kind of sex we'd previously had (hand sex using gloves, using condom wrapped dildos) was all very very very low risk. I figured that it was her choice and didn't ask questions.

Brad and I spent an amazing weekend together at the November event and our connection started deepening. We talked a lot about what we had available and about what might get in the way of healthy relationships on each of our parts. I found myself opening to him and wanting more time and connection with him.

Two weeks before I was scheduled to leave for Portland for Claire's birthday weekend, Claire messaged me again to tell me she felt "sick" thinking about me leaving Brad's place to head to her birthday party. She said she couldn't find a way to be okay with me continuing to see Brad after they had broken up. She made some comments implying that she didn't understand why I would continue to see him after her breakup, much less deepen the connection. She acknowledged that her feelings weren't in line with how she wanted to handle things, but I was uninvited from her party.

Because I wasn't willing to break up with Brad, because I didn't see things the same way she did about Brad's choices, I was no longer welcome at her party or, as time went on, in her life.

When Person 1 is dating a person we either wanted to date or had a challenging transition with (Person 2), it can be tempting to take our frustration and anger out on Person 1, particularly if they are close to us. After all, we've already learned that Person 2 won't give us the satisfaction we want, so why not see if we can get it from Person 1 instead?

Why is this a problem? While it's certainly impossible to not let any feelings bleed over from one connection to another, this pattern often emerges from monogamist ideas about "bro code" or "girl code." Like slut shaming, this pattern also often uses the language of sexual risk to cover our real feelings.

What should you do instead? Put the effort into understanding and naming what your feelings are and who they're actually related to. If you notice that feelings are spilling onto bystanders, think about how you would feel to be punished for the "sins" of your partner in their relationship with someone else. Also, check your assumptions - are you assuming the dynamic you had with this partner is the same with all of their other partners? Are there any factors at play here that might make these dynamics less global than you think? Can you find a way to honor that everyone gets to make their own decisions and to decenter yourself from those decisions?

Special Non-Monogamy Situations

● ● ● ● ● ●

As you move into your exploration of non-monogamy, you may find yourself in some novel situations that are particular to segments of the non-monogamous world. While lots of the challenges and strategies for non-monogamy are universal, there are some special circumstances that I want to make sure to address. These may not be particularly common, or may have their own set of very specific challenges. Each of the segments of this section touches on something a little different. While I'm not diving particularly deeply into any of them, this should at least give you an overview.

Navigating Sexual Spaces

When you talk to people about non-monogamy, many people imagine a life filled with nightly orgies featuring a rotating cast of beautiful strangers. While that's rarely anyone's reality, sexual spaces, such as sex clubs and sex parties, can offer you an opportunity to take one step closer to this feared (or dreamed) reality.

Before I talk about sexual spaces I want to make one thing super clear - not everyone who is non-monogamous wants to, or even does, go to sexual spaces. You're not "bad" at non-monogamy if you don't want to have group sex or have sex in front of other people. You're not "more enlightened" or hotter if you go to a new sex party every weekend. Just like whether you like the theater or baseball games, your choice about whether or not to attend sex-related events is unrelated to whether you do non-monogamy.

If you're someone who wants to explore sexual spaces, you're in luck. While 30 or 50 years ago you might have struggled to find a group of like minded folks, these days even relatively small cities have swinger clubs, and large sex-affirming events, like Naughty in Nawlins or the Swingset Desire Takeover, are plentiful. In addition, online communities like FetLife and Kasidie make it ever easier to find either a group of people or a public club to indulge in your wildest semi-public sex fantasies.

People find themselves interested in sex clubs and parties for a variety of reasons. For some people, they want a place they can go to watch other people having sex. Others want a space they can play with their established partners either with others watching or on specialized equipment (e.g. St Andrew's cross, spanking bench, stripper pole) that they don't have at home. Still others want to find new people to explore and play with, whether for that night or for a longer time.

Sexual spaces tend to fall into two rough categories:

Private play parties - Often by invitation only and kept to relatively small numbers (often 10 to 50, but sometimes as big as 150), these parties are held at hotels and private residences. Folks usually get invited when they meet someone in the social group or community. These parties may be more or less structured depending on who throws them and the group norms. Some play parties are like any other social gathering except that sex might happen there, others have dedicated opening activities to help everyone get on the same page about the space and the rules there.

Sex clubs - While sex clubs often require a "membership" in order to bypass laws about lewdness or nudity, they are public spaces that people can go to for sex or kink play. Different clubs will often have different focuses, whether related to type of non-monogamy (e.g. Swinger clubs), orientation (queer clubs vs more heteronormative ones), or type of play (e.g. BDSM clubs). Clubs will generally have rules and waivers you'll need to sign and agree to. Once you enter, you may be given a tour or you may just be left to your own devices. There are generally designated play areas and areas where play is discouraged. Some clubs have bars where you can buy drinks, some ask you to bring your own beverages, and some have no alcohol allowed. Some have food, others don't. Cover charges for the clubs may vary by gender or whether you're coming as a couple or as a single. Finally, some clubs have theme nights while some are more generic.

Selecting which kind of sexual space to go to is largely a matter of personal preference. If you've never been to one before, you may need to try out a few before you find one that fits for you. You may also find that it takes going to a particular club or party a few times before you start to make connections with the people there. As with any other hobby or activity, it can take some time to make new friends and for folks to get to know you. This can be especially true in sexualized spaces, where there is often some apprehension that someone might be there for less than positive reasons.

Whatever kind of space you choose, there are a few general tips that will help you have a better time

1) High possibility, low expectation: It's easy when we're going to a party or club to bring all of our anxieties and hopes and fears in with us. Sometimes, we decide that we'll only have a good time at the space if certain things happen. The higher our expectations, the more likely it is we'll be let down. One San Francisco area party group sums this up in language that encourages people to treat play parties as a high possibility, low expectation space. The more that we can approach our parties as a place where things COULD happen not where things MUST happen, the more likely it is that we'll be able to relax and have a good time.

Expectation also tends to make us feel more needy and less centered or confident, which in turn makes it LESS likely that people will play with us. It can kick off a self-fulfilling prophecy where we become upset that "no one" wants us, then we are sullen, which makes us harder to approach, which makes us more sullen, and so on.

The more that you enjoy the opportunities you get and treat them with genuine gratitude, the more people will be drawn to interact with you and the more likely it is you'll find yourself with people to play with.

2) Consent: Being really good at consent, both asking for it and respecting a "no," is one of the best ways to build a good reputation and make sure you're not hurting anyone. Ask before touching people, ask everyone involved in group play before joining the group, ask before each new activity (e.g. touching a butt, a breast, kissing). Some folks say that consent is sexy, but really it's more that consent is the absolute bare minimum for things to not be terrible. (I mean, you wouldn't say that the reason a restaurant has amazing food is because the chefs wash their hands after they go the bathroom.) When you're new to these kinds of approaches to consent, they can feel a bit forced or awkward. However, think how hot it is to make someone actually ask you for what they want - the possibilities for tease and denial abound!

3) Substances: In different communities, people may engage in play with different substances on board. These can include alcohol and cannabis or others like nitrous, LSD, and MDMA. If you don't like being around substances, try to get in touch with party organizers to see what kind of party they throw. In general, if you're going to be playing with substances, be sure to let anyone else you're getting sexual or kinky with know what you're on so that they can judge whether they feel good about playing with you. Be sure to consume substances within your own range of control, because if you're not clear enough to drive you're probably not cognitively clear enough to give good consent either. If someone seems like they're altered, you may want to evaluate whether you can trust that they're able to give you good consent in that moment.

4) Going together vs going alone: If you're going to a sexual space with a partner, it's helpful to negotiate before you get there how you want to act towards each other during the night. Some folks expect their partner to stay with them at all times if they go together, others expect that they'll touch base during the night and leave together but not much else. You can't know until you talk about it, so be sure to negotiate clearly to avoid any conflicts. In addition, it may be

helpful to come up with a code word or gesture you can use if one of you is uncomfortable and needs support.

If you're going to a sexual space alone, it may be helpful to have a friend or partner you can check in with either at the party or over the phone or messenger before and after the party. It's also helpful to have a buddy at a party or venue so that if you need someone to check in with because of having strong feelings or needs for reassurance you've got a person there.

5) Self-care: When you're surrounded by hot, sexy people or having a super hot sexy time yourself, it can be easy to forget to do basic self-care. It's unfortunately common at parties for people to end up dehydrated, or with low blood sugar, because they got too distracted with all of the fun. So be sure to drink water, bring some snacks, and monitor how your body is doing. Pro tip: Electrolyte supplements are a great way to keep yourself in play shape. You can get tablets to add to water or pills to take, look for supplements designed for athletes/runners.

Choosing Conscious Monogamy

Sometimes you do all the work of challenging the fairy tale myth of monogamy and find out on the other side that you want to do monogamy. That's great! More self-knowledge tends to be a good thing. And, once more, there's nothing wrong with monogamy. Maybe you're choosing monogamy because the partner you love wants to be monogamous, or maybe you're choosing monogamy because that's just what fits best for you. Whatever the reason, there are a few tips from the non-monogamous world that might help you in practicing conscious monogamy.

Just as with a non-monogamous relationship, remember that monogamy is a system that only works when everyone involved is making a free choice to participate. The work on unlearning the monogamy mindset that non-monogamous folks do can actually help you practice better monogamy, as it helps you center consent and autonomy in your relationships. If anyone sends any judgment your way for choosing monogamy, know that it's about them and not you.

As the ethics chapter discussed, the form of your relationship is far less relevant to how healthy it is than the way you execute that form. Conscious monogamy is totally possible and a great choice for those who want to go that way!

Married and non-monogamous

Whether it's just a piece of paper or a spiritual joining, deciding to get married can have some effects on how non-monogamy works for you. If you are married and doing non-monogamy, you may need to have more specific conversations about how your marriage intersects with your non-monogamy. Sometimes, people have assumptions about what marriage means - that it necessarily means hierarchy, that you must practice veto, or that it gives your spouse more say than other partners. While you may choose to include those elements in your structure, none of them are necessary. Kevin Patterson, of Poly Role Models and Love's Not Colorblind, and his wife are both relationship anarchists, so trust me, your married non-monogamy can be done in any way you prefer.

If you're choosing to practice your non-monogamy in a non-hierarchical fashion, you may need to do extra work to be sure that unequal power distributions don't happen accidentally. The kind of legal involvements wrapped up in a marriage may mean that it's more challenging for you to break up with a partner or that they may have a more direct financial or other influence over you. This isn't necessarily a bad thing; after all, one reason to choose marriage is to reinforce your commitment to making a particular relationship work over time. It's just important to be aware of how that may impact other relationships.

When dating others, if you're married check in with them about their assumptions about what your marriage means. Some folks may assume that you're making different choices than you are, so don't hesitate to correct their assumptions. Let them know how marriage works for you and whether it means anything about what's available from you in other relationships.

Finally, because multiple marriages are illegal in many countries, you may not be able to legally marry all of the people you might want to marry. Some folks choose to not get legally married at all because of this restriction, while others will call multiple people their spouses although they're only legally married to one of them. You can always throw a wedding for any relationship, even if a legal marriage isn't available, so that you can express your commitment for anyone that you'd like to.

Asexual, Demisexual, and Megasexual issues

For folks on the far ends of the sexual desire spectrum, non-monogamy might look a little bit different.

Asexuality/Demisexuality: Folks who are asexual (or "ace") are people who don't experience spontaneous desire for sex. They may still choose to engage in sex or masturbation, or may just do masturbation, or may be sex repulsed, or any combination thereof. Folks who identify as grey asexual ("grey ace") are somewhere on the spectrum between sexuality and asexuality, so they may sometimes have sexual desire or may have specific situations in which they experience desire. People who are demisexual ("demi") are people who only experience sexual desire in the context of a loving, intimate relationship.

There is no reason that people who are ace, grey ace, or demi can't practice non-monogamy. For some folks on this end of the spectrum, they like that non-monogamy offers their partners a way to get their sexual needs met from someone else. Others like being able to flirt and date and kiss with multiple partners. If you're someone on this end of the spectrum, jump on in to non-monogamy! Be clear with your partners about what you have available for them, but don't listen to anyone who says there isn't room in the non-monogamy tent for you.

If you encounter someone who is on the ace side of the spectrum, don't shame them. These orientations are just as real as queerness, and deserve just as much understanding and support. Please don't be the person who makes folks feel like they don't belong or like there's something wrong with them because they're different than you are. This doesn't mean you're ever obligated to date someone who you think isn't a good fit for you, but you also don't necessarily know whether you can be happy dating someone on the lower end of the desire spectrum until you give it a shot.

Megasexuality: On the opposite end of the desire spectrum is megasexuality. Rebecca Hiles of The Frisky Fairy and I created this term to describe the way we classify ourselves when it comes to sex and love. Megasexuals ("megas") are people who tend to not experience a romantic desire or connection unless there is a sexual connection. In other words, megas need to experience sex with someone before they can know whether dating a person will work for them. This doesn't mean that they're shallow or that they're just perverts or only want casual sex. For me, I genuinely feel like I don't know someone well enough to date them until we've had sex.

Unfortunately, megas often encounter stigma in the non-monogamy community. Those who are perceived as men are often thought of as "players" or told that they're heartless. Those who are perceived as women are slut-shamed, even though you'd hope that the non-monogamy community would be better than that. For me personally, there are a lot of people I can have sex with, but very few I want to date. And trying to date someone without having sex with them just doesn't work for me. I've tried! I really have! There have been some lovely people who just moved at a slower pace than works for me, and I ended up losing interest. This doesn't mean that the only thing I want from people is sex - on the contrary! I want really big, deep love in my life too.

Like folks who are ace and demi, megas need our understanding and inclusion too. Just because you can't understand how or why their attraction and interest cycles work, that doesn't mean that their experiences aren't as real for them as yours are for you.

Monogamous/non-monogamous relationships

What happens if you're non-monogamous and someone you're seeing is a monogamous person? Since non-monogamy is still relatively uncommon, many folks in non-monogamy find themselves seeing or dating people who aren't themselves practicing non-monogamy. Can a relationship between a monogamous person and a non-monogamous person work? Maybe.

This area is particularly complicated to talk about because so much of whether it functions well or not depends upon the people involved. If you have a monogamous person who is not particularly prone to jealousy or possessiveness and who supports their partner doing what they want, then that's an easy relationship to manage. More often, though, what you're struggling with is a cultural conflict, where two contradictory belief systems clash with each other creating misunderstandings and difficulties for everyone involved.

When I think about monogamy and nonmonogamy, I think of it as a spectrum (or multiple spectra; see the chapter on desires, page 33). On this spectrum, some people are naturally more monogamous than others, just as some are naturally more non-monogamous than others. In the middle is a big group of people who could theoretically go either way, but who tend to move towards monogamy because of the huge cultural pressures towards it. As such, there are likely a number of people who are monogamous now who could either choose to be non-monogamous or be accepting and affirming of a non-monogamous partner.

In general, if a monogamous person tries to convince you to leave non-monogamy, especially using shaming or threats or manipulation, that is unlikely to be a successful long term relationship unless you too want to be monogamous. If the monogamous partner views your non-monogamy as something you are "doing to them" or "taking" from them, or harming them with, that mindset will likely have to change before you can have a healthy relationship.

Just as when we talked about selling non-monogamy to other people, it can be helpful to have your own ideas and beliefs about non-monogamy clear in your mind before you negotiate this type of relationship. Likewise, it's important for both partners to be clear on what their wants, needs, and boundaries are and to be committed to holding those, even if they know it might end the relationship. Finally, it's important for both of you to work on challenging your own beliefs about relationships, sexuality, partnering, and love. Most of us will have plenty of beliefs that we're operating on that function just outside of our consciousness; you can usually identify those whenever you feel pulled to say "it's obvious" or "of course it's this way" or "everyone/no one/always/never/should/ought." When these beliefs come up, try to take some time to figure out what the actual belief is and whether that works in this connection.

Realistically, long term successful relationships between monogamous and non-monogamous people are challenging and prone to not working out. Often, the monogamous person feels slighted by the non-monogamous person's unwillingness or inability to be monogamous for them. In some situations, the monogamous person will tell the non-monogamous person that they'll end the relationship if they find someone to be monogamous with, putting the relationship in a constant state of risk. If you find these dynamics developing, ask yourselves whether this relationship is actually a fit. Many people say to me that "the heart wants what it wants" or that they love someone as a reason to continue a relationship that is hitting challenges. To that I say, "Love is Not Enough." Mark Manson wrote a great article on why love is not sufficient for a relationship to thrive. While love can feel great, our emotional sense of connection is often not reflective of whether the relationship is healthy or compatible. After all, people in abusive relationships often love their partners deeply.

In the end, whether this kind of relationship works depends almost entirely on whether you are both able to find spaces of mutual respect and affirmation. If you can love each other exactly as you are, it's possible for this to be successful,

Queer Non-Monogamy

BAD JOKE:

What does a lesbian bring to her second date?

A U-Haul.

What does a gay man bring to his second date?

His new boyfriend.

Shockingly, it's not just straightish, heteronormative, cisgender folks who do non-monogamy. Although almost all mainstream media depictions feature a man and woman couple, where the woman is bisexual and the man is straight, non-monogamy of all flavors is still something queer folks can do. Perhaps one of the loudest and most well known voices about non-monogamy in the queer community is Dan Savage. He coined the term "monogamish" to describe the relationship structure he has with his husband, and he frequently encourages people to accept that strict, 100% monogamy is not necessarily achievable over the long run.

In some queer communities, monogamy and the heteronormative mainstream relationship model have always had challenges. After all, to be queer is to challenge and reject what society tells you to do. After the push for gay marriage, some queer communities have been attempting to return to more monogamous models, perhaps as part of the respectability politics employed by the PR campaigns for equal rights to marriage for gay folks.

In terms of non-monogamy communities, queer folks tend to have somewhat separate circles within non-monogamy than folks who are largely hetero- aligning due to issues discussed earlier relating to homophobia, cissexism, and others.

Bi-phobia and bi erasure also have facets within the non-monogamous queer world. Many gay and lesbian identified people will not date bi or pansexual people. Some people assume that all bi folks are into threesomes or group sex. Some people assume that if someone identifies as pan/bi they want to have sex with everyone and don't ever say no.

Bisexual men and most trans/non-binary folks tend to be particularly singled out in non-monogamy worlds. While bi women are largely accepted, bi men are sometimes met with revulsion in more hetero-leaning communities, and with skepticism and patronization in queer communities. For instance, most swinger clubs won't allow "single" men into play spaces, swinger resorts won't allow "single" men, and men who aren't accompanied by a woman at sex clubs are often charged much higher fees for entrance.

For trans/non-binary folks, dating in general can be like navigating a field of landmines while blindfolded. The risks of violence and shaming and rejection are significantly higher for people who aren't cisgender. Figuring out which non-monogamy communities are affirming of trans/enby folks may take some research, and even then it's possible to run into prejudice.

Gay men, particularly in major metropolitan areas, often have a lot of opportunities for engaging in casual/public sex and often stick to their own communities made up solely of gay men. Bathhouses, certain gyms, and gay clubs/bars tend to cater to the needs of this demographic. Lesbians may have more difficulty finding affirming spaces. In areas with large concentrations of queer folks, gay male spaces often aren't particularly welcoming to lesbians. Heteronormative spaces often operate on the myth that lesbians just haven't "found the right man" or that they would appreciate the opportunity to have sex with a cis man.

All of these factors add a new layer of complexity to those attempting to do non-monogamy while queer. This isn't to say that you can't, after all most of my personal community is queer, but it may take more work to find people who are like you and who practice non-monogamy in a way that works for you. If you're in a bigger area, there may be specific meetups or munches for queer non-monogamous folks. If you're not, you might start inside of the queer communities and then work to find non-monogamous folks within them.

Sex

We live in a world where we are constantly surrounded by sex but generally unable to speak frankly about the specific sex we're having with the real people in our lives. Almost all of us are steeped in mores that tell us sex is dirty and wrong and we should save it for the one person we love and marry. How does that make any sense? We talk about sex as a hugely important thing that is used to sell everything and simultaneously tell people that sexual problems aren't a "big deal" or enough to consider changing or ending a relationship over.

Compounding these problems are our norms for discussing sex. We have baseball metaphors, terms like "smash" and "destroy," and slurs like "slut" and "whore." People socialized as men in our culture are encouraged to get a yes through whatever means necessary, to overcome obstacles and "score." People socialized as women are encouraged to stay pure but to also be a great lay for that one person they really love. You need to be a chaste (future) wife in the streets and a porn star in the sheets.

Men aren't empowered to use their no for sex and often can't identify sexual assault as something that happened to them, even when they describe someone having sex with them against their will. Women aren't empowered to use their yes without shame or guilt and some get drunk so they can have an "excuse." Finding someone who knows how to have open and honest conversations about sex in this culture is a huge challenge because all of these factors work against us.

Even within non-monogamy circles plenty of people talk about how it's "not just about the sex" as a way to sound more respectable. And yes, it is not ALL about the sex, but that's not really the point. Rather than responding to allegations that us non-monogamous folks are all horny pervs with a response of "Some of us are, and sex is fun, and some of us are less horny and that's great too" even the non-monogamous clutch their pearls and squeal "It's about love!"

And yet, for most of us (not necessarily the asexual or demisexual folks) sex is a part of why we do non-monogamy. We all want different things and - as long as they're grounded in good consent - they're all perfectly wonderful and glorious. Whether you're one of the slutty pervy types (like me), someone who likes an occasional thing, or someone who prefers cuddles, what you want is totally normal.

So then how do we get what we want? Now that there's a whole wide world of non-monogamy in front of us, how do we get a plate to take to the buffet? The answer is with our words - you have to open your mouth (or your messaging app) if you want your fantasies to become realities. Using our words can be really intimidating, especially when we're new to it, but practice makes it easier.

Lucky for you, I'm including my "Ultimate Guide to Talking Dirty" to help get you started. What does dirty talk have to do with getting the sex you want? Well, would you rather someone you play with walk up to you and in a flat tone state "Would you like to know about the sex I like?" or have them look at you and, with a slight growl in their voice, say "I've been fantasizing about some things we can do together. Want to hear?" Dirty talk can be a great tool for helping us improve the skills we need for negotiation about the sex we want to have. This worksheet also includes a huge bank of words you may or may not want to use but which can get you started on your own dirty talk fill in the blank game with a partner or 2 or 3.

Your Ultimate Guide To Talking Dirty

1. Set the scene
   - 💜 Ask them for consent
     - 💜 Make sure they want you to talk dirty to them and/or send pics
     - 💜 Make sure it's the right time to do it
     - 💜 "I'd love to talk dirty to you, are you into it?"
   - 💜 Talk about terms
     - 💜 What words are off limits? What words do they love? What do they want you to call their sexy body parts?
     - 💜 "I hate the word cunt but I love pussy"
     - 💜 "I love the work cock but dick just sounds silly to me"
   - 💜 Establish any boundaries
     - 💜 Do they only have a certain amount of time? Do they want words, pictures, both? Is there anything they don't want you to talk about?
     - 💜 "I love talking about you fucking me, but I don't want to talk about having condom-less sex"
     - 💜 "I want to talk about spanking but not PIV sex" (PIV = penis in vagina)
     - 💜 "That sounds super hot and I've got 15 minutes for it"

2. Start slow
   - 💜 Start the talk the same way you would start an in person encounter
     - 💜 Kissing /Touching / Removal of clothes / What you want to do

3. Build anticipation
   - 💜 Enjoy the journey, not just the destination
     - 💜 Don't be afraid to tease for a bit

4. Let them know what you're enjoying and how much
   - 💜 Tell them how your body is reacting
     - 💜 "I'm so wet/hard"
   - 💜 Let them "hear" your responses
     - 💜 Moan/Grunt/Whisper/Scream
   - 💜 Ask for more
     - 💜 Yes /Please/Harder/Faster/Deeper
   - 💜 Tell them when you're there
     - 💜 "I'm cumming"/"I just came"

5. Thank them and plan for next time
   - 💜 Let them know what you loved
   - 💜 Tell them whether/when you'd be up for more
     - 💜 Can they message you anytime? Do they need permission first?

Download the worksheets at www.buildingopenrelationships.com

Dirty Talk Cheat Sheet

Hot Buttons

faster	need
harder	please
more	begging
slower	don't stop
yes	keep going
deeper	fuck me
give it to me	

Adjectives

hot	tasty
wet	erect
warm	loud
moist	quiet
hard	muffled
soft	fast
smooth	slow
rigid	intriguing
excited	enticing
hungry	irresistible
luscious	amazing
delicious	tight

Verbs

	pull
stroke	massage
touch	tease
tantalize	tickle
graze	squeeze
grab	thrust
hold	writhe
pin	slide
press	wrap
push	ram
slam	ravage

Things to talk about

breath
skin
lips
hands
fingertips
tongue
voice
mouth
waist
curves
muscles

sounds
moan
scream
breathing
skin slapping

Words for Orgasm

cum
explode
wave of ecstasy/ pleasure/etc.
fill (him/her/ them) up
squirt
gush
release
climax
ecstasy

Words for sexy parts

vulva/vagina
slit
pussy
cunt
(adjective) hole
snatch
wetness
heat

penis
dick
cock
hard on
member
rod
hardness

butt
ass
rear
derriere
booty
behind

scrotum/testicles
nuts
balls
sack

Section 2:
Established in
Non-Monogamy

Here you are! You've jumped into your exploration, had some talks, gone on some dates, maybe even found a new sweetie or 2 or 3 or 4. So . . . what now? Unfortunately, a lot of the non-monogamy resources out there focus heavily or solely on people just starting out and, in some ways, that makes sense. People just starting have a whole world of ideas and terminology and feelings to work their way through. However, those of us who have been at this a while also need help sometimes.

In this section, I'll focus on the kinds of problems and situations that you find yourself in after you gone through the "this is so new!" phase of non-monogamy. As with Section 1, you might not need everything in here - that's great! Keep what works for you and feel free to let go of the rest.

Communication:
Beyond the Basics

● ● ● ● ● ●

In Section 1, we covered communication strategies that everyone can use to set themselves (and their partners) up for success as much as possible. Over time, however, you might find yourself in some communication situations that are more specific to those actively practicing non-monogamy. Here are some of them!

When are you talking/sharing TOO much?

As I'm sure you can tell by reading this book, I'm a BIG proponent of communication. I think that most folks don't talk nearly often enough about nearly enough things. I think this lack of communication leads to lots of the most common problems we see in relationships, and that increasing communication is one of the (on the surface) easiest steps you can take to improve your relationships. However, you can end up in a situation where you're sharing TOO much and creating more problems.

What is too much? That will vary from person to person. I've had some partners who wanted to hear a full on blow by blow of my hottest sexual experiences. I've also had partners who reacted poorly to me sharing more than a general "I hooked up with so and so." There's no right way here, only ways that are better or worse for you. For me personally, I talk about my sex life on my podcast, Life on the Swingset, and on the internet, and in places like this book. I also prefer to have partners who enjoy hearing stories of my fun with other lovers and who enjoy telling me their stories. Therefore, I'm likely to do better with people who want more communication rather than less.

Issues of over communication can also arise when it comes to relationship conflict or problems. Sometimes, the best thing to do about a small slight or concern is to let it go rather than to talk it out. If you find that you're spending more time processing your relationship than having it, it's worth checking in about whether all of this processing is actually necessary. After all, our relationships are supposed to be sources of comfort and joy, not sources of stress and struggle.

So in short, calibrate your sharing and communicating to ensure that everyone's needs are being met. And if you find yourself spending most of your relationship talking about your relationship, it may be time for a check in.

Explaining non-monogamy to others

The longer you do non-monogamy, and the more out you are, the more likely it is you'll have to explain non-monogamy and how you do it to other people. Your first challenge will likely be explaining (or selling) non-monogamy to people you'd like to date and have relationships with. Next, you'll want to consider talking about how you do non-monogamy with your doctor and other medical professionals. Finally, you may move towards discussing non-monogamy with your friends and family.

Selling non-monogamy to monogamous folks

In an ideal world, everyone would be able to freely choose between monogamy and nonmonogamy and there would be robust, diverse dating pools for all the different relationship structures. In reality, many people have never heard of non-monogamy or considered trying it for themselves. So when you try to date, the odds are high that you'll end up at one point or another having to explain this whole non-monogamy thing to someone you like and who you'd like to have join you on this journey.

As with most things, people tend to respond best to arguments that emphasize benefits and positives over ones that emphasize negatives. So, while it can be tempting to deliver your soap box screed about the evils of monogamy and mainstream dating as a part of your explanation of why you, yourself, are not monogamous, this approach is likely to make the person receiving it feel defensive of the life they still largely identify with.

So take some time to think about what you think the biggest benefits are of non-monogamy. If you could paint them a picture of why this thing you do is so fantastic and makes you so happy, what would be the highlights?

When people ask me why I do non-monogamy, I light up with excitement and joy. This is a chance for me to let them in on the things that have been giving me so much life! Here are some things I might say: I'm someone who loves to have a lot of sex with a lot of people and who likes to have deep, meaningful intimacy, even with my one night stands. There are so many amazing, beautiful, interesting people in this world and being non-monogamous means I get a chance to get to know so many more of them more deeply!

I get to be my whole, true self and not worry that someone will judge me for how slutty I am with my body or my heart. And some of my best friendships have come from people who I didn't work well with for dating but who have been my best wing person or cheerleader. I love that I can be fully honest and transparent, even about the super hot sex I have with other people, and that this honesty brings us closer and closer every time.

Knowing your own highlights so you can focus on them more effectively is a great way to paint non-monogamy as a feature in your life rather than a bug or a hindrance.

Common benefits folks talk about are:

- ♥ Independence

- ♥ Freedom

- ♥ More love around you

- ♥ People to enjoy all the parts of your life

- ♥ More honesty

- ♥ Deeper, more connected community

- ♥ More sex

Now you know how to talk about what's great for you in non-monogamy. If figuring out how to package the benefits of non-monogamy is one side of the coin, preparing to answer their questions is the other. We've all had the experiences where someone asked us questions that hit us wrong or that put us on the defensive. The thing is, you've had a lot of time to come to the idea of being non-monogamous and to understand what it means for you and your life. If this is someone else's first experience hearing about non-monogamy, they're going to have questions that may sound "stupid" to you or that may come off as hurtful.

Questions are a normal part of understanding a new world view and, since most of us are pretty attached to our current world view, the first phase of those questions tends to be oriented mostly towards proving this other world view is "wrong" or "bad" rather than truly understanding it.

Just like you came up with a plan or a sound bite for why non-monogamy works well for you, it's helpful to come up with some canned responses to common questions by folks

who aren't themselves non-monogamous.

- ♥ Does that mean you don't do commitment or relationships?

- ♥ You mean like cheating?

- ♥ But what about jealousy?

- ♥ How can you love more than one person?

- ♥ You mean you just want to play the field?

- ♥ But don't you ever want children?

- ♥ Does that mean you just have lots of group sex?

- ♥ What about STIs?

- ♥ What if your partner falls in love with someone else?

Overall, while it may sound cheesy, what you're doing here is akin to a sales or public relations job. Your goal in these conversations is to be honest in such a way that it is persuasive. You shouldn't lie or be dishonest, but you do want to be aware of how you select your wording. Let's see two examples of how you could respond to "What about STIs?"

Example 1: It sounds like you assume that I'm teeming with disease. I get tested every 3 months! I can show you my test results if you want. But I'm telling you, I'm clean. I work really hard to make sure I'm not spreading things around. Not everyone in the community does that, you know! And yeah, there are some people I wouldn't have sex with cuz they'll just have sex with anyone, you know? But I'm really good about what I do.

Example 2: That's such a great question! I'm glad you're focusing on taking care of your own health, that's such an important trait. I understand why it might seem from the outside like folks who are non-monogamous have a greater risk of STIs. After all, they have sex with more people! What the research tends to show is that people in consensually non-monogamous relationships tend to have lower rates of STI transmission than the general population.

There are lots of possible reasons for this trend. First, we get tested more frequently than most monogamous folks, which means we would know something has changed early on before it spreads. Second, we tend to speak more openly about STIs in general and about our recent testing and results, so this increase in communication and honesty helps each of us make more informed decisions. Third, use of barriers and prevention measures is common and people tend to explicitly negotiate use of condoms and even gloves and dams, which means we're taking more precautions than most monogamous folks. Finally, we're really honest with each other about what sex we're having with other people.

Research has found that one of the biggest causes of STI transmission in monogamous folks is infidelity (of course combined with lack of barrier use and poor communication), so since we know up front what sex our partners are having, we can be sure to adjust our own behaviors to the level of risk that feels good to us.

So in the first example, it's pretty clear that the person is feeling personally attacked and defensive about how they personally handle STIs. They're also using some language (e.g. "clean" and "dirty") that indicate they have some internalized stigma and shame around STIs. While their intent is clearly to convince this person that they personally are a safe risk, their defensiveness could easily raise more questions than it answers.

In the second example, the speaker focuses on giving objective information and data that answers the actual question asked. Ideally, this answer is given with a friendly, happy tone that invites the listener in rather than a haughty, snobby tone that excludes the listener. The second answer doesn't assume where the listener is coming from or that there is any malicious intent on the part of the person who asked the question. Instead, it treats the question like one that makes sense and even gives encouragement for asking it.

The more you make people feel like their experiences are normal and understandable, the more you reflect what you're seeing in them, the more likely it is they will hear what you have to say. After all, as social creatures, one of the most powerful drives humans have is to see and be seen by each other. When you give someone validation, you make it more likely that they will want to understand and validate you in return.

Now this tips in this chapter may help your conversation go more smoothly, but they can't guarantee that any given monogamous person will be open to considering dating someone who is non-monogamous. Unfortunately, being non-monogamous tends to narrow your dating pool some. This can suck at times - I mean, if someone were to draw a diagram of the non-monogamous community members' sexual connections, it would show just how much overlap there is! While it can narrow your dating pool, you can sometimes find monogamous folks who are willing to give it a shot. After all, most of us who do non-monogamy were once monogamous ourselves!

Benefits of non-monogamy

Sometimes, it helps to take some time to figure out why we like something before we start talking about it with other people. This worksheet can help you clarify what you get from non-monogamy and make those conversations far easier!

What makes you happy about non-monogamy?

What benefits have you found that you didn't expect?

- ♥ Independence
- ♥ Freedom
- ♥ More love around you
- ♥ People to enjoy all the parts of your life
- ♥ More honesty
- ♥ Deeper, more connected community
- ♥ More sex
- ♥ Folks to help with kids/finances

What were your worries when you started?

How have those worries ended up playing out? Did the worst happen?

How do you think you've grown by doing non-monogamy?

What are the things about your life that you wish others could understand?

Talking to your Doctor (and medical professionals) About Non-Monogamy

Why in the world would I recommend you tell your medical team that you're non-monogamous? I mean, how is that any of their business?

The thing is, most medical professionals assume that you're monogamous, and make guesses about your needs and risk profile based on that assumption. If you're married, for instance, your doctor will assume that you don't need to be checked for STIs, since (monogamous) married people don't have any risk for STIs according to the assumptions of many doctors. Thus, when you're seeing your primary care team, you may have to actively work to let them know that you're not following their assumed risk profile.

As a disabled veteran, I get my medical care through the VA.
Whenever I go to see a new doctor, they ask me either if I'm married/ in a relationship or how many people I've had sex with over a given period of time. I use this as an opportunity to say that I'm polyamorous and have multiple partners. I also tell them that I have sex with men who have sex with men and with sex workers because this changes the kinds of tests they are likely to approve for my STI panel.

While I'd love to say that I don't feel scared about their judgments, I do. Every time, I worry what kinds of looks I'm going to get, what they're going to write in my notes, and what they're going to say about me with other staff behind closed doors. However, I do it anyway, because I would rather get accurate care than pretend to be more "socially acceptable" and not get the care I need.

When talking to medical professionals about your non-monogamy, here are some tips to keep in mind:

1. Your tone as you talk about it will affect how they view it. If you act ashamed, they'll follow your lead. If you present it as totally normal, they're more likely to take it that way too

2. Volunteer information rather than waiting to be asked. They may not even think to ask you the questions that you need them to ask to get the information about you. If you think it could even possibly be relevant, volunteer it.

3. Let them know about your risk aware sex practices and about what kinds of activities you do. If you do anal play, and tell them you do, you're more likely to get approved for a site-specific test than if you just request a "full panel." Telling them about your risk aware sex practices also helps them judge what level of risk you might be exposed to and can help to justify more frequent and in depth testing.

4. If they judge you, find someone else. Their decision to judge their patient has very very little to do with you and a lot to do with them. If you otherwise really like them, or if you don't have other options, you can decide to educate them and give them any of the number of resources available online to help doctors understand non-monogamy. The National Coalition for Sexual Freedom is a great starting place for these resources.

5. Don't be afraid to ask! Ask all the questions you can think of. If they don't know the answers, ask them to look into it. Utilize your medical care providers to help you make better decisions and be more informed.

Explaining non-monogamy to friends and family

Humans are social creatures - we require community to thrive. Our friends and family are often the people upon whom we rely for comfort, support, and a sense of belonging. So it makes sense that anything that might cause a rift in these relationships is something that would give us pause. However, as we talk about in the outness section, keeping something important about you from the people you care about isn't a way to foster greater closeness.

If you filled out the Benefits of Non-Monogamy worksheet (page 214), you're already well on your way to getting this conversation on the right path. Your friends and family want the best for you - they love you! If you present your non-monogamy as something that enriches your life, they're more likely to be able to follow your lead. Remember that it might take them a while to come to terms with this change - after all, you've been thinking about and doing non-monogamy for how long? - So if they struggle at the start, or say some hurtful things, take a breath and understand that this is a journey not a single conversation

I came out to my parents as non-monogamous shortly after leaving the military. I offered to buy them a copy of More Than Two, but my mother told me she didn't want to read it and had no interest in learning more. That hurt, but I told myself that she had come a long way about my queerness and maybe this could change too.

Just over 2 years after our first conversation about my non-monogamy, I was visiting my family again and told my mother about this book. I talked about how excited I was to be writing it and how much I wanted to be able to help others succeed in non-monogamy. She told me she didn't approve of anything I was doing. In the past, when she had said things like this, I would have shut down and just walked away, sure that she couldn't change or understand.

But this time, I took a chance instead and told her how sad it

made me that she didn't want to know more about my life and who I am. I cried and shared my hurt, and that moved her to share her sadness that I wouldn't ever experience the happiness she had in her monogamous marriage. We were then able to talk a bit more about things and she was able to ask some questions and listen. We're still not quite on the same page, and she still sometimes says she hopes I find the "one man for [me]" or that I "won't give up on monogamy," but it feels like progress.

In reality, letting people know that you're different always runs the risk that you'll lose some connections. That loss hurts, no doubt. And, in the end, the people with whom you really belong are the ones who will make the effort to understand you and love you exactly as you are.

For more information about talking about non-monogamy with friends and family, look at the section on outness and coming out (page 261).

Handling changing levels of seriousness

● ● ● ● ● ●

Though most of us struggle to admit it, very few relationships in our lives maintain the same level of seriousness over time. Whether it's the friendship that was super close in high school but fades once you leave to college, or the casual fuck buddy who somehow you find yourself seeing all the time and falling in love with. The only constant in life (and relationships) is change. Human hearts are messy and complicated and don't tend to respond particularly well to attempts at control by the brain. So while we often enter any given relationship with certain goals or hopes or plans, the reality can end up being far different.

And yet, almost no one explicitly discusses with those in their life how they will handle "level" changes in the relationship. I mean, have you sat down with your new partner and discussed how you want to break up? I get it, that conversation sounds ridiculous. But how many times have you ended up wishing you knew how to ask someone if they like you or like like you? How often have you wondered how to help someone transition to a different kind of relationship because what you have isn't working for you anymore?

I've roughly titled these sections "Upleveling" and "Downleveling" since in mainstream dating understandings, more seriousness/entwinement/commitment is considered "moving up" and less of those is considered "moving down." As your resident solo poly who dabbles in relationship anarchy, I wanted to give one quick note about this language. Most of us learn about relationships and how they should go from a mainstream, heteronormative, mononormative model of relationships that Amy Gahran (aka Aggie Sez) calls the relationship escalator. She uses an escalator as a metaphor for the ways that popular culture assumes all relationships must go, best exemplified in the children's rhyme "First comes love, Then comes marriage, Then comes the baby in the baby carriage." Escalators only have one direction. You cannot stop part way up and decide to stay there. In the relationship escalator, higher levels are always preferable to lower ones (particularly for those socialized as women). You know a relationship is "successful" if it gets to the top of the escalator and ends in death. If a relationship doesn't work out as it goes up the escalator, then it's a "failure" and you need to start over at the bottom with someone new, discarding the old person from your life entirely.

Thinking about relationships as having "levels" often encourages us to try to fit the people in our lives into boxes rather than just allowing what happens between the two of us to find its own shape.

One of the recent times I found myself needing to transition with someone was when I had not followed my own advice about handling NRE (see page 114). When high on lovey dovey neurotransmitters, I made a whole load of promises to the person I was dating; remember Troy? Although I was already someone who identified as solo poly, who had previously determined that cohabiting with partners was hard for me, who didn't necessarily want to get married and maybe didn't want to have children, I became a whole other person once NRE hit.

I asked Troy to be my "primary" in all but name, made plans for how we would handle marriage proposals, talked about potential future kids, and eventually asked him to move across the country for me. Yes, I did all of that in the first 3-4 months of our relationship. To make it even worse, Troy and I had never even lived in the same city, so the only time we'd had with each other was "vacation" time, not real life, hard work, day to day living time.

Well around month 8, shortly after Troy moved from Georgia to California at my request, I started to have some . . . changes of heart. We were living together, sharing a bedroom, and spending almost all of our free time together. I felt trapped and suffocated. I started nitpicking everything he did, taking out my resentment and regret on him, my feelings coming out warped and sideways. We started fighting, more and more frequently, each fight leading to me pushing him away and him trying to chase me to get back to the closeness we had shared. We became each other's (and our own) nightmares.

Around 11 months into the relationship, I left for a long trip out of the country. I was hoping to get some distance and recalibrate myself so that I could figure out what I actually wanted and needed in my business, my life, and my relationships. How did Troy and I handle my absence? Well, we fought. Hard. In fact, while I was at my last stop on the vacation we had a fight that was so bad that I knew things had to significantly change. If I was going to save this relationship, we had to transition to a place of less expectations, less shared time, and less shared space. Shortly after I returned home, I told Troy I needed him to move out if we were going to be able to continue seeing each other.

The move took some time - after all, housing in the SF Bay Area is hard to find at reasonable prices - and we spent that time further struggling to each get our own needs met without actually telling the other what those were. I started exercising more and more independence, he kept trying to find ways to reconnect. Shortly after he moved out, we broke up. We hadn't been able to "stick the landing" on our transition enough to salvage a relationship that worked for both of us. Neither of us had been able to ask for what we wanted in a way the other person could hear and we hadn't been able, as a duo, to negotiate what our new relationship would look like.

The good news is that Troy and I, after a few months of distance, were able to find the new level that works for us. We're good friends, just like we had been before, and we still sometimes have sex when it feels right for both of us. We both grew significantly out of that break up and, honestly, if we were to meet and date today I think we'd do far better than we did when we first started dating. It took a breakup, but we found the "level" that works for us. We also finally learned how to talk to each other about what we want.

Once upon a time, I read a great piece about re-envisioning different relationship structures as different areas at a big campground (I've tried to find the author and the post and have come up with nothing - so please let me know if you find it!). Some people end up in a cabin, some are by the lake, some are high up on the mountain, and some are in tents by the river. None of these is necessarily "better" than the others, but some may be better fits for the campers.

So when we talk about these kinds of transitions, know that it's not "better" or "worse" to be more or less serious/entwined/committed. Those are just different campsites and the only "right" campsite is the one you and the person(s) camping at it want to share.

Upleveling

Ah, the dreaded question - "So, what is this? Where are we going?" How many of us have spent hours chatting with friends about how to figure out whether the person we're seeing wants to "go steady" with us? Who hasn't felt the anxiety and fear the moment the question escapes our lips?

Calling the question of whether a relationship is going to more towards greater levels of commitment or entwinement can be intimidating for even the most veteran daters. When we look to the mainstream cultural scripts about how to do so, we often see that this question tends to be posed by the woman in a heterosexual relationship, and is a question to agonize over for a significant period of time. If the person being asked does not immediately respond with enthusiasm, then the relationship as a whole is doomed and you must end it immediately. This pattern - agony, anxiety, fear and then either success or failure - sets most of us up to view conversations about asking for more as huge, serious, and overwhelming.

What if we could, instead, just ask for what we wanted from our partner with as much clarity, openness, and level headedness as we ask them if they want pizza or Indian food for dinner?

There are several common problems folks run into when they're starting these "upleveling" conversations. As we've discussed in other chapters, the way you start a discussion and the emotional tone you bring to it strongly influences how the person you're talking to is likely to respond. If I bring a topic to you with fear and shame, part of your brain is going to be thinking it MUST be scary or shameful. If, however, I bring the topic up with excitement and openness and with the ability to negotiate from a place of centered calm, it's far far more likely that the person I'm talking to will be able to do the same.

Another common issue comes from the pressures we may exert on the conversation. Often by the time we start an "unleveling" conversation, we have already within ourselves done lots and lots and lots of thinking and debating and considering of what we want. We've often built hypothetical futures in our heads of what the other person might say or of what our lives might look like when we get a yes (or a no) from that person. Then, when we actually start the conversation with them, we already have the pressure of our hopes and dreams and wishes bearing down on the conversation.

We may expect a final answer immediately or have trouble talking about the variety of options available because we've become attached to one particular outcome. It might behoove us, then, to instead talk about leveling the same way we deal with other conversations - early and often.

In addition, when having these conversations we can often think of them as black and white options - we're going to be primaries now or not, we're going to cohabitate or not - rather than as the beginning of a shared trip to a buffet of relationship choices. After all, what does being a primary mean? What are the expectations and responsibilities inherent in that? If someone asks me if I want to be their partner, the first thing I always ask them is what does that actually mean in terms of how our relationship will change?

Each of us thinks we know absolutely what these terms mean, but we can forget that not everyone shares our definition. After all, even monogamous folks can't agree on what is or isn't cheating! So rather than asking about title changes in isolation, it can be helpful to think about what that means in terms of your relationship. Does it mean more time together? Does it change what information you each need from the other? What expectations are tied to this relationship label for you? What behavior changes are you asking for when you ask for this change in level?

Finally, consider what aspects of this change are things you need and which are negotiable. If the person isn't available for more time, is that a deal breaker? Would that mean staying at your same level, downleveling, breaking up, or upleveling in a different way? When we become too attached to one specific way of doing things, we make it hard for the richness and complexity of the real people with whom we're relating. Just because you like to see partners 3 times per week when you're boyfriends doesn't mean that they do, and does that mean one of you is doing it "wrong?" Not necessarily. Find spaces for flexibility and be open to new solutions that you might not have thought of before. Remember that you are both negotiating this relationship together, so the more you try to cram someone into the space you want them to fill, the harder it will be for them to bring their true self to your relationship.

Overall, when thinking about asking for a change in this direction, take some time first to clarify what it is you're asking for, what different options are available, and be ready to negotiate. Open the conversation from a space of excitement and openness and be sure to schedule it for a time when you'll both be able to bring your best selves and think creatively. Approach it as a creative collaboration rather than a promotion/demotion conversation. And, most importantly, remember to bring your best tools for handling challenging emotions if they don't want what you do.

What do I want/expect from this relationship?

If you start a trip before you know where you're going, you're less likely to end up where you want to be. The same is true of relationships! We can't assume that our partner knows what we want or what we don't want, so take some time here to clarify what it is you want from a given relationship. (P.S. - it's okay if what you want changes over time! This is just a snapshot to get a conversation going)

How much time do I want us to spend together? What's the minimum for me to be happy?

How often are we messaging/texting/talking?

What do we call each other? What do we mean by those titles?

What information do I need to know? When do I need to know it? *(i.e. Do I need to know about dates before they happen? After? What about new sexual partners? How about if someone is considering moving or changing jobs?)*

How do we navigate and handle priority levels between the people we're seeing? If two folks request the same time, how will we decide?

Would this person be my emergency contact? Would they visit me in the hospital?

If I got seriously ill or injured, would I want/expect this person to help me out?

What do I want/expect from this relationship?

How do we handle holidays and family events?

Who knows about this relationship? What do they get to know?

What kinds of PDA (public displays of affection) do we do?

How often do I want us to be having sex? What's the minimum amount? What's the maximum?

What kinds of sex are we having?

What words/pet names/titles are we using with each other? Are any of them exclusive to this relationship?

What kinds of long terms hopes/dreams am I having about this connection?

What kinds of longer term steps are likely off the table for me? *(i.e. Cohabitation, marriage, kids, mixing of finances)*

Downleveling

While conversations about transitions to more seriousness can be stressful, conversations about transitions to less seriousness can feel impossible to successfully execute. No one I know of enjoys upsetting, hurting, or disappointing someone they care about. Outside of relationship transitions due to abuse or significant harm, most of our "downleveling" happens as a result of changes in fit. Many of us struggle with tendencies towards people pleasing and perfectionism and can find ourselves trying to force something to work, even when it's not the right fit for us, because we don't want to let the other person down.

Downleveling conversations can come from changes in our life circumstances, changes in priorities, changes in each of us as partners, or as a result in poor proactive management of NRE (see the chapter on NRE for tips on this!). Sometimes what we thought we wanted ends up not being the right fit, or sometimes we grow and change in ways that make the things that used to be a fit no longer a fit.

The same way that many of us cling to that one piece of clothing that we've had for years and we're sure will look GREAT on us once we lose 20 pounds/gain some muscle/whatever, we can sometimes find ourselves reticent to acknowledge that a relationship isn't working for far too long. Why is that? Well, multiple factors come into play.

First, most of us never really learned how to downlevel with love and kindness. If we look at how mainstream dating treats breakups, they are always huge, emotional blow outs that leave people crying for days/weeks/months. They're often tinged with anger and resentment and many couples go out with a bang - but not the sexual kind. We don't see many transition conversations that involve two people sitting down, talking about the reality of their changing needs, and figuring out what a good fit would be for them going forward.

The number one tip I would give for these kinds of conversations is to talk about them early on in dating someone. Ask the person you're seeing how they handle downleveling. Do they prefer in person or in writing? Do they want it scheduled or spontaneous? Is it best at a public place? Their place? Yours? Try as much as you can to find commitments the two of you can make about how you will handle any downleveling that comes up in the future.

I know, you think I'm weird for recommending you talk about breaking up as you're getting together. I get it. I do. It sounds ridiculous. However, as humans we tend to do much better at figuring out these sorts of needs and commitments when we're happy with each other than we do when we're already upset or frustrated. Talking about how you'll handle the bad times when you're in the good times is the best way to set yourselves up for amicable conversations.

For macro level tips, remember to come at this conversation, as most conversations, with as much kindness as you can muster. Even if the reason for down leveling is that the person has done something that pisses you off, there are ways to be kind and set firm boundaries at the same time (See the chapter on boundaries –page 58– for more!). The way you show up for the tough things reflects more greatly on you than how you show up when it's easy. Remember who you want to be and bring that person to the conversation.

Just like we talked about in upleveling conversations, think of this discussion as a creative collaboration session. What is it that you're available for with this person? What are you not available for? What's negotiable? Coming to the table with plenty of options empowers both of you to create something new that fits your needs. Don't worry about sticking to standard societal models here - there isn't one right way to downlevel or one right outcome to come to. Is sexual intimacy still available? Emotional? What kind of time is available? How do you want to interact when you run into each other? How do you want to talk to other people in your life about the down leveling? You can fill out the Forming Your Downleveling Conversation worksheet (page 232) for help clarifying your answers to these kinds of questions.

Be prepared for the other person to have strong emotions come up. After all, you've had time to think about and plan this and they may not have known it was coming. Figure out ahead of time how much bandwidth you have for supporting them in these emotions and what it is you would do if their emotions are more than you have bandwidth for.

Most of all, know that it's okay to have these conversations. You don't need to keep squeezing yourself into a dress that doesn't fit. You don't have to keep a suit that's now 5 years old (and looks it) just because you keep really really hoping it'll somehow fit you now AND look the way you want it to. Wanting a downlevel is totally okay, for any reason or for no reason. You get to do what fits for you.

Be sure to plan for some self-care for after the conversation. Even if the conversation goes well, it's likely to bring up some stress and fear for you, so having a good self-care plan in place will make it easier to recover and move on.

When to change levels

So how do you know when it's time to look at moving to a new campsite? Well, sometimes there are changes in circumstance or context that may prompt a reevaluation of your relationships. For this category, any major life event that might have you checking back in about where your life is going would probably be applicable.

> ## Events such as:
>
> ♥ Death
>
> ♥ Divorce
>
> ♥ Moving
>
> ♥ Birth of a child
>
> ♥ Breakups
>
> ♥ Start of new relationships
>
> ♥ Loss of a job
>
> ♥ Got a new job

Other reasons for evaluating where you've pitched your campsite might be less about external events and more about internal experiences.

These could include:

💜 Coming to the end of NRE

💜 Feeling dissatisfied

💜 Noticing resentment

💜 Frequent fights and conflicts

💜 Feeling a desire for greater closeness

💜 Feeling "smothered"

💜 Falling in love

💜 Feeling stuck

💜 Feeling inspired

💜 Noticing you're preventing yourself from saying things to the other person (good, bad, or otherwise)

Finally, it might be helpful to do regular check ins about how your relationship campsites are suiting you. Things change over time and it can be easy to get caught up in the changes of our life without paying attention to whether the relationships we still have are working for us the way they did before. How often should you do this check in? Well, I think that depends on how quickly things change in your life and how quickly you notice yourself moving towards or away from partners. If you're a fast mover, you might want to check in every quarter; if you're a slower mover it might be every 6 months or every 12. Doing a check in doesn't obligate you to change anything, it's more like getting a regular oil change - maintenance that lets you know early if something needs attention.

Forming your downleveling conversation

If you're noticing that you want to transition your relationship towards lower degrees of seriousness, use this worksheet to help you form the conversation you'll have with your partner about it.

What do you enjoy about the connection or have you enjoyed?

What elements of the relationship would you like to keep?

What elements of the relationship do you want to look different? How would you like them to look?

How would you guess your partner would best receive this news?

How much are you available to hold their feelings and process this change with them?

Who can you turn to for support around your feelings related to this transition?

How much time do you need to adjust to the change? How can you make space for them to take time to adjust to the change?

Special Circumstances in Established Non-Monogamy

● ● ● ● ● ●

Just as there are some topics that tend to come up for folks starting out, there are some special situations that come up for those who are practicing non-monogamy longer term. Some of these may apply to you right now and others may not, but it's worth thinking about all of them.

Living off the escalator

Within non-monogamy, some relationships maintain more similarities to mainstream models than others. For those of us who venture way, way, way out from the standard script, the challenge of figuring out our path can be even more challenging

I started identifying as solo poly in 2014 after finding the

definition and discovering the ways in which I wanted to center autonomy in my relationships. In a lot of ways, I think this decision came out of the personal work I did while deployed in Afghanistan. You see, while you're deployed, you have a LOT of time to think about things. For me, I decided to spend that time focusing on two questions - what if I never get married again, and what if I never have kids.

Going into the deployment, I thought that the non-monogamy I wanted was an open relationship, with one strong central partnership that would lead to marriage and children and other outside sex without deep feelings. As I prepared to leave for Afghanistan, though, I found myself grappling with the question of whether I should just go ahead and have a kid on my own, or whether I should focus my energy on finding a marital partner if marriage was what I wanted. I had come out of a broken engagement at the start of 2012 to a string of relationships with lovely people with whom who it just didn't work and I was starting to panic. I had turned 30 without a good marriage prospect in sight. So I decided to give myself the space to see if marriage and kids were things that I wanted or things that society had told me to want.

I read Why Have Kids? by Jessica Valenti, Outdated by Samhita Mukhopadhyay, and memoirs by Chelsea Handler and Caitlin Moran. I spent hours and hours letting myself consider a future without that secure, mononormative blanket of couple privilege and having babies. By the end of my deployment, I had discovered solo polyamory and come to the conclusion that I didn't need children or a marriage and that what I did want was to be free to be myself while having deep loving relationships.

I came to my conclusion and then heard a resounding question in my head "So . . . what does that even look like?" I had no idea how my life would work if I didn't want to follow the script. Would anyone want to date me? Would I want to live with someone? What if they wanted kids? What does an adult life even have in it if not these structures?

So I started experimenting. I found that things that don't work for me are people who assume they get my time, sharing a bedroom with a partner, dating people in hierarchies, people who say they want one thing but act in another way, and folks who want me to prove that I'm into them. Things I found that do work for me were long distance relationships, slut referral networks (where happy slutty people introduce each other to their favorite happy slutty people), dating other solo poly folks, and having lots of casual loving connections. I also found my shorthand for how I do relationships - I like to have several deep, loving connections that center autonomy. That is, no one gets to tell me what to do with my body, my heart, my mind, or my time.

When we try to answer the question of what life looks like off the relationship escalator, there's no one answer. Every one of us who jumps off will find our own way of navigating the world of relationships and life. And, to be frank, you're likely to have to do a fair amount of trial and error to figure out what works for you.

Here are some areas to consider:

💜 What does commitment mean to you outside of a relationship escalator model? (Check out the section on commitments back in the first half of the book! page 43)

💜 What kind of living situation works best for you?

💜 How do you want to handle finances? Would you combine them with a partner?

💜 How do you best negotiate time and scheduling? Do you like to have regular weekly dates? To schedule a month worth of dates at a time? To do only spontaneous hangouts?

💜 Where do you stand on local vs. long distance connections? What makes each better or worse for you?

💜 What kind and frequency of communication works for you?

💜 What time/energy/etc. do you need to take good care of yourself?

💜 Do you want kids? How would that look? What would make that more or less appealing for you?

💜 How do you feel about dating people who generally do relationship escalator relationships?

💜 What are the reasons you're choosing life off the escalator?

💜 What are the biggest benefits of being off the escalator for you?

💜 What are the biggest hurdles you face in living off the escalator?

💜 How do you want to explain what you do?

💜 Who can you talk to when you have dilemmas about life off the escalator?

Being a better metamour

In non-monogamy, we have the unique opportunity to expand our worlds, communities, and chosen family by connecting with the people our partners bring into our spheres. In this section, we're talking all about how to be a great metamour, the skills, mindset, and tools you need to help build the best metamour relationships possible.

A metamour is the partner of my partner. So if I'm dating Jo and Jo is dating Sarah, Sarah is my metamour. While someone people feel apprehension about metamours, I think they can be one of the best parts of non-monogamy. Some of the best humans I've met have been metamours, and I've been lucky enough to develop lasting friendships with many of them!

Unfortunately, some folks (particularly cisgender men) don't put much effort into being a good metamour. Can you imagine if your best friend went away to college and came back with their new friend and you didn't make any effort to get to know that friend? Or even worse, if you started trying to undermine their relationship so you could get your friend back from them? Our metamours are people who enrich our partners' lives, so I like to think of us as all being on the same team. We all want our shared partner to be happy and thrive, and we'll support that best when we're able to work together.

Different people prefer different styles of metamour relationships. Some folks prefer a family style approach, where everyone is close with each other's partners, almost to the point of requirement. Some folks want very little contact with metamours, or none at all. Folks also fall everywhere between these two extremes. As with relationship styles, there's no right way here, but there are some ways that are more ethical than others.

In general, every person should get to choose how close they become with any other person. With metamour relationships, it tends to work best when metamours can at least be in the same room (I call this birthday party style - can you be at your shared partner's birthday party together?) Any style that requires relationships with one person to have relationships with another person is probably less ethical, and infringing more on autonomy, than one that doesn't have that requirement.

So how can you be a better metamour? Being a good metamour is like being a good friend or building a new friendship. Be in contact with your metamour, ask them questions about themselves that don't just relate to your shared partner. If you have shared hobbies, think about hanging out with them without your shared partner there. If you're having concerns about them, talk with them directly rather than playing telephone through your partner.

Now you may occasionally have metamours who aren't available for a friend-type relationship - that's okay. In that case, treat your metamour with as much kindness and caring as you can manage. We can't control someone else or force them to have the kind of relationship we want, we can only control ourselves. Be sure that the way you interact with your metamour is within your values and you're set.

Long-distance relationships

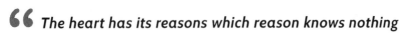 **The heart has its reasons which reason knows nothing**
of... We know the truth not only by the reason, but by the heart."
- Blaise Pascal

In a perfect world, everyone we love and want to spend time with would live very close to us. Like within walking distance maybe! And yet be totally okay with the amount of space vs closeness that we require. Unfortunately, it's a great big world filled with really fantastic people and you may from time to time find yourself in a relationship with someone who lives far from you. Enter the oft-maligned long-distance relationship.

While mainstream dating culture seems to think that long-distance relationships (LDRs) are doomed to failure, that doesn't have to be the case. It's true that in some ways long-distance relationships are more challenging - you have to be on top of more logistics, scheduling is more complicated, and some love languages may be harder to get met than others. However, LDRs do offer some benefits. For those who lead busy lives or tend to become polysaturated, an LDR can be a connection that is easier to fit with/into/around the rest of your life. Because you can't just immediately move in together during NRE (I know nothing about this), LDRs force you to get to know each other better and over a longer period of time. You're more likely to do lots and lots of talking instead of lots and lots of fucking (though phone and video sex can be great too!).

If you're thinking about entering an LDR, it's important to be realistic with yourself and your partner about what you can offer them. If you know that you tend to struggle to maintain interest if you're not seeing someone regularly, that's something to discuss up front. If sex is important to you, problem solving about how to get that need met is going to be essential. And, if you just don't know yet whether you can do long-distance, be honest about that and just keep your partner posted about how things are going for you.

As with everything else, there's no one right way to do LDRs. As long as you're honoring your values and your partner's needs and autonomy, you can create whatever fits best for the two of you. Maybe that's daily texts and calls every other day, or maybe it's a monthly video-sex-athon. Whatever feels best for you is a great option.

Problems
for Established
Non-Monogamists

• • • • • •

When you see messed up stuff

It would be great if the world of non-monogamy was a utopia, free of the problems of the regular world. Sometimes, we like to think that our own personal communities, the people we know, could never be like the "bad guys" or "monsters" we hear about in the news. We think to ourselves, "We're great at consent and communication and boundaries! We would never have a Weinstein or Cosby in our community!"

The reality is that even "monsters" have friends and family, and there are no clear monsters. Each and every one of us, over a long enough timeline, will hurt someone else badly. We will all end up coercing someone, we will all end up coerced. We will all be toxic towards a partner, we will all have partners who are toxic towards us. All of us grow up in a culture built on rape culture and coercion and control, founded on the idea of power over rather than power to or power with. As such, none of us escape the same programming that told Weinstein he was entitled to the attention of and sexual interaction with all of those women; we just may enact it in smaller degrees.

In her books, Brené Brown talks often about how everyone is doing the best they can with the tools they have. This means that there are (almost) no movie-worthy bad guys, just flawed humans who were likely gravely hurt themselves, enacting hurt on others.

To add to this mess, we all are raised in carceral models of responding to wrongs. In the carceral system, things are black and white - someone is innocent or guilty, the victim or the perpetrator, worthy or worthless. If someone does something bad enough, they are ruined forever and no longer worth our understanding or care. They become disposable, locked away forever or executed, or released back into the civilian population with a record that will make getting a job or housing exceedingly difficult. Many of us feel like those who do wrong "deserve" these punishments, particularly when the wrongdoers are people we're not close to. And yet, when someone you know does something unacceptable, or you do, I'm willing to wager that you find some empathy and understanding and no longer see things as quite so black and white.

Restorative and transformative justice approaches arose out of the communities of indigenous people and people of color as a response to the carceral model that disproportionately harms people from these communities. In these approaches, they instead posit that no one is disposable and that solutions must be more complex than punish harshly or do nothing. In restorative justice, the process centers the needs of the harmed party - what do they need to be restored to how they were before the harm? In transformative justice, the process looks at how the community and context contributed to the harm, to how they created a situation in which a person would act in this way.

In these approaches, the focus of the response process is on increasing safety and care for those harmed, humanizing those who did harm, and brainstorming a wide array of possible responses before settling on one. These processes may include monetary ways of making amends, apologies, coursework or other learning exercises, therapy/counseling, removal from certain events or activities, or other options altogether. In transformative justice in particular, there is a focus on understanding what the community at large must do to enact lasting change.

Working from restorative and transformative justice mindsets is much harder than working from a carceral mindset. After all, things are no longer quite so clear cut - people aren't villains or victims, they're nuanced, messy creatures. These approaches force all of us to confront the pieces of ourselves that we see in those who caused harm and to examine how we may have contributed to systems of harm and oppression. Self-reflection of this kind is always far less easy than distancing oneself as "not like that."

From a community perspective, however, creating a system where anyone who messes up is either exiled and publicly shamed or has nothing happen will make it far far harder for us to admit our own mistakes and to deal with the mistakes of others. In Conflict is Not Abuse, by Sarah Schulman, the author argues that in this system we require things to be very very bad before we will pay attention since admitting something happened invokes such severe consequences. Instead, she asserts, we should create communities that encourage us to talk about harm at much lower levels of severity and open up our solutions process to more options.

Imagine if you could openly talk about how you had messed up and get the support of your community in changing and doing better. Imagine if you could talk about the people who have harmed you in small ways, not just huge ones, and help them learn to grow and be better. These are the kinds of communities I would like us to build - ones that respond to harm with caring, support, accountability, and kindness for all involved. After all, kindness is not the same as niceness - sometimes the kindest thing we can do is call someone on their shit from a place of compassion.

So, with this background, what kinds of messed up stuff might you see in non-monogamy and how might you handle it?

Abuse in Non-Monogamy

When most of us think about abuse in a relationship, we imagine screaming and throwing things and hitting. While those are definitely abusive behaviors, abuse can be much more subtle than that as well. Isolation, control, manipulation, and coercion are all parts of abusive dynamics that we may have trouble spotting from the outside. There are some great resources available about what abuse looks like and where it comes from - Why Does He Do That by Lundy Bancroft is an excellent book about the mindset of those who abuse others (though I disagree with his assertion that it is mostly men who abuse women).

In non-monogamy in particular, abuse can be much more challenging to pinpoint. If a person has several relationships without abusive dynamics and one relationship with them, we are likely to explain away the problems we see because the abuser isn't like that with their other partners. Furthermore, we may have trouble believing that someone who has one or more well liked and respected partners may be acting in abusive ways because of how highly we think of the people around them.

Abuse in non-monogamy can also play out in the ways that one person influences and controls their partner's actions with that partner's metamours. For instance, Joe may tell Pat that he's fine with Pat dating other people and thinks it's great, but every time Pat has a date Joe ends up in an emotional emergency and tells Pat that if she really loved him she would stay home and help take care of him. Or Joe might insist that he can read every message Pat receives from someone else in the spirit of "transparency."

Because abusive dynamics can get more complex in non-monogamy, it's important to be aware of the underlying dynamics that make something abusive or potentially abusive. Abuse is pattern that undermines or overrides the autonomy and boundaries of the person being abused. In abusive dynamics, consent (with regard to any given area, not just sexual) is disregarded or overridden. There are plenty of behaviors that are hurtful or harmful that are not abuse, and some behaviors that would be abusive if part of a larger pattern are just shitty when done once. For instance, calling your partner a name in anger is shitty; doing it consistently over a period of time is abuse. Some specific articles to look at for more information are in the Resources list.

Everyone is problematic

Everyone, each and every single one of us, is raised in a culture that plants all kinds of problematic stuff in our brains. Racism, sexism, homophobia, cissexism, ableism, classism - we are stewed in the soup of oppression whether we like it or not, and none of us gets out unscathed. No matter how much we work at unlearning oppressive mindsets, the shadows of these cultural lessons linger behind, haunting us and requiring constant vigilance and a need to continually work to do better.

As the internet will tell you, all your faves are problematic. But this actually expands even further - everyone is problematic. You, me, your partners, everyone. We are all products of a culture of horrors, and to think that any of us is ever "past" those horrors is a fantasy.

Therefore, as you move through the world of non-monogamy, you are bound to encounter folks who are at different stages in their journey through anti-oppression work. This includes some folks who are barely on the start of the path, to folks who you expect the best of but end up disappointed by. The people we put on pedestals, in this community or any other, are flawed individuals just like us. None of us are immune to messing up.

So what do you do when you encounter problematic behavior in your community? The answer to this question is hotly debated among anti-oppression activists. Some advocate for calling out, immediately and with vigor pointing out how someone has acted in a problematic way so that they can learn and correct themselves. Some argue for calling in when possible, a more personal, intimate way of talking about a behavior that is about centering your connection with the person. Yet others explore how else we might talk about these problems in ways that are as humane as possible, even to those who have acted in ways that perpetuated oppressions.

Personally, I enjoy the work of Tada Hozumi, The Selfish Activist. They are a genderqueer POC and a therapist doing body-centered work. Their work explores how to understand the realities of the human brain and to work towards change. They also offer a group for people who want to work on authentic allyship.

In general, when you see something problematic, take a moment to consider how you would want someone to tell you that you had messed up. What would help you receive it well? What support would you want in changing? What kinds of things might make you shut down or get defensive? This isn't to say that how you deliver a message about someone being problematic is more important than them changing, or that it's always your responsibility to be nice to people who mess up. It is to say that when we react from our places of anger and hurt, we may not be as effective in getting change from the other person as we would prefer. So consider all of the options available to you, and don't be afraid to take some time to come up with how you want to approach them.

Since you're also a messy human mired in oppression, it's helpful to work in advance on creating systems to help you do better when you mess up. Identify who the people are who you can talk to about messing up and who might tell you truthfully about your actions rather than just being "on your side." Read as much as you can about unlearning oppression and put in the work. When someone tells you that you've messed up, try to receive it with as much openness as you can, and figure out how you can continue to work towards being better in an ongoing way.

Responding to harmful stuff in your community

is this something harmful or is it something different. Are the choices this person is making hurting others? Are they mistreating others? Are they spreading dangerous misinformation? If you cannot locate any actual harm, it might be worth asking yourself whether what they are doing is actually "wrong." If it is creating harm, then it's even more important to take a step back and get a clear look at what is happening. What specifically are they doing that is wrong? What are the precise behaviors or beliefs that are causing harm? What is the nature of the harm they are causing?

Next, you'll need to think about what it is you want to do about the harm. Do you have enough of a relationship with these folks to talk to them directly about it? Is there a community leader who might need to be involved? Is this something that you personally have to be involved in calling out or correcting or is there someone who is a better fit to handle it?

If you are the person who chooses to be involved in talking about it, and are not the person being directly harmed (we'll get to this in a bit), the next step is to take some time to try to understand and empathize with the other folks. What might be driving these choices? How can you find some caring and compassion for them? Can you see them as full, complex humans and not just defined by this behavior? How might they best receive feedback? What kinds of factors might be influencing the choices they are making? How might they react to what you're going to tell them? How might they feel in this conversation? What kinds of support or help might they need to handle this conversation and to effectively make change?

After this, it's time to consider all of the different options you can think of for how they can make amends and demonstrate accountability for causing harm. It's important here to do some preliminary brainstorming, even though when you have the conversation you're going to give them a chance to brainstorm as well, because it's so easy to get mired into one or two options. When you brainstorm, be sure to come up with some "solutions" that you would never actually choose as this can help loosen up your thought processes.

For instance, if the harm the person caused was mistreatment of one of their partners, you could have them put in a pillory in the public square and pummeled with rotting produce as someone yelled "Shame!" over and over. You need to spend a good chunk of time letting your brain come up with options because it'll want to stop after one or two, especially your most preferred options, but the bigger your response buffet is, the more likely it is it'll have a dish everyone can agree on.

The next to last step is to move forward with the conversation. With as much kindness and caring as you can muster, let the person know what they did and what the harm was. Let them have their initial reaction - most of us feel upset and defensive and hurt when we are called out about something. Show them understanding, and let them know that you want to find a solution together. Ask them what different solutions they can come up with, help them brainstorm with you. Let them know what you think accountability and change might look like and see if you can find common ground. Then come up with a plan for what happens moving forward.

The last step is to implement the plan and check in on how it's going. Is the person honoring their commitments? Do things need to change? How are they responding?

Responding to harmful stuff in your

Are the choices this person is making hurting others?

What are the precise behaviors or beliefs that are causing harm? What is the nature of the harm they are causing?

Is this something that you personally have to be involved in calling out or correcting or is there someone who is a better fit to handle it?

If you are the person who chooses to be involved in talking about it, what might be driving these choices? How can you find some caring and compassion for them? What kinds of support or help might they need to handle this conversation and to effectively make change?

What are all of the different options you can think of for how they can make amends and demonstrate accountability for causing harm?

After implementing the plan: is the person honoring their commitments? Do things need to change? How are they responding?

Messiness of Loss in Non-Monogamy

● ● ● ● ● ●

One of the biggest benefits to non-monogamy is how much more love and joy and pleasure you have the opportunity to experience. So many people, activities, and opportunities for growth! The flip side of that coin is that there can sometimes be more loss as well. In this chapter, we're covering the different ways loss can show up in non-monogamy and ways that it can be messy.

In general, mainstream white US culture (like most Northwest European cultures) is pretty terrible at dealing with loss. Our most common mental approach to losses is to pretend they will never happen. We will always be happy! Things will always go well! Or, if you have anxiety, you may find yourself in the opposite boat, preoccupied with all you have to lose as each new relationship opens. All this to say that this chapter may be challenging for folks to read and may stir up some of your own patterns and fears of losses of different kinds. If that happens, that's perfectly normal. Just take a breather and come back.

Breakups

Every relationship you have will end, either through death or through a breakup. We've got lots of good information in this book already about how to handle these relationship transitions between the transitioning partners, but this chapter is more about how you as an individual cope with the loss and how it impacts your other relationships.

A unique situation in non-monogamy is like follows:

I had been seeing Carl for about 4 months when I started seeing Jerry. While Carl was long distance and hierarchical and therefore necessarily limited in some ways, Jerry was local and not engaged in any serious relationships. Plus, Jerry was super cute and he was very very into me. When we started seeing each other, I had serious NRE and we started talking very early on about the intention to be foundational/anchor partners to each other. Jerry even got a weekly recurring date in my calendar and an entire weekend of my time booked.

Things were great at first, but Jerry was relatively new to polyamory and hadn't yet really honed his skills. In particular, Jerry started acting in a way that hits one of my biggest buttons - he would be clearly upset, but when I asked him about it, he would say he was "fine." The first time he did it, I asked him if he was sure and reflected what I was seeing. He said "No, I'm fine." So I said "okay" and went on about what I had been doing. Jerry then stopped me and said "Sometimes you'll need to pull it out of me," indicating that he would need me to push him into sharing what was going on with him. I set a firm boundary with him that since my work involves digging out what people aren't saying I didn't feel good about doing that in romantic/ sexual relationships. He agreed to work on voicing his wants and needs or to tell me he wasn't ready to talk if I asked and something was going on.

Sadly, Jerry continued to struggle with these skills. We had more and more arguments, getting harder and harder, until eventually I sat him down, in person, to tell him that I needed us to "downlevel" so that I wouldn't keep expecting more of him and getting disappointed. Jerry seemed to take it well and we scheduled a date for about 3 weeks out. Five days before our scheduled date, Jerry texted me to say he didn't want to see me anymore.

Throughout all our troubles, I was talking to Carl and asking his thoughts and advice. He was also someone who helps folks with relationships, so I felt grateful that he had the bandwidth to support me through it. However, there were some days where almost all of what Carl and I were talking about was related to Jerry. While the relationship between Carl and I was going great, the stress coming from my relationship with Jerry bled in and made me more irritable and difficult with Carl.

In non-monogamy, the "blast radius" of problems is significantly larger than in monogamy. When one of your relationships is struggling, that can add stress into the relationships that are doing well. That stress can then spread to the relationships your partners have with others. Depending on how closely entwined a network is, problems in one relationship can ripple out two, three, or more degrees.

While it makes sense for the people we care about to support us when we're struggling, even when what we're struggling with is another partner, we have to be aware of how we're impacting others with our choices. Be sure to check in regularly to make sure your other partners have the bandwidth to support you, and encourage them to use their "no" when they need to. If you're the supporting partner, you need to be on top of your boundaries to be sure that you aren't taking on more than feels good for you. If you notice yourself feeling stressed or resentful, that's when it's time to take a break and check in. You don't ever have to be the person supporting your partner through their relationship troubles.

Overall, if you find yourself doing more relationship processing than relating, that's probably a good sign that it's time to re-evaluate and see what would need to change or whether it's time to do some transitioning.

Most of the time, our breakups will be spaced apart. You'll have several relationships, then one will end, then new ones will start, then another might end. However, sometimes our breakups all line up at the same time. So what do you do when you go from dating a bunch of people to suddenly single?

While you might think that being non-monogamous would make it easier to become single, having multiple relationship losses stack on top of each other often feels worse than one monogamous relationship ending. Sometimes breakups will have a cascade effect, especially if the catalyst for a breakup is something you did wrong. After all, in our small communities people talk. If you mess up big in one relationship it's not unusual for that word to spread and for it to negatively affect other relationships.

Taking several hits in a row can be especially demoralizing. If you have insecurities or fears, stacked transitions can feel like your worst nightmares coming true. Your brain might tell you stories like you're undateable or you ruin everything.

When you find yourself in this position, it's important to have good intimate (but platonic) support networks. In our culture, most women and non-binary folks have several close friends with whom they can talk about their emotional lives. Those socialized as men, particularly those who identify to the masculine end of the spectrum, may have fewer of these connections. Mainstream culture teaches men that they cannot talk about their feelings - they can yell at sports, they can show anger, and they can drink. Maybe, if they're lucky, they can tell their partner (usually assumed to be a woman or femme) about their feelings and she will help them understand and hold and manage his feelings. This socialization pattern means that cisgender, masculine men (especially those who are straight) who find themselves in a breakup cascade sometimes find themselves without anyone to support them.

Regardless of your gender, if you find your insecurities or fears flaring more than usual in a stacked breakup, it's never a bad idea to seek out professional help. That can be in the form of a therapist or coach, or could be in the form of medication depending on your medical provider's assessment. There is no shame in letting someone else help you with this burden. If one break up is bad, two is that badness squared, three is that badness cubed, and so forth. This stacking has a logarithmic function curve, not a simple multiplicative one.

Give yourself time and space as well to determine what you want to do about dating going forward. If your relationships ended because you messed up, how do you want to be better in the future? If they ended for other reasons, can you see any common elements? What did these transitions teach you about what you need in relationships and how you can be better as a partner going forward?

While you can do some of this processing and date at the same time, sometimes it's best to stay single for a while. It's often hard to get clear reads on our own wants, needs, and direction when we're entwined with others. Though I understand why some might want to "get back on the horse" as soon as possible, my professional opinion is that most people have never taken as much single time as they need. Dating will always be available to you, but singleness may not be. So cherish this opportunity to take all of the building blocks of your life and your self concept and see which ones you still want and how you want them to fit together.

Messing up other relationships when one ends

When a relationship ends, sometimes we find ourselves diving into the deep end. We may be bitter and resentful and angry, we may be inconsolable and sad and hopeless, or we may be insecure and feel worthless. While our other partners generally are available to comfort us, sometimes it does happen that we end up needing more help than they can provide. Or, even worse, we may end up sabotaging our other relationships because we are so consumed by the feelings and stories we have about the break up.

In these situations, we compound loss on loss, reinforcing any narratives we have about our inability to do relationships right, or that everyone will leave us, or that no one loves us, or that people are awful. I mean, think about it, how long would you want to stay with someone who kept telling you that no one loves them? Or that they're unworthy of love? Or that people are all terrible? Not very long, I imagine.

If you're lucky, your other partners will give you a hard reality check before you hit their breaking point. Even then, though, there's often already damage that's been done. None of us is capable of holding someone else's self-destruction indefinitely, and we each have our own point at which we cannot do it anymore.

So, if you find yourself spiraling down after a relationship ends, be sure to keep checking in with your other partners about how they're doing. If you notice that you're really struggling - having trouble sleeping or eating, having trouble with personal hygiene, or other serious impairments - I would strongly recommend you seek out professional help. While not all breakups lead to serious mental health issues, some can, and it's better to get help so you can come back from it than to struggle alone. Plus, your partners aren't ever going to be able to replace the help of a therapist (yes, even if your partner is a therapist).

Death

Yes, I'm really going to talk about death here.

I get it, you want to skip this section. You want to just flip to the next thing because this sounds so depressing. And after all, this won't happen to you for YEARS, right?

I was 34 years old, dating a 47 year old. His name was El and I was smitten with him. So deeply, fully in NRE that just seeing his name pop up on my phone forced a huge grin onto my face. El seemed healthy, he was muscular, and was doing hard physical labor renovating his house. Yes, he smoked, but he seemed perfectly fine. He was full of life - or at least that's what we all kept saying at his funeral.

I would have never thought that, at 34, I would lose a partner to death. I thought that certainly I was too young, he was too young, there was no way. Because I was so certain that death was far down the line, I hadn't really prepared myself. Even though I knew I was SO INTO EL, I agonized over whether what we were doing was dating. I struggled with the question of whether I should even be open to seeing him given that I had JUST chosen to be single before we started seeing each other. The moment he died, all of those petty mortal quibbles fell away. Of course we had been dating, of course I had feelings for him, of course I should have opened myself to the possibilities and joy he brought to my world. It took losing him to see how afraid I'd been and how much distance that had put between me and what I really wanted.

None of us can know when death will touch us closely. And while it is tempting to plug our ears and say "La la la, not listening," it behooves us to think about what we would want if someone close to us were to die or if we were to die.

Death becomes extra messy in non-monogamy when folks aren't out of the closet. Imagine if someone you loved died, and no one in their family knew you as anything other than a friend. Imagine going to their funeral and having no one understand or acknowledge your place in their life. Imagine not being able to tell them because you can't out the deceased.

Non-monogamy can make death far more complicated. Our losses ripple out and leave unintended consequences. If our families don't approve, they may try to bar the people closest to us from our memorials. If there is conflict between our partners, that may create extra stress after our death.

Because what we are doing doesn't follow mainstream scripts, we have to do far more logistical work to be sure things aren't a mess when we die.

Here are some things to consider:

💜 Who would you want to be personally notified if you died

💜 Who is your legacy contact on Facebook and other social media

💜 Who would would want at your funeral/wake/memorial

💜 What do you want done with your body

💜 What kind of funeral do you want

💜 How will folks access your passwords and accounts

💜 Have you set up a will

💜 Have you talked to your partners about your wishes when you die

💜 Have you talked to your partners about THEIR wishes when they die

💜 What are the things you would want to have if a partner died? (i.e. A picture of you together, a recording of their voice, a shirt they had worn)

💜 What kind of support will you need when a partner dies?

💜 How would you support your partner if one of their other partners died?

When I found out El was dead, there was only one person I felt fully comfortable talking to about it. I knew I was going to fall apart and while I might seem like a very open person, I tend to hold those kinds of things very tightly. I called Carl, even though were were in a strange place between dating and not dating. Carl listened to me cry and let me say whatever I needed. He held space for me because he loved me and I am so thankful that he had the bandwidth to do that.

After the initial wave of grief, I was able to reach out to another lover, Ray. I sent him a message asking if he could, literally, fuck some of the

grief out of me. Ray was happy to hold space for me, to lick my tears off my face, to give me an orgasm that ended in sobbing and to help end some sobbing with orgasms. He helped me find my way back into my body, to feel things all the way through, and to get the air I needed to start breathing again.

After El's death, things were a mess. He didn't have a will. No one knew his passwords to access his bank accounts so that they could finish the construction on his house. He didn't have a legacy contact on Facebook, so the company owned his profile as soon as they discovered he was dead. I found out he died over Facebook messenger, and almost no one in his life knew we were dating because it was so new. His family dissolved into fighting and squabbles over resources. When I went to his house for the first of his 2 memorials, once his family found out who I was they kept telling me to take anything of his that I wanted. I had no idea what he would want me to have. I didn't have any pictures of us together, I didn't have a recording of his voice. All I have are memories, and those, sadly, fade with each day.

There is no going back and fixing things AFTER someone dies. I wish that it hadn't taken El's death for me to understand all of the things I needed to prepare for and plan for. I hope that you, by reading this, will consider doing the planning and preparation I didn't and that you might save yourself some of the heartache so many of my friends have experienced in the wake of El's death.

Preparing for deaths

Thinking about and preparing for death may seem morbid or like it's not necessary yet. However, we never know when death might come for us. Here are some questions to consider:

Who would you want to be personally notified if you died?

Who is your legacy contact on Facebook and other social media?

Who would would want at your funeral/wake/memorial?

What do you want done with your body?

What kind of funeral do you want?

How will folks access your passwords and accounts?

Have you set up a will?

Have you talked to your partners about your wishes when you die?

Have you talked to your partners about THEIR wishes when they die?

What are the things you would want to have if a partner died? *(i.e. A picture of you together, a recording of their voice, a shirt they had worn)*

What kind of support will you need when a partner dies?

How would you support your partner if one of their other partners died?

Find more resources to help you prepare for your (and someone else's) death at https://sexpositivepsych.com/mortality/

Outness

● ● ● ● ● ●

The biggest misconception about coming out is that it's a one time decision. As if someone wakes up one day, says "Okay, I'm ready to be out" and then walks out the door and is now OUT. In reality, coming out is a daily, minute by minute decision about how much information we share about ourselves with others. For instance, do you tell your coworkers that you LARP (do Live Action Role Playing games)? Do you let your boss know you're an atheist? How much do your parents need to know about your food preferences and that you've never been super into their leftover soup (where all the leftovers become a soup)?

Coming out is something we tend to associate with marginalized identities, especially identities related to sexual orientation and gender. That's partly because these identities are often some of the easiest to hide. If I'm queer but I look "mainstream" and no one ever sees me kissing someone who looks like "my" gender, they may never know that I'm queer. If I'm genderqueer but largely present in gender conforming ways, folks may not be able to tell what my true identity is. The same is true of those of us who are non-monogamous. Aside from someone seeing us at a party or on a date with multiple people, they can't necessarily know from looking at us that we're "not like other people."

Most people are nervous about coming out, and sometimes that's for good reason. In some places, you can lose your job, your kids, and all your friends if they find out you're non-monogamous. Some states have even been known to revoke the licenses to practice of professionals (like psychologists) because of dubious morality clauses in licensing legislation. And for a lot of people, the closet is pretty comfortable.

Couple privilege (which was covered in depth back in Section 1 – page 147) is a term that describes the benefits afforded to folks who are perceived to be in a monogamous couple. These benefits can include people treating you like you're more mature and grown up, greater perceived stability, an easier time paying bills and buying property, and greater social acceptance. Many parties allow a "plus one" and lots of people assume that a person's partner is invited when they invite that person to an event. Couples who blend in get benefits that those who stand out don't have access to.

If we zoom all the way in to you as an individual, you always have 100% of the choice in whether you come out as non-monogamous or not. You know your life better than anyone else does so far be it from me to think that I know what's right for you.

However.

In my experience, most people think that the consequences of coming out will be far worse than they end up being.

I first came out as bisexual/queer when I was 17. I told my mother shortly after I started the process of coming out and she threw a big screaming crying fit. And then, the next day, it was like nothing had happened. I came out to her several times over the next few years before it finally stuck. The time it stuck, my mom threatened to disown me AND to divorce my dad if he didn't do the same. She even asked me if I had sex with trees or animals because obviously as a bisexual person I just don't discriminate at all.

Fast forward to 13 years later, and my mom wished me a happy pride when I marched in the SF Pride Parade with my then partner who was genderqueer and AFAB (assigned female at birth; see glossary). All this is to say that people often come around, even when their initial reaction is highly negative.

The reality is that the more of us who are out about non-monogamy, the easier it'll be for all of us. When no one knew anyone who was gay (or at least thought they didn't) it was much easier to think gayness was a fad or a disease. Once more and more queer folks came out, it became harder and harder to make those assertions or hold those beliefs.

Humans, in general, are afraid of things they don't understand or have experience with. If someone has never in their life met anyone who was non-monogamous, at least to their knowledge, then it's easy for them to assume people who do that are sick perverts. If their buddy Joe from the office is in a polyamorous relationship though, things start to be different.

I know that we can't all be trailblazers or activists or spokespeople. And I recognize that those who take the risk to be on the front lines often end up taking some hard knocks. Overall, though, living in the closet necessarily means hiding pieces of yourself and that tends to be painful and challenging over the long term.

Here's a flowchart you can walk through when deciding whether or not to come out to someone about something. First, take a minute to brainstorm all of the benefits you get from staying closeted (respect, ease of interaction, etc.). Next, ask yourself what the consequences or negatives might be of staying closeted (e.g. secrets, fear of exposure). Third, brainstorm the risks you face when coming out (Could you lose your job? Are you in the midst of a divorce where it could be used against you?). Fourth, try to think of all the benefits you might get if you came out.

The last step is to think about your social capital. Social capital is a shorthand I use for the positive feelings and trust we earn when we develop good relationships with others. If someone really cares about me, I'm going to have more leeway to do something challenging than if I'm brand new at a company. So think about what social capital you have and whether you want to "spend" it on the coming out process.

Again, at the end of the day, only you can decide how out to be. Some folks are out to their friends but not family or coworkers. Some of us talk about our sex lives on the internet under our real names and with our real faces. There's no right answer. Every time you have the option to come out, you can make a new decision about what feels right for you.

Coming out decision-making worksheet

(Start here!) Benefits of staying closeted →	Consequences of staying closeted ↓
(End here!) Benefits of coming out 	Risks of coming out ←

What is my social capital and do I want to spend it?

Do they need to know?

Talking to your kids about non-monogamy

Let's start by tackling some common assumptions people have about how non-monogamy affects kids. Dr. Elisabeth Sheff , a non-monogamy researcher, has found that kids from non-monogamous families often fare better than their counterparts in monogamous households. Kids in non-monogamous families have more loving, caring adult figures around them, giving them a great backing and more resources to call upon. More love from responsible adults tends to be a good thing for kids, so having more than two standard parent types tends to lead to better outcomes. There's little to no evidence of non-monogamy harming kids or leading to them having greater risk taking behavior when it comes to sex.

If you practice non-monogamy and have kids, at some point there will be conversations you need to have with them. Everyone handles these issues differently - some try to keep the reality from their kids for as long as possible, some start telling kids age appropriate information from the start, and everything in between. In general, when dealing with kids and sex and relationships, the best advice is to answer questions in an honest, age appropriate way. Most kids have no problem understanding that mommy and daddy love other people too.

The difficulties here come from ways that your kids then interact with society at large. In some areas, being non-monogamous might be enough to get CPS called on you. If you're going through a nasty divorce, non-monogamy might be used as a way to establish that you're an unfit parent. If the parents of your kids' friends find out, they may not want their children associating with yours anymore. These realities of a prejudiced world make the question of how to handle conversations with kids about non-monogamy far more challenging.

As you talk with your kids about your non-monogamy, you may have to include conversations with them about what they share with other people. This sucks, a lot, both for you and your kids. It's never a great idea to tell kids that something is a shameful secret, but conversations with kids that don't talk about how things might be affected if they tell others can lead to serious consequences for everyone.

It's important for you to evaluate what information you think your kids can handle and how out you are willing to be with them, especially if they share the information with other parents, schools, sports teams, etc. This is a very delicate balancing act that no one has the right answer to. Only you can figure out the best answer for you and your family.

Check the Resources section for several books and websites focused on issues for non-monogamous families.

Navigating social media while non-monogamous

In the age of social media, relationships become much more complex. After all, is a relationship real if it's not on Facebook? Do you need to post a couple selfie to Instagram?

For those coming from the world of monogamy, or for those who are closeted or more private, navigating social media can be even more complicated.

> *Example: Ry and Jim have been dating for 6 months and are polyamorous. Jim has recently started dating Jean. While Ry is pretty reserved on social media about who they're seeing, Jean likes to post a lot on social media about their dating life. After they've been dating a month or so, Jean posts about their new relationship with Jim on their social media accounts, including several photos and sweet "couple" type posts. Ry gets upset with Jim for allowing Jean to "rub it in my face" that Jim and Jean are dating now. Ry feels like Jean is trying to claim territory or push Ry out of Jim's life.*

As you can see, if Ry and Jim and Jean never actually talked about how to handle social media, every person in this situation could have reason to be upset. To Ry, Jean has overstepped; to Jean, Ry is being unreasonable; to Jim, they're caught in the middle of something no one actually negotiated.

When thinking about how to handle social media, it's important to have these conversations early and often. Develop a plan for social media with each of your partners to make sure that you aren't caught off-guard by their decisions.

Here are the important questions:

💜 How do you personally handle social media when it comes to relationships?

💜 How do you feel about being tagged on social media?

💜 How do you feel about photos of you and your partner on social media?

💜 How do you feel about your partner posting about their other partners?

💜 How do you feel about your metamours posting about your partner?

💜 What guides your decisions about social media? (Fear, privacy, openness, etc.)

💜 What are deal breakers for you around social media?

When The Shit Hits The Fan

● ● ● ● ● ●

As in all things, it is not if something will go wrong, but when. And as the saying goes, those who fail to plan, plan to fail. When things are going well, or we're starting out a new connection, we may not want to even consider that things could go wrong. After all, things are so good right now! But if you don't come up with strategies to deal with problems before they arise, your likelihood of dealing well with those problems is significantly reduced.

So to get you started with your relationship disaster preparedness plans, here are examples of common situations where the shit hits the fan:

Misagreements/poor communication

One of the most common times that we end up in a problem is when everyone in the relationship thought they were agreeing to the same thing but had different meanings for that thing.

> **Example:** Pat and Sam agree that they will let each other know when they "start dating someone." To Pat, this means that before

they go on the first date they will let their partner know. To Sam, this means that when you know that you want to continue dating the person you'll let them know, which might be after the 3rd or 4th date. Sam goes on two dates with Alex and then tells Pat that they want to continue dating Alex. Pat gets upset because Sam broke their agreement.

You can see how the lack of clarity about agreements here created a big problem. As far as Pat is concerned, Sam broke the agreement. For Sam, though, this seems like Pat is being unreasonable and holding them to a standard they never agreed to. This situation is one that Jeana Jorgensen, sex educator and folklorist, calls a misagreement. Both parties were certain they understood what they were agreeing to and thus didn't fully negotiate out their terms.

Part of how human brains tend to work is that we assume most folks think and work the same way we do. Since we are creatures that take as many shortcuts as possible mentally, we will often find ourselves skipping steps in discussions. We think to ourselves, "Of course they think this means the same thing I do! It's obvious!" when in fact the terms we're using contain multiple meanings and plenty of nuance.

To avoid this pitfall, be sure to clarify fully what terminology means to you in your agreements and rules. You may feel silly or like you're over-clarifying for a while, but it's usually better to be more explicit than you think you need.

Now if you find yourself in the middle of a misagreement, try to take a step back and think about whether the agreement was as clear as you both assumed it was. If the agreement wasn't clear, try to find a place of compassion and curiosity and as much as possible avoid blaming and punishing your partner. Use each time you find a misagreement as an opportunity to check in on the rest of your agreements to make sure that you're both on the same page.

In these situations, one or more folks may want an apology or be asked to give an apology. The most helpful book I've found on this topic, Why Won't You Apologize, by Harriet Lerner, discusses how to apologize effectively, even when you don't agree with all of what you're being asked to apologize for. She also discusses how to most effectively ask for an apology.

Different styles of dating/love

As we talked about in the misagreements section, we all tend to think that others do things the same way we do or that the way we do things is the "right" way. However, when it comes to sex and relationships, there is no one right way to do things.

> *Example:* *Cameron and Peyton have been dating for about 6 months. Cameron's version of non-monogamy is to have one very deep, serious relationship and several other more casual connections, so they have been really happy focusing the majority of their energy on Peyton. Peyton, however, prefers to have multiple deep, loving relationships and tends to continually meet and date new people as they have time and energy available.*
>
> *Cameron spent the first several months of the relationship believing that as soon as their relationship became closer and more committed, Peyton would eventually settle down more and stop dating so many people. Peyton, on the other hand, expected that Cameron would soon tire of "nesting" and get back into the dating world.*
>
> *As time passed, Cameron became increasingly frustrated that Peyton is so "distracted" by these other connections and felt like Peyton would slow down if they really cared about Cameron. Peyton, for their part, didn't understand why Cameron was frustrated. Each time Cameron got upset, Peyton asked what Cameron wants from them that they aren't getting, but Peyton feels like nothing they do will work unless they do things exactly Cameron's way.*

Some of us are very very slutty with our hearts and bodies. Some of us prefer a few connections. Some people are asexual. None of these ways of doing things are necessarily better or worse than the others. However, some may be better or worse fits for others. In the above example, Cameron and Peyton do things very differently. Both of them then feel like their partner is doing things that hurt them, whether it's Cameron's resentment or Peyton's continued dating.

When we're newly falling for someone, we assume that over time our differences will be small problems. Through the lens of NRE, we see rose colored visions of futures that somehow magically fit. However, it almost never happens that something that is a mismatch becomes less stressful as we exit NRE. So what do you do once you find yourself deeply caring and not matching up?

Ideally, you would have conversations early on about what relationship style you practice and about what your dating tends to look like over the long run. If those conversations didn't happen, or if NRE clouded them to the point that you couldn't tell what you'd want, this is the time to sit down and have a serious conversation about what will and won't work for each of you.

I think of building a relationship like building a structure together where you're both creating the blueprints. At first, every building starts with a foundation, so you don't necessarily need to communicate a ton beyond knowing how big the foundation should be. Most buildings have walls around the outside, so again you may not need to be super clear about what you need. However, there comes a point where the two of you need to get more clarity about what it is that you're building. If you don't, you end up one day in the middle of building a huge kitchen for your restaurant when you run into the doors your partner is setting up for their emergency room. So do you have a hospital with gourmet food? A really dramatically themed restaurant?

These kinds of conflicts are a serious gut check for all involved and often end up pointing out the expectations and wants and needs we've been leaving unspoken or unacknowledged, even to ourselves. Each person should take some time to figure out what those things might be. Maybe, in this case, Cameron thinks that Peyton's approach means that Peyton doesn't really care about Cameron. Maybe Peyton thinks that Cameron's expectations are about sex shaming and slut shaming. Peyton may have a belief that freedom is key to good relationships, where Cameron may believe that we sacrifice for those we love. Take some time to uncover not just what you want, but also the why. Then come to each other and see if there's a way you can find something that works well for both of you.

New partners

In the mainstream, monogamous dating world we expect that our partner being interested in someone new would automatically create problems in a relationship. It's forbidden! How dare they! In non-monogamy, we would assume that this kind of reaction might be less common or severe. And yet, the introduction of new partners has the potential to create conflict within established relationships, even those that are the MOST open.

> *Example:* Rory and Sydney have been in a serious, cohabitating, committed, non-hierarchical, polyamorous relationship for 3 years. Rory has been with their other partner Val for 1 year and Sydney has been with their other partner Dakota for 6 months. Recently, Sydney met Eli and has been falling for them fast, spending a couple of days a week with them. Rory is worried about the speed with which things are moving between Sydney and Eli, and has, started talking to Val who also has concerns. One day, Val and Rory sit Sydney down to tell her that they think Eli is bad for their relationships with Sydney and that Sydney needs to reconsider what she's doing and spend more time with her more established partners (Val and Rory).

Seeing your partner get smitten over someone new can bring up lots of fear and insecurities. What if they like this person more? What if I'm not young/pretty/smart/sexy/kinky/whatever enough now? What if they stop spending time with me? As a friend of mine often says, the insides of our heads can be a very bad neighborhood; we will get mugged in there, and sometimes we help the muggers.

In general, new folks coming into your poly network or "polycule" are normal, regular people just like you who happen to like the same person you do. Most of the time, they are not trying to hurt or ruin your relationship or to steal your partner away from you. While these things can happen, they are pretty rare and, frankly, a person can't really be "stolen" unless they agree to it.

If you're finding that your partner is having lots of NRE, maybe it's worth going back over the NRE section for more ideas on how each of you can handle this time. If you find that you're struggling with lots of insecurities, look over the section on insecurities and self-care while your sweetie dates to see if there's anything helpful you can try out. And, if you genuinely feel like the new person is doing something problematic or unethical, use the tough conversations sheet to figure out how to talk with your partner about it in as constructive a way as possible.

Differences in desire

How often do you want to have sex in a relationship? What kinds of sex do you want to have? What is Great Sex to you? (Great Sex can change the world!) These questions seem simple enough, particularly when posed in the theoretical. However, a difference in desires is one of the most common problems in relationships.

Shortly before my 22nd birthday, I met Dan. I was at a swing and blues dancing event in St. Louis when I heard that the instructor, organizer, and dreamboat Dan was newly single. I was taken to a friend's house and saw Dan walk out of the shower wrapped in a towel. He was strong and confident and his skin had the sheen of water recently wiped from it. His bald head was shiny in the light and his smile was wide and ringed by thick, beautiful lips. Dan looked like a snarky, trickster version of Taye Diggs and I wanted nothing more than to dance with him, and maybe even feel a kiss from those lips.

Over the course of that weekend, we danced several times and each time it was electric. He was such a good leader, and I could hear the music through the movements of his body. He got me so excited and I was surprised that someone like him could possibly be interested in someone like me. We saw each other again a few weeks later in New

York and when he asked me to walk outside with him, and then asked to kiss me, I was on cloud nine.

The first few months of our relationship were a hot long distance buildup. We talked on the phone and over messenger. When I flew out to see him, we had hot sex multiple times a day, every day of my trip. I was intoxicated by his touch and I was still so surprised that he was for some reason interested in seeing me. We had several more trips to see each other over the next few months and then, after I graduated college in May, I moved out to California in part to be closer to him.

The first several months of living in the same state saw us having sex a couple of times a day when we saw each other on weekends. Then he moved out to the Bay Area and we went to 3-4 times per week. That felt like a pretty good pace for me as I have a fairly high libido but also a busy schedule. As we moved in together, got engaged, and got married over the next 8 months, though, the frequency and quality of sex began to drop significantly. By two to three years into our relationship, we were having sex 3-4 times a month, if that, and none of it was particularly satisfying. The only times that we had sex that was good was when one or both of us was drunk.

I tried to talk to him multiple times about how much I wanted us to be having more sex and he would say he wanted it too, but even if I tried sexting him or tried putting on lingerie or tried indicating my desire, nothing seemed to be the right way to reignite that spark. I was miserable, and I grew more and more resentful. I needed sex, and he either didn't want me or didn't want sex in general. Either way, the desire gap nagged at me every day, making me question my attractiveness and sex appeal, and fueling my frustration at the state of my relationship.

One of the best analogies I've heard for differences in desire is this: If you had a relationship where one partner wanted to eat three times a day and the other wanted to eat once a day, there's no good way for them to compromise and eat all of their meals together. Either one person is eating when they don't want to, or the other person is not eating when they want to. The person who wants to eat three times may feel resentful that their partner is starving them; the person who wants to eat once may feel like they don't even have time to get hungry before their partner is badgering them to eat again.

It's not common for differences in desire to be masked by NRE or by the difference between dating someone casually and dating more seriously. So when relationships progress, we often find ourselves with someone who wants to eat significantly more or less than we do and no good way to start negotiating a meal schedule. While some might say that the beauty of non-monogamy is that you can "eat" with other people, sometimes that doesn't actually fulfill the desire you have for any one specific partner.

So when you find yourselves with different desires, it's important to sit down and talk openly and honestly about what each of you actually wants and needs. Is it particular activities? A certain frequency? What needs to happen for you to feel like you've gotten what you want? Is orgasm necessary? What pieces can you get met elsewhere and which ones do you want specifically from this partner?

If you're the partner with higher desire, it's particularly important to be aware of any ways that coercion or control are slipping into your interactions. It's easy when we're really really hungry to be a jerk about the person we think should be feeding us. As I've talked about before, we are all raised in a culture that excuses using pressure or persistence in the name of "persuasion" to get our sexual needs met, particularly for cisgender men, so keeping things fully consent based can be really hard. Try to remember that your partner isn't "starving" you or doing something on purpose to hurt or upset you.

For the partner with lower desire, there can be temptation to just "lie back and think of England." Unfortunately, engaging in sex you don't enjoy can serve to further reduce your overall desire in the long term. Lots of people with less desire than their partners can feel guilt or shame so be sure to remind yourself that having lower desire isn't actually a BAD thing, it's just a difference.

Some of the best writing on desire and how to access it comes from Emily Nagoski's book Come As You Are. While the book is mostly about women's sexuality, the basic concepts are applicable to people of all genders. This book has great worksheets for identifying what helps with desire and what hinders it. With the help of these worksheets you may be able to find ways to help meet somewhere closer to the middle.

Sometimes, however, there just isn't going to be an acceptable compromise. At that point, it may be time to consider whether there needs to be some kind of relationship transition.

Differences in cleanliness

I know, I know, I talk about dominant culture paradigms a lot and how the kyriarchy messes with our relationships. This area in particular is one that tends to be profoundly affected. Those socialized as women are often socialized to be much more aware of and proactive about cleanliness. Even as children, people tend to hold those they perceive as girls to a higher standard when it comes to cleaning than they do those they perceive as boys. In many households, the "men" are allowed to do little to no cleaning and their spouses and sisters and other relatives are expected to do the cleaning for them.

As such, many people socialized as men don't notice or feel a responsibility for some kinds of mess. I don't think I need to explicitly tell you how I feel about these gendered standards. However, since we are all surrounded by this culture, we will all bear some marks from it that we must work actively and specifically to undo.

In relationships, it is likely that partners will have different standards of cleanliness. These differences often don't become a problem unless partners cohabitate or spend significant amounts of time at each other's homes. When they do arise, though, we tend to see that everyone involved thinks they are in the right. For the cleaner partner, they think that of course their partner should be willing to meet their standard. For the less clean partner, they think their partner is an unreasonable nag who should just calm down and let it go.

When this problem comes up, it's best to address it early on. Folks to tend to let resentment build for quite a while before addressing the issue and that, as we've covered elsewhere, is generally never a good idea. So as soon as you notice there may be different standards, it's helpful to get ahead of the issue.

For the cleaner person, you may have to accept that things will not always be to your standard. You may have to walk your partner through what clean looks like for you, how often you would like things cleaned, and come up with a system to help them remember to do cleaning. While this feels unfair and can be a significant amount of work, a partner who just doesn't see the messes you do or doesn't have the same ideal cleaning schedule may not be able to independently come around to things on their own. Hopefully, this phase is like a short instruction and expectation setting phase and does not become the permanent way of life. Be sure to be explicit about how long the two of you are taking to figure out this system and get on the same page and come up with ideas about how to handle it if/when the less clean person forgets to follow through on their end of things.

For the less clean person, you may have to work on taking more initiative. Just because something doesn't seem like a big deal to you doesn't mean that you can't learn to notice and change something. Let your partner know what might help you meet them in the middle, and be real with them about how the two of you can find a mutually agreed upon level of cleanliness. Once you know what your partner expects, don't wait for them to point something out before you do it - make a point of looking for things every day or two to see if there's something happening that your partner might appreciate you taking care of. You can think of this like a game or like an act of service or like a deposit in your love bank. The more you manage to be proactive and clean things before they even notice, the more grateful your partner will likely be. If you don't know how to clean things to their standard, ask them if they'd be willing to teach you. Sometimes super clean people have neat tricks and tips that help them get to a cleaner place easier and more quickly. It'll also give them the chance to show you how much effort and work they've been putting in that you may not have realized.

And, like many of the issues in this chapter, this conflict can become a deal breaker for some people. For some less clean folks, they may feel like their partner's standards are just too high - more effort or work than they want to put in. For some cleaner folks, they may feel like their partner just can't get it right. If this happens, it may be worth discussing either a division of areas (e.g. the entertainment cave can be sloppy but the bathrooms must be clean clean clean), hiring professional cleaning help, or considering the option of no longer cohabitating. Choosing not to cohabitate doesn't mean you have to break up, it just means you won't live in the same space. For tips on this, see the section on relationship transitions (page 219).

Different risk aware sex protocols

For people around my age (Oregon Trail generation, Gen X), we were raised in an era that talked about how risky sex was because of how fatal and dangerous AIDS was. The systems that taught us about safe sex shamed those with STIs and shamed those who decided not to take every possible precaution. As such, many of us carry internalized beliefs that those who might choose to have unbarriered sex are necessarily wrong or a problem or deserving of the shame that was drilled into us.

However, every person gets to make the decisions they want with their own bodies. We don't need to necessarily have sex with people who make decisions that are riskier than we want to engage with, but what we often do when encountering these differences is to make our decisions "right" and their's "wrong" in a way that isn't helpful and that doesn't respect the autonomy of the other person.

> *Example: Adam and Brian have been seeing each other for 6 months and are both polyamorous. Over this time, they have grown very close and are talking about moving away from using barriers for their sex with each other. Part of why they want this change is because they want to feel closer to each other and share something special in the form of unbarriered sex.*
>
> *Adam has always been very risk averse, so he uses all possible*

barriers with all partners - gloves for hand play, dams for oral on vulvas or anuses, and condoms for penetrative sex with penises or dildos. Brian is willing to accept some risks in his sexual practices, so he always use condoms for penetrative sex, but sometimes don't use gloves or dams depending on his risk assessment in a given situation.

As they talk about being fluid bonded, Adam expresses a worry that Brian's less strict practices would expose Adam to risks. Brian hears Adam's concern and offers to provide him up to date information about what new risk factors are introduced. Adam tells Brian that he would prefer for Brian to use gloves and dams for all other partners because of Adam;s concerns around STIs. Brian tells Adam that he's willing to consider this change, but would prefer to stay at his same protocols, and lets Adam know that they can return to using barriers at any time in their own relationship if Adam feels uncomfortable with the risks from Brian's other partners. Adam leaves the conversation feeling like he was issued an ultimatum and Brian leaves the conversation feeling like Adam is trying to control him.

When people in a relationship disagree about what risk aware sex protocols to use, it can be tempting to try to convince the more risk tolerant partner to adopt the practices of the less risk tolerant partner. However, this may not always work, You may find, especially over time, that this compromise leaves the more risk tolerant partner feeling constrained or controlled. Instead, you may need to negotiate what boundaries and risk aware sex practices you need to have if the more risk tolerant person does not want to change their practices.

The biggest blowouts on this topic tend to be when the partners in a relationship want to stop using barriers for emotional or commitment related reasons and meaning. In this case, the less risk tolerant partner may feel more urge to "convince" the more risk tolerant person to adapt stricter practices so that the less risk tolerant person can feel good about engaging in unbarriered sex. While I understand this urge, it's really easy for this process to veer into coercion.

During these negotiations, it's important for everyone involved to remember that there isn't any objectively "right" level of risk management to choose. Even when the two of you disagree, it's important not to shame each other over your differences. Someone who wants to use all the barriers isn't "paranoid;" someone who chooses to not use some or all of the barriers isn't "reckless."

If you can't come to a space of understanding and agreeing with each other about risk aware sex practices, it might be worth re-examining the underlying beliefs and fears that are driving each of your positions. In addition, sitting with the meaning of using or not using barriers and talking with those meanings with each other can help you find out whether there are unspoken desires or expectations that are impairing the discussion. Finally, if none of this helps, figure out what each of your boundaries are and see what fits for both of you. It may not be what each of you wanted, but it will mean less resentment in the long run.

An agreement stops working

How many cliches are there about when plans don't work? When we're building a relationship, we do our best to create agreements that we hope will last. We do our best to guess what we will need over the long term. While some of these agreements are easy to renegotiate, some of them are more difficult to change. And yet, any agreement we cannot renegotiate is destined to create misery in at least one of the people following it. Change is the only constant in our lives, and sometimes that means that the agreements we made no longer fit us.

For tips on how to re-negotiate an agreement, look at the agreements chapter (page 62). If the agreement is one that cannot be renegotiated, for instance if the solution one person wants isn't acceptable to the other, it may be time to transition. For more on that, you can check the transitions chapter (page 219).

Unable or unwilling to meet a partner's wants/needs

In a perfect world, we would all be eager and able to meet whatever needs our partner had. Sadly, sometimes what our partner wants or needs is something that either doesn't fit for us or would actively make us unhappy. If we are centering empowerment in our relationships, we cannot expect our partners to compromise their own happiness for ours.

So where do we go when a partner cannot give us what we want or need? What happens when what would make us happy doesn't work for them? First, it can be helpful to take some time to figure out what it is that you actually need. Which parts of that are negotiable and which parts aren't? When you boil it down, what are you trying to get? Next, use the tough conversations worksheet (page 91) to discuss it with your partner.

If at the end of the day they cannot provide it and you cannot find a suitable solution, it may be time for a transition conversation (page 228).

Availability

The mainstream monogamy model tells us that we are supposed to have a fairly high amount of time available for our romantic relationships. Weekly dates are usual at first, progressing to seeing each other 2-4 times per week, then eventually moving in together and seeing each other daily. What do we do in non-monogamy, then, when our partners have multiple other partners and cannot, by the laws of reality, have 4 dates available per week for each of their 3 partners?

While availability may seem like something easy to negotiate, you may be surprised how commonly it leads to major problems.

Usually, when I start dating people, I do a good job of setting expectations in terms of availability. For people I'm just starting to *see, I usually have time to see them once per month. If I really like them, I might see them two or three times in a month. I thought I had been pretty clear with Ralph when we started dating about what time I had available.*

After our fourth date, Ralph messaged me to tell me that he felt frustrated that I hadn't made more time for him. I had seen him four times in less than a month! Since we liked each other and wanted to develop a deeper relationship, he wanted the option of spending multiple days a week together. He compared our connection to his connection with another partner who spent 2-3 days per week with him. I told him that I didn't have that available. He told me that wasn't acceptable.

We broke up after that conversation, at my prompting. I didn't want to stay with someone who was unhappy with what I had available or who would try to guilt me for the realities of my schedule.

Sometimes we have flexibility in how much time we have, and sometimes the amount of contact or interaction that makes us feel good doesn't feel like enough for our partners. When this conflict comes up, take the time to figure out if there's any creative solution. If not, this may be a situation where a transition conversation is needed (page 228).

Emotional availability

Like time or interaction availability, sometimes we do not have space in our hearts for what others would like from us. Maybe we've had a recent trauma, maybe we're already spending a lot of our emotional energy at work, or maybe we're just not feeling a deeper emotional connection with that particular person.

Even in non-monogamy, people tend to struggle with communicating openly about their emotions for others and about what they want from others in terms of emotional investment. After all, admitting that you are emotionally invested in someone is a move towards vulnerability. And, in some ways the more emotionally invested partner is the one with the least power.

It's important to work on undoing patterns that discourage talking about feelings. A great blog to read about this is Casual Love by Carsie Blanton. If you're developing feelings for someone, let them know. If you don't have much available for feelings, let your lover know if you feel like they might be falling for you. Different levels of emotional availability don't have to be a terminal issue for a relationship, but it does involve very careful negotiation. Be sure to use the tough conversation worksheet to figure out what it is you need from them emotionally and how you can find ways to meet each other's needs.

Different levels of attachment

Related to different levels of emotional availability, it unfortunately sometimes happens in relationships that one person feels more emotionally attached than the other does. While it would be lovely if people always fell in love equally, sometimes we fall harder for someone than they do for us (or vice versa). In the monogamy fairytale model, a discrepancy in attachment means that a relationship is doomed. That may not need to be the case in non-monogamy if you don't want it to be.

Much of the conflict in these situations comes from the ways in which we conflate depth of emotional attachment and expectations about relationship entanglements. In the monogamous world, the person you love the most is obviously the person you are in your monogamous relationship with, who you will marry and live with and have children with. In non-monogamy, we may want more entanglements from those who we care more deeply for, or we may not. We can choose to care deeply for someone and yet not have deeply committed relationships with them. Or we can care deeply for someone who likes us a lot but isn't attached to us in the same way.

Sometimes, this difference is one we can learn to accept and work with. Other times, it's something that feels too hard for us. If you find yourself in a position where a difference in attachment isn't working for you, it's worth trying out a conversation about it. You can use the Tough Conversations worksheet (page 91) to help you get your thoughts together. If that doesn't help, read through the transitions chapter (page 219) to see if it might be time for a transition.

Bad boundaries

Honestly, I think that this may be the most common cause of problems in relationships. If you don't use your "no" appropriately, it's easy to end up in a place where you've gotten past where your boundaries should be. Having good boundaries is the best gift you can give yourself and your partner.

If you're bad at boundaries, review the boundaries chapter (page 58) and go back through the boundaries questions. It might be helpful to let your partners know that you sometimes struggle with setting your boundaries and enlist their help in keeping you on top of setting the boundaries you need. For particularly bad cases of this, enlisting the help of a coach or therapist can be key to making a lasting change.

If your partner struggles with boundaries, fill out the tough conversation worksheet (page 91) to determine how to talk to them about how their poor boundaries are affecting you and what you need from them going forward. When dating a partner with poor boundaries, you may feel like you're in a trap or like you're expected to be a mind reader. If you feel like you keep getting in trouble for something you didn't know you had done wrong, this might be a sign of your partner not adequately communicating their boundaries to you.

> ### Some questions you can ask your partner when you're feeling like you might be hitting an unstated boundary are:
>
> ♥ Hey, it seems like you're asking me for something but I don't know what that is
>
> ♥ Is this statement information or a request
>
> ♥ You said yes, but it doesn't seem like you're really a yes. Am I reading too much into it?

> 💜 I feel like I'm having trouble trusting your yes and no because sometimes you say yes and then seem really upset about it. Can you help me figure out a solution?

Not asking for what you want

Not using your ability to ask for your wants/needs is almost as common and problematic as not setting your boundaries. Unfortunately, our partners aren't mind readers, so in order to get what we want, we have to take a chance and ask for it. If you don't, you're doing both yourself and your partner a disservice. For most of us, asking for what we want is really challenging. Taking a chance to ask for what you want is necessarily a vulnerable act.

When we're in a relationship and we don't ask for what we want, it is likely we won't get it. A lot of folks, especially people who are new to non-monogamy, are really worried about being so brash as to ask for what they want. They worry about "What if this person says no?" and, I think, they worry also about "What if this person says yes?" For many of us, the thought of getting all the things we want is almost as scary as being shot down.

So often, we reject ourselves before anyone else gets a chance to; we assume they will say no so we don't even ask. We don't ask that person on a date. We don't ask our partner to go down on us. Yet, almost all of us want nothing more in the world than to make our partners happy. We want to take care of ourselves, we want to take care of our partners. And the thing is, you can't do that very well if you don't know what your partner needs.

Not asking for what you want will also build resentment. When we don't ask for what we want, we often end up wondering why our partner hasn't just given it to us already. The monogamy fairytale tells us that our partners should automatically know what we want; after all, how many people in movies or TV shows tell their partner how to pleasure them?

I know it's challenging to ask to ask for what you want but you can totally do it. If you're worried about how to ask for what you want, try the tough conversation worksheet (page 91) or the dirty talk guide (page 202). Reid Mihalko also has a great difficult conversation formula.

If you want to get it, you have to ask for it. Someone can't say "yes" to you until you ask. If you ask, there's at least a chance that they can say "yes." If they say "no," then at least you have the information you need to make a good decision.

Someone's "no" can also give us very helpful and necessary information. For instance, if I tell someone that I go on dates with other people and they say that that's not okay with them, I know that person isn't a good fit for me. If I'm noticing that the way someone is playing with my genitals isn't actually working very well for me and I give them that feedback and they won't change or respond, that's not someone who's going to be a good sexual match for me.

If you ask for what's important to you and that person can't give it to you, that's okay. Now you can make new choices about your relationship. Maybe the style of relationship changes, maybe there are new things you have to negotiate, maybe this is the time for your relationship to transition. But regardless, you aren't going to get what you want until you ask.

Major life events

Sometimes, life kicks you in the teeth. You get fired, someone dies, a child is born. Anytime a huge change happens, it is likely to bring change to our relationships with it.

Remember El from the section on death? Losing El was a huge hit to my dating life. I had ended all my other relationships before he and I started seeing each other (for totally unrelated reasons), and for the time immediately after his death, I felt too fragile and scared to say yes to any dates.

After three or four months, I began considering dating again and noticed all of the new fears I had in the wake of El's death. As much as I wanted to find some love and deep connection, I felt the fear of the loss of those connections more acutely than ever before. The idea of falling simultaneously excited me and made me so so scared. So, each time I met someone who seemed promising, I had to let them know why I seemed to be pushing them away while pulling them in.

We cannot avoid life's big changes; the best we can do is be honest about what is happening for us and how that impacts the ways we show up in relationships. If you or your partner(s) have had a major life event, take the opportunity to check back in with each other about your expectations and agreements to see if they still fit. (See page 226.) Check in with yourself when a major life event happens to see what you have available as a result of this change.

In Closing

● ● ● ● ● ●

You've made it! Here you are, all the way at the end of the book. Once you've gotten here, it doesn't have to be your end with this book. Remember, the skills and worksheets we covered together are here for you anytime.

As you come to the end of this resource, take a moment to congratulate yourself - you did something huge. You took the time and energy to invest in learning more. You took a chance - on this book, sure, but more importantly on yourself. Where you go from here is up to you. I hope that you'll find your own way to live that is authentic for you. And I hope that you'll find the relationships that fit for you and enrich your life.

Now, if you made it to the end of this book and you feel like you need more help, there are lots of fantastic professionals out there who can help you on your exploration. Non-monogamy friendly therapists and coaches are ever more readily available. The Kink Aware Professionals list is one place to look, as is the Open List at openingup.net.

I also offer coaching and classes to help folks out. If you want to know more, check out my website - sexpositivepsych.com.

Good luck, bon voyage, and may your life be filled with love.

Glossary

● ● ● ● ● ●

AFAB – Assigned Female At Birth. A person who was labeled a girl when they were born.

Agency – The ability of a person to act in a given environment.

Agender – Someone who identifies as having no gender agreements – Agreements are an element of a relationship setting up conditions. They are renegotiable by anyone affected by the agreement.

Allosexual – Someone who experiences sexual desire

AMAB – Assigned Male At Birth. A person who was labeled a boy when they were born.

Asexual – Someone who does not experience spontaneous sexual desire.

Autonomy – The ability to self-govern, that is to make one's own decisions

BDSM – An acronym to describe the variety of activities often considered in the realm of "kink." The acronym is actually several concepts: Bondage and Discipline, Domination and submission, Sadism and Masochism.

Bigender – Someone whose gender identity includes two genders.

Bondage – The act of restraining someone, generally in an erotically charged fashion.

Boundaries – Boundaries are the lines we draw around how others can interact with our own bodies, hearts, minds, and time. Boundaries are only about you, so you cannot have a boundary about someone else's behavior with someone other than you.

Cisgender – Someone whose internal perception of their gender agrees with the gender they were assigned at birth. For instance, if when you were born the doctor said "it's a boy" and you internally feel like a boy/man, you are cisgender.

Compersion – Joy for another person's joy. Sometimes called the opposite of jealousy, but can co-exist with jealousy. When you feel happy because a friend gets promoted, that's compersion.

Demisexual – Someone who only experiences sexual desire when they have a strong emotional connection

Discipline/protocol – A subset of kink that involves the Dominant setting rules for the submissive to follow. Protocol may include specific guidelines about service to the Dominant and other interactions.

Domination and submission (D/s) – An erotically charged situation where one person (the submissive) gives up control over some or many aspects to another person (the Dominant). In D/s, the "s" is generally lowercase and the D is generally uppercase.

Fluid bonding – A shorthand term for people who have decided not to use barriers for some or all sexual activities.

Full swap – When a swinger couple allows for intercourse as well as other activities.

Genderfluid – Someone whose gender flows between more masculine and feminine feelings and expressions.

Genderqueer – Someone whose gender does not fall within the gender binary.

Grey asexual/grey ace – People who fall on the spectrum between allosexual and asexual

Heteronormative – A term to describe the way that our current culture enshrines a world view that promotes heterosexuality as the normal or preferred sexual orientation.

Hierarchical polyamory – A style of polyamory with strict levels of partnership that involve power imbalances between the levels. Those at "higher" levels of the hierarchy are given power over relationships at lower levels in the hierarchy.

Impact play – A kink activity involving striking with implements in an erotically charged way.

Intersex – A person whose reproductive or sexual anatomy doesn't conform to typical ideas of male or female due to any number of chromosomal or gestational reasons.

Kyriarchy – A social system or set of connecting social systems built around domination, oppression, and submission.

Megasexual – Someone who tends to not develop romantic or emotional connection without sexual connection

Metamour – The partner of your partner.

Monogamish – A coin termed by Dan Savage to describe a relationship that is generally monogamous but which may have rare sexual interactions outside of the relationship.

Mononormative – A term to describe the way that our current culture enshrines a world view that promotes monogamy as the normal or preferred sexual orientation.

Non-hierarchical polyamory – A style of polyamory that does not have strict levels or that does not include power imbalances between kinds of partnerships. People may still give certain partners priority and do not necessarily have the same relationships with all people involved.

Non Binary/enby – A person whose gender does not fall within the gender binary.

NRE – New Relationship Energy. The cascade of chemicals, feelings, and urges one experiences when beginning a new relationship.

Objectification – The act of degrading someone from a person to an inhuman object. This can be part of consensual BDSM play, but is more often something done to disempower another.

One penis policy (OPP) – In a heterosexual couple, a rule that both partners will only date other women, generally asked for by the man.

PIA – Penis in anus sex, sometimes called "anal."

PIV – *Penis in vagina sex, sometimes called intercourse or (less precisely) sex.*

Poly-saturated – *When a polyamorous person is at the point that they are not available for new connections because of the number of existing connections.*

Polyamory – *The practice of having multiple sexual and/or loving relationships at the same time with the knowledge and consent of all involved*

Polycule – *A term to describe the network of connections in a polyamorous dating group. This can be fairly contained or more widespread.*

Polyfidelitous – *A closed, exclusive relationship between 3 or more people.*

Primary partner – *In a hierarchical polyamorous relationship, the primary partner is the person at the top of the hierarchy. This partner has the most closeness and priority and (in a true hierarchy) has the ability to make rules about other lower level relationships.*

Queer – *An umbrella term for a variety of sexual and gender minorities to indicate the person is not straight and/or cisgender. As queer is a reclaimed slur, it should only be used as a descriptor when someone self-identifies as queer.*

Relationship Anarchy – *A style of relationship in which people do not put friendships and sexual or romantic relationships in different categories but instead allow each relationship to find its own level. People who practice relationship anarchy may or may not be non-monogamous. Relationship anarchists often do not use rules or agreements in their relationships.*

Relationship escalator – *The idea about how mainstream relationships work described by Amy Gahran. The idea is that mainstream relationships assume a general, upward, inflexible progression for relationships.*

Rules – *In a relationship, a condition agreed to by two or more people is a rule if there are people affected by it who do not have the ability to renegotiate it. A common example is veto power.*

Sadism and Masochism – *The pleasure found in giving (Sadism) or receiving (Masochism) pain.*

Secondary partner – In a hierarchical polyamorous relationship, the secondary partner is below the primary partner on the hierarchy. In a true hierarchy, some aspects of their relationship are dictated by the primary partner of their partner.

Soft swap – When a swinger couple agrees to not engage in penile penetration of a vagina or an anus, but allows for oral or manual/hand sex.

Solo Poly – A form of polyamory that centers autonomy and agency. For more information, see solopoly.net or Joreth InnKeeper's piece But What Does Solo Poly Even Mean.

Swinging – A form of non-monogamy, generally practiced by couples, that allows for sexual contact and relationships with others but generally does not allow for emotional or romantic relationships with others

Top and Bottom – In BDSM, the top is generally the one performing the action or running the interaction and the bottom is generally receiving the action.

Transgender – Someone whose internal perception of their gender does not agree with the gender they were assigned at birth.

Unicorn hunting – The practice of a couple, generally a heteronormative couple, looking for a third partner, generally a "hot bi babe" (attractive bisexual woman) to "complete" their relationship. Often characterized by objectification and power imbalances.

Veto Power – A rule sometimes found in hierarchical relationships where a partner can unilaterally end any of their partner's other relationships. E.G. John and Cindy practice veto power, so John told CIndy she had to break up with Brad because Brad made John uncomfortable.

Wobbles – The anxious, insecure feelings you can sometimes get when a partner interacts with other people.

Resources

● ● ● ● ● ●

In the event that these links change or more resources come out, I've created a page on my site for updates. Please visit https://sexpositivepsych.com/book-resources if you're reading this past the publication date of July 2018.

Books

Braving the Wilderness by Brené Brown

Come As You Are by Emily Nagoski

Conflict is Not Abuse by Sarah Schulman

The Dance of Anger by Harriet Lerner

The Dance of Connection by Harriet Lerner

The Dance of Intimacy by Harriet Lerner

Daring Greatly by Brené Brown

Designer Relationships by Mark A. Michaels and Patricia Johnson

The Ethical Slut by Janet Hardy and Dossie Easton

The Five Languages of Apology by Gary Chapman and Jennifer Thomas

The Five Love Languages by Gary Chapman

The Game Changer by Franklin Veaux

The Gifts of Imperfection by Brené Brown

How to Be a Woman by Caitlin Moran

The Husband Swap by Louisa Leontiades

The Jealousy Workbook by Kathy Labriola

The Joy of Conflict Resolution by Gary Harper

Love's Not Colorblind by Kevin Patterson

Messages: The Communication Skills Book by Matthew McKay

More Than Two by Franklin Veaux and Eve Rickert

The New Bottoming Book by Janet Hardy and Dossie Easton

The New Topping Book by Janet Hardy and Dossie Easton

Nonviolent Communication by Marshall Rosenberg

Off the Relationship Escalator by Amy Gahran

Open by Jenny Block

Opening Up by Tristan Taormino

Outdated by Samhita Mukhopadhyay

The Polyamorists Next Door by Dr. Elisabeth Sheff

Relationship Agreements by Eri Kardos-Patel

Rewriting the Rules by Meg-John Barker

Righteous Discontent by Evelyn Brooks Higginbotham

Rising Strong by Brené Brown

Sex at Dawn by Christopher Ryan and Cacilda Jethá

Sex From Scratch by Sarah Mirk

The Smart Girl's Guide to Polyamory by Dedeker Winston

Stepping Off the Relationship Escalator by Amy Gahran

Stories from the Polycule by Dr. Elisabeth Sheff

What Love Is and What It Could Be by Carrie Jenkins

Why Have Kids? by Jessica Valenti

Why Won't You Apologize by Harriet Lerner

Websites

General Websites

More Than Two (Blog) - Morethantwo.com

Solopoly (blog) - Solopoly.net

Kimchi Cuddles (non-monogamy comics) - kimchicuddles.com

Cuddlist (professional cuddling) - cuddlist.com

Polyamorous Misanthrope (advice) - polyamorousmisanthrope.com

I'm Poly and So Can You (advice) - IAmPoly.net

The Radical Poly Agenda (blog) - radicalpoly.wordpress.com

The Selfish Activist (social justice) - selfishactivist.com

Sex-Positive Psych (my site!) - sexpositivepsych.com

Polyamory in the News - polyinthemedia.blogspot.com

Joreth InnKeeper's site (blog) - https://joreth.dreamwidth.org/

Dr. Elisabeth Sheff's site - Elisabethsheff.com

Talking About Sex (resources for those with kids) - talkingaboutsex.com

Off the Relationship Escalator (blog and solopoly information) - offescalator.com

The Frisky Fairy - friskyfairy.com/wp

National Coalition for Sexual Freedom (NCSF) - ncsf.org

Open Relationship Resources and the Open List - openingup.net

Specific Posts

Joreth's Relationship Commitments
joreth.dreamwidth.org/386617.html

The Word Privilege is Being Used in Two Ways by Siderea
siderea.livejournal.com/1180897.html

Why It's Painful And Scary To Talk About Transformative Justice, and Why It's Time by Andy I
medium.com/@AndyEyeballs/why-its-painful-and-scary-to-talk-about-transformative-justice-and-why-it-s-time-6123b35d45fd

Building Up, Not Tearing Down by Franklin Veaux
morethantwo.com/blog/2014/12/wlamf-no-30-building-not-tearing

Polyamory and Statistics, or "Why haven't we found our third yet?" by Maxine
emanix.livejournal.com/28752.html

Love is Not Enough by Mark Manson - markmanson.net/love

Dr. Evelin Dacker's STARS model for safer sex conversations
evelindacker.com/2017/06/08/stars-safer-sex-talk-for-everyone/

Reid Mihalko's safer sex elevator speech - reidaboutsex.com/elevator

But What Does Solo Poly Even Mean by Joreth InnKeeper
https://joreth.dreamwidth.org/356434.html

Can Polyamorous Hierarchies Be Ethical? Part 1 by Eve Rickert
https://www.morethantwo.com/blog/2016/06/
can-polyamorous-hierarchies-ethical-part-1-tower-village

Can Polyamorous Hierarchies Be Ethical? Part 2 by Eve Rickert
https://www.morethantwo.com/blog/2016/06/
can-polyamorous-hierarchies-ethical-part-2-influence-control

Confronting Abuse in Polyamorous Relationships by Rebecca G. Power
https://psiloveyou.xyz/confronting-abuse-in-polyamorous-relationships-
f9e35eea4546

Yes, Abuse Can Show Up in Polyamorous Relationships by Ginny Brown
https://everydayfeminism.com/2015/05/abuse-in-poly-relationships/

Abuse in Polyamorous Relationships by Shea Emma Fett
https://medium.com/@sheaemmafett/
abuse-in-polyamorous-relationships-d13e396c8f85

The Misagreement by Jeana Jorgensen
http://www.patheos.com/blogs/foxyfolklorist/the-misagreement/

Podcasts

Life on the Swingset

Polyamory Weekly

Multiamory

Disability After Dark

American Sex Podcast

Sex Gets Real

Bawdy Storytelling

Modern Love

Death, Sex & Money

Sex Nerd Sandra

The Dildorks

Chronic Sex

Swingercast

Sex Out Loud

Carnalcopia

Risk

Loving Without Boundaries

Polychat

About the Author

Dr. Liz believes that great sex can change the world. She is on a mission to help you have more meaningful, pleasurable relationships in life and work, as well as the bedroom. She's a coach and licensed psychologist (CA 27871, OR license pending) helping couples and singles develop self-confidence and authenticity in their relationships, whether conventional or non-traditional. Dr. Liz has made multiple media appearances, including as a co-host as on the Life on the Swingset podcast, Cosmopolitan, Playboy, and on the Canadian Broadcasting Corporation radio show Ideas. As a sex educator, Dr. Liz has spoken on many stages internationally including the American Association of Sexuality Educators, Counselors, and Therapists Annual Conference, the Guelph Sexuality Conference, and the Woodhull Sexual Freedom Summit. Dr Liz believes that being confident in who you are is the gateway to great relationships and great sex - and great sex, according to Dr. Liz, can change the world. Learn more about Dr. Liz at sexpositivepsych.com, Sex-Positive Psych on YouTube and Facebook, and @sexpospsych on Twitter.

Keep up with Dr. Liz
Twitter: @sexpospsych
Facebook: Sex-Positive Psych
Youtube: youtube.com/c/SexPositivePsych
Email: openbook@drlizpowell.com
Join the Sex-Positive Psych mailing list: bit.ly/sexposemail

For more on non-monogamy, love, and relationships, visit Dr. Liz online at sexpositivepsych.com

Made in United States
Orlando, FL
21 April 2023

32322191R00172